CANNABIS

MOVING FORWARD
PROTECTING HEALTH

For access to digital chapters and other
eproducts, visit the APHA Press bookstore
(www.apha.org).

CANNABIS

MOVING FORWARD
PROTECTING HEALTH

David H. Jernigan, PhD
Rebecca L. Ramirez, MPH
Brian C. Castrucci, DrPH
Catherine D. Patterson, MPP
Grace Castillo, MPH

de Beaumont
BOLD SOLUTIONS FOR HEALTHIER COMMUNITIES.

APHA PRESS
AN IMPRINT OF AMERICAN PUBLIC HEALTH ASSOCIATION

American Public Health Association
800 I Street, NW
Washington, DC 20001-3710
www.apha.org

Georges C. Benjamin, MD, Executive Director

Printed and bound in the United States of America
Book Production Editor: Blair Reynolds
Typesetting: KnowledgeWorks Global, Ltd.
Cover Design: Alan Giarcanella
Printing and Binding: Sheridan Books

Library of Congress Cataloging-in-Publication Data

Names: Jernigan, David, author.
Title: Cannabis : moving forward, protecting health / by David H. Jernigan,
    PhD, Rebecca L. Ramirez, MPH, Brian C. Castrucci, DrPH, Catherine D.
    Patterson, MPP, Grace Castillo, MPH.
Description: Washington, DC : American Public Health Association, [2021] |
    Includes bibliographical references. | Summary: "This book does not take
    a position on whether expanded legal use of non-medical cannabis should
    continue. It seeks to provide a consolidated source for the evidence,
    issues, challenges, and experiences with legalized cannabis for
    non-medical use and the lessons learned from America's long history with
    alcohol and tobacco control. It seeks to provide guidance for those who
    are and will continue to be in positions to struggle with the issue of
    cannabis control"-- Provided by publisher.
Identifiers: LCCN 2021008716 (print) | LCCN 2021008717 (ebook) | ISBN
    9780875533179 (paperback) | ISBN 9780875533186 (ebook)
Subjects: LCSH: Cannabis--United States. | Marijuana--United States. |
    Marijuana abuse--United States. | Drug legalization--United States.
Classification: LCC HV5822.C3 C366 2021 (print) | LCC HV5822.C3 (ebook) |
    DDC 362.29/52610973--dc23
LC record available at https://lccn.loc.gov/2021008716
LC ebook record available at https://lccn.loc.gov/2021008717

Contents

Foreword

In 1933, just as the 21st Amendment to the US Constitution passed, repealing the 18th Amendment and ending the prohibition of alcohol in America, Raymond B. Fosdick and Albert L. Scott published *Toward Liquor Control*, a blueprint for alcohol regulation that continues to have relevance today. It was commissioned by John D. Rockefeller Jr. In his Foreword, Rockefeller admits to being a teetotaler who "sought to support total abstinence when its achievement seemed possible." However, while this was Rockefeller's aspiration, he was a realist. Recognizing the failure of alcohol prohibition, he turned his attention to temperance. Rockefeller recognized that the repeal of prohibition would create other problems and that "a study of the practice and experience of other countries would be of genuine service." Rockefeller greatly underestimated the importance of the study he commissioned. Much of America's alcohol policy and state-based regulatory system can be traced back to or has at least been influenced by *Toward Liquor Control*.

Nearly 90 years later, America is again struggling with the legalization of a previously illicit substance—cannabis. Much like the years following the end of alcohol prohibition, there are different opinions and beliefs about the wisdom of nonmedical cannabis use. The debates can be as intense as those of the "wets" and the "drys" during prohibition debates. There are obvious economic benefits that include increased tax revenue, increased jobs, and savings from reductions in arrests, trials, and incarcerations, which may be increasingly expedient as states look to rebuild from the economic losses post the COVID-19 pandemic. However, others have concerns about the consequences of legalization for nonmedical use, citing the potential impacts of long-term, heavy use and exposure to passive marijuana smoke; the dangers from unregulated growing, production, and testing; and the potential effects on children through exposure and unintended access.

While the debate may persist, the momentum for nonmedical legalization is undeniable. According to the National Conference of State Legislatures, as of November 2020 only three states (Idaho, Nebraska, and Kansas) fully prohibited public access to cannabis. On December 4, 2020, in a historic vote the US House of Representatives approved a legalization bill (though it was not taken up in the Senate). The election of President Biden with the Democrats holding both houses in the 117th Congress may signal that the push toward at least decriminalization if not legalization may accelerate.

While the decision to legalize cannabis for nonmedical use may seem like a simple binary choice, it is far from it. Legalization for nonmedical use creates a complex web of questions that include employment and occupational safety; proper levels of taxation; production practices; manufacturing quality and consistency; marketing; alternative cannabis products such as flowers, concentrates, oils, and edibles; and regulation of growers, producers, and testing labs. Social equity questions pertaining to existing cannabis-related criminal records and incarcerations, righting the wrongs of the racist war on drugs, and inclusivity in the production and sales in this emerging market further complicate nonmedical legalization. This book addresses these and many more pertinent issues.

This book does not take a position on whether expanded legal use of nonmedical cannabis should continue. It seeks to stand on the shoulders of John D. Rockefeller Jr and *Toward Liquor Control* by providing a consolidated source for the evidence, issues, challenges, and experiences with legalized cannabis for nonmedical use and the lessons learned from America's long history with alcohol and tobacco control. It seeks to provide guidance for those who are and will continue to be in positions to struggle with the issue of cannabis control.

However, like Rockefeller, my coauthors and I recognize the need for thoughtful debate about cannabis control. As is detailed here, the federal designation of cannabis as an illicit substance has restricted research into its harms and benefits, leaving an absence of evidence and information for policymakers and regulators. Legalization of cannabis for nonmedical use will not wait for the evidence, and influence will be exerted over the regulatory process. Protecting the public's health and well-being may mean erring on the side of caution rather than on the need to catalogue future harms.

As we attempt to follow in the footsteps left by Rockefeller, Fosdick, and Scott, we can only hope that *Cannabis: Moving Forward, Protecting Health* will have even the most modest portion of the impact of *Toward Liquor Control* by contributing to the creation of effective, fair, and safe state-based regulatory systems. If the legalization of cannabis for nonmedical use is a reality, then we must, like Rockefeller, pivot to provide appropriate controls to protect the public, ensure quality products and ethical practices, and maintain safety.

Brian C. Castrucci, DrPH
President and CEO, de Beaumont Foundation

Acknowledgments

We want to acknowledge and thank the individuals who were interviewed by and shared their expertise with the authors: Dave Berry (Alberta Liquor and Gaming Division), Jason Blanchette (Boston University School of Public Health), Michael Botticelli (Grayken Center for Addiction at Boston Medical Center), Shawn Collins (Massachusetts Cannabis Control Commission), Steve Davenport (Aperture Research), Adrienne Epstein (New England Treatment Access), Cynthia Hallett (Americans for Nonsmokers' Rights and ANR Foundation), Will Humble (Arizona Public Health Association), Neal Insley (National Alcohol Beverage Control Association), Lara Kaminsky (The Cannabis Alliance), Beau Kilmer (Drug Policy Research Center at RAND), Robin Legun (The Cannabis Corner), Leslie McAhren (New Mexico medical cannabis dispensary owner and public health researcher), Tim Naimi (Boston Medical Center), Justin Nordhorn (Washington State Liquor and Cannabis Board), Paul Pisano (National Beer Wholesalers Association), Craig Purser (National Beer Wholesalers Association), Mitchell Rosenthal (Rosenthal Center for Addiction Studies), Steve Schmidt (National Alcohol Beverage Control Association), Lynn Silver (Public Health Institute), Mitzi Vaughn (Altoterra Capital Partners, Ltd.), and Lauren Zeise (California Office of Environmental Health Hazard Assessment). They generously shared their experience and knowledge, providing us with lessons learned and food for thought for future policy considerations.

This book would not have been possible without the reviewers who provided substantive comments and feedback on specific chapters, including Frank Chaloupka, Gail Christopher, Ziva Cooper, Jim Fell, Beau Kilmer, Clarence Lam, Leslie McAhren, Jonathan Samet, Steve Schmidt, Michael Sparks, and Monica Valdez Lupi. While their comments and review helped improve the content and accuracy of the book, the authors alone remain responsible for any errors or oversights.

We would like to thank Jim Mosher, an attorney/researcher and leader in the alcohol policy field for more than thirty years, who provided substantial contributions and feedback to Chapter 4. David and Rebecca are forever grateful for the mentoring that Jim provided them over so many years to help frame our thinking around lessons from the alcohol policy field with respect to cannabis.

Finally, this work would not have been possible without the support of the de Beaumont Foundation staff, especially Grace Guerrero Ramirez, Rachel Locke, and Dr. Rachel Hare Bork; Dr. James B. Sprague and the de Beaumont Foundation Board of Directors; and, as always, thank you, Pete.

Introduction

In 1933, the United States ratified the 21st Amendment to the Constitution, repealing the prohibition on "manufacture, sale, or transportation of intoxicating liquors." The 21st Amendment left how to accomplish regulation of alcoholic beverages almost entirely to the states and limited the power of the federal government to interfere. Overnight this created a vacuum in state policy, a vacuum into which strode industrialist John D. Rockefeller Jr, who commissioned a slim volume called *Toward Liquor Control*.[1] This book analyzed both the US experience prior to national prohibition and what other countries had tried and learned in regulating alcohol to lay out models for how the states could implement alcohol control systems while avoiding the excesses that had led to prohibition.

Nearly a century later, states are in an analogous situation regarding cannabis.* Public sentiment has largely turned against cannabis prohibition. A wide range of claims about health benefits of cannabis has led to laws allowing medical use in 35 states and four territories across the country, despite the continued presence of a federal prohibition. Growing numbers of states are experimenting with full legalization, medicalization, or some combination of the two. A vacuum exists, however, in public health research–driven guidance regarding how states that decide to legalize adult use of nonmedical cannabis can do so while still safeguarding public health and safety.

That is where this book comes in. The aim here is not to take a position for or against legalization but to bring together, in one place, what has been learned over the past 100 years, in the US and elsewhere, about how best to regulate a complex substance, which may have health benefits but is also potentially intoxicating and addictive. This book focuses on regulation of those parts of the cannabis plant that are clearly more intoxicating and addictive than others. There are many lessons to glean from public health research into tobacco and alcohol regulation as the most prominent other legal and potentially addictive substances in the US marketplace. There is also a lot to learn from efforts by other countries to make cannabis more widely available in a relatively safe manner.

---

*While the terms *marijuana* and *cannabis* are often used interchangeably, for the purposes of this book we will use the term *cannabis*. *Cannabis* is a broad term that can be used to describe all products derived from the *Cannabis sativa* plant, and the National Academies of Sciences, Engineering, and Medicine report states that *cannabis* is the standard terminology used within scientific and scholarly fields. We will also use the term *medical cannabis* for states in which cannabis was allowed for medical reasons and the term *cannabis for nonmedical use* in states that have legalized cannabis for use among persons 21 and older.

This book assumes continued federal prohibition of cannabis, although this could change. However, if it does, the odds are good that the federal government will follow a path similar to what it did with alcohol, leaving most control and much discretion in the hands of individual states. The guidance in this book will then be even more relevant, as every state will need to find a way forward that is acceptable to its citizens and protects public health and safety.

Health policies and policymakers are priority areas of focus for the de Beaumont Foundation, which took the role of Rockefeller in commissioning this report. Much remains unknown about cannabis as a plant, a medicine, and a commercially available commodity. However, as states and possibly the nation embark on yet another national experiment to control an intoxicating substance, it is important to recognize what we do know, both about cannabis itself and about what science can tell us regarding effective methods of regulating it. This book draws on a comprehensive scoping exercise, including literature reviews, as well as interviews with a wide range of subject-matter experts, from public health researchers and local and state health officials and regulators, to members of both the nonmedical and the medical cannabis industry. The goal of the report is to insert a strong public health voice and perspective, based in research and experience, into current debates over how to regulate cannabis for nonmedical use.

WHAT IS A PUBLIC HEALTH PERSPECTIVE?

In 2002, the Institute of Medicine (now the National Academy of Medicine) defined the mission of public health as "fulfilling society's interest in assuring conditions in which people can be healthy."[2] From this perspective, if cannabis availability is to be broadened, the key question is, "What are the conditions under which people can be healthy *and* cannabis can be more widely available to adults for nonmedical use?" The first portion of this book reviews what we know about cannabis use, cannabis users, and the health impact of cannabis use in the United States. This public health perspective seeks to work from the best available data, and these early chapters provide the basis for later discussion of specific structures and policies that show promise for preserving people's potential for good health as cannabis availability expands.

From the available data (presented in more detail in these early chapters), there is a general agreement that cannabis use is not healthy for young people. There is also a consensus that overconsumption of cannabis is unhealthy for users and for those around them. Public health goals for cannabis regulation—distinct from the goals, for instance, of private industry, maximizing state revenues, or rectifying the injustices caused by cannabis prohibition—include

- Preventing youth cannabis use;
- Controlling the prevalence, frequency, and intensity of cannabis use;

- Reducing cannabis-related harms to individuals and communities;
- Ensuring accurate information about the risks of cannabis use; and
- Minimizing the influence of a profit-driven cannabis industry in setting cannabis policies.

BUILDING AN EFFECTIVE CANNABIS REGULATORY SYSTEM

After the first three scene-setting chapters, the remainder of the book takes on the question of how to operationalize these goals. Leaning heavily on experience and research from alcohol and tobacco regulation, Part II begins with Chapter 4 by looking at the big picture of state-level cannabis regulation, describing the current status of state cannabis laws and other relevant policies, reviewing the regulatory models available for nonmedical cannabis, and making recommendations regarding the kinds of cannabis control systems states may want to consider from the perspective of protecting public health.

The ensuing chapters go further into more specific aspects of cannabis regulation. The enforcement of cannabis prohibition in this country has led to severe and unjust consequences for Black and Latinx communities in particular, specifically in terms of mass incarceration, reduced opportunity, and resulting family and community impoverishment. As a critical preface to exploring the specifics of cannabis regulation, Chapter 5 summarizes research on this legacy of social injustice, looks at efforts states have made and are continuing to make to rectify this, and makes recommendations for the way forward.

For alcohol, the World Health Organization has identified three areas where regulation has the greatest potential for being both effective and cost-effective.[3] The next three chapters examine these areas as they apply to nonmedical cannabis. After reviewing regulatory options for cannabis products themselves, Chapter 6 summarizes research and policy options regarding cannabis marketing and promotion. Chapter 7 focuses on the physical availability of cannabis through retail outlets, including the potential impact of outlets on crime and regulatory options for addressing the risks of overconcentration of outlets in certain neighborhoods. Chapter 8 focuses on pricing and taxation of cannabis cultivation and products. Chapter 9 then summarizes monitoring, surveillance, and enforcement needs, including how best to monitor and prevent driving under the influence of cannabis; current data systems available for monitoring and surveillance of cannabis use and policy effectiveness more generally; and the need for additional data and evaluations to assess and stay abreast of the impact of cannabis on individuals and communities as this experiment proceeds.

Each of Chapters 4 through 9 closes with public health–focused recommendations regarding best practices for regulation of what has been described in that chapter. The final chapter outlines a way forward based on the evidence presented in earlier chapters, summarizing the policy recommendations from each of the chapters and providing a blueprint for next steps.

REFERENCES

1. Fosdick R, Scott A. *Toward Liquor Control.* New York: Harper and Brothers; 1933.

2. Institute of Medicine Committee on Assuring the Health of the Public in the 21st Century. *The Future of the Public's Health in the 21st Century.* Washington, DC: National Academies Press; 2002.

3. World Health Organization. Technical Annex (Version dated 12 April 2017). Updated Appendix 3 of the WHO Global NCD Action Plan 2013–2020. 2017. Available at: http://www.who.int/ncds/governance/technical_annex.pdf. Accessed April 5, 2021.

I. CANNABIS IN THE UNITED STATES

Cannabis Use and Users

SUMMARY AND INTRODUCTION

- Past-month cannabis use by youth ages 12–17 has fallen since the beginning of this century, but use rose slightly from 2018 to 2019. Past-year, past-month, and daily or near-daily use has risen steadily nationwide in the past decade among youth ages 18–25 and adults age 26 and older.
- As of 2012–2013, daily or near-daily users accounted for 75% of cannabis purchased and 60% of dollars spent on cannabis. More recent surveys report that those using cannabis daily or near daily still make up 80% of consumption and 71% of the days of use.
- These most frequent cannabis users are disproportionately likely to have lower incomes and less education than the general population.
- Youth cannabis use rates have remained relatively stable or increased slightly over the last 10 years. However, youth have become less likely to perceive cannabis use as risky, which may result in greater youth use as availability of cannabis increases.
- While it may be too soon to tell, early studies of the effects of legalization of non-medical cannabis suggest that adult use increases in its wake; findings on effects of legalization on youth use are mixed.

A public health approach to cannabis requires data on the plant itself as well as on patterns of use and harm. Data in this realm are a moving target—the cannabis plant produces more than 100 cannabinoids, and there are many gaps in our understanding of the plant and its components in part because cannabis has for decades been a Schedule 1 drug at the federal level.

That said, the central concern of this book is a public health approach to regulation of cannabis as a psychoactive and potentially addictive substance. As such, the book focuses on those parts of the plant that have this potential. While one cannabinoid—cannabidiol, or CBD—is on the market in a wide and growing range of products, it is not known as an addictive or intoxicating substance and thus receives only passing mention in this report. Rather, we begin by looking at the cannabis plant itself and then describe current prevalence and patterns of use of the forms and portions of the cannabis plant that have the greatest implications for public health.

WHAT IS CANNABIS?

The dried leaves and flowers of the cannabis plant, also known as marijuana, have been used across the globe for thousands of years for medicinal and psychosocial effects; other parts of the cannabis plant have been used for industrial purposes. The principal psychoactive ingredient in cannabis is delta-9-tetrahydrocannabinol (THC),[*1] which is nonpsychoactive when in the plant itself but is converted to a psychoactive by drying and heating.[2] The potency of THC varies based on plant type, parts of the plant harvested, and growing and processing techniques. Trichomes (tiny hair- or crystal-like stalks on the surface of the plant) have the most psychoactive content, followed by flowers (buds). The leaves have some THC, and the stalks and stems have very little.[2]

The cannabis plant has three principal strains or varieties: sativa, indica, and ruderalis, all of which may be crossed with each other to produce hybrids and different products.[3,4] Sinsemilla (or sensemilla) is high potency cannabis produced by keeping female plants unpollinated and seedless. These plants generally yield products of between 10% and 20% THC. Hashish, which comes from the dried resin of mature flowering and unpollinated female plants, can exceed 40% THC.[2] Extracts, often used in dabbing (described in Chapter 3), can raise THC levels to 75% or even higher.[5,6]

As mentioned, CBD is generally thought to be nonintoxicating, although one study found that users reported feeling intoxicated by very high-dose vaporized CBD administered without any THC.[7] There is some evidence that CBD can blunt the anxiety sometimes produced by high doses of THC.[8] Cannabis with a lower THC-to-CBD ratio may pose less risk of overintoxication and dependence; however, low doses of CBD may potentiate intoxication from THC, underscoring the complexity of the THC-CBD relationship and how much still remains to be learned.[7-9]

Understanding the therapeutic effects of CBD independent of THC is the subject of a growing body of research.[10,11] The 2014 Farm Bill provided protections for hemp research, and the 2018 Farm Bill extended these protections and took another significant step, allowing general cultivation of hemp (cannabis plants that do not contain more than 0.3% THC) for the first time since 1937, pending each state department of agriculture submitting a plan to the US Department of Agriculture. The 2018 Farm Bill also included hemp under the Critical Agriculture Materials Act, thereby defining it as of strategic and

---

[*] The acronyms THC and CBD are defined in this chapter but not in the rest of the book, since they are terms commonly understood in the field of cannabis studies.

industrial importance to the nation. However, the 2018 Farm Bill did not legalize CBD, leaving it under the jurisdiction of the Food and Drug Administration, which has thus far approved just one CBD-derived medication. Despite the proliferation of CBD-derived products in the marketplace, aside from this medication (Epidiolex), all are illegal in interstate commerce.[12,13]

Cannabis has in the past been most frequently ingested through smoking, but methods of delivery are rapidly changing in the wake of legalization. These can include vaping, eating, drinking, and dabbing (heating a metal element with a blowtorch and inhaling a highly concentrated cannabis extract).[14] These new delivery techniques can have different health effects, which are discussed in more detail in Chapter 3.

PREVELANCE OF CANNABIS USE IN THE UNITED STATES, 2019[*]

According to the annual National Survey on Drug Use and Health (NSDUH), in 2019 an estimated 48.2 million Americans age 12 or older had used cannabis in the past year (with no distinction between medical and nonmedical use). This number corresponds to 17.5% of the US population age 12 or older and varies by age group (Table 1-1).[15] About 3.5 million people age 12 or older used cannabis for the first time in the past 12 months. This is the equivalent of approximately 9,500 new cannabis users each day. Almost 75% of these new users were between the ages of 12 and 25.[16,17]

Table 1-1. 2019 Cannabis Prevalence in Millions

	Past Year (%)	Past Month (%)	Daily or Near Daily in Past Year (%)	Daily or Near Daily in Past Month (%)	Initiation
Population 12+	48.2 (17.5)	31.6 (11.5)	10.1 (3.7)	13.8 (5.0)	3.5
12–17-year-olds	3.3 (13.2)	1.8 (7.4)	.28 (1.1)	.45 (1.8)	1.4
18–25-year-olds	12.0 (35.4)	7.7 (23.0)	2.5 (7.5)	3.3 (9.9)	1.2
Age 26+	33.0 (15.2)	22.0 (10.2)	7.3 (3.4)	10.0 (4.6)	.89

Source: Adapted from Substance Abuse and Mental Health Services Administration.[15]

---

[*]Data on cannabis prevalence come from national surveys based on self-reports, which are vulnerable to what is known as social desirability bias, the tendency for people to skew their answers based on what they think others may think of them. For instance, heavy drinking is often stigmatized, and people routinely underreport their alcohol consumption. However, for products like alcohol, it is assumed that people underreport consistently over time, so surveys are useful for tracking trends. Public opinion about and the legal status of cannabis are in flux; in this context, people could be becoming more likely to report both cannabis use and related consequences. Trends in both need to be viewed with this in mind.

Table 1-2. 2019 Past-Month Use by Demographic Category in Thousands (%)

	Age 12+	Age 12–17	Age 18–25	Age 26+
Male	18,614 (13.9)	981 (7.7)	4,171 (24.7)	13,461 (12.9)
Female	12,993 (9.2)	856 (7.0)	3,578 (21.3)	8,559 (7.6)
Not Hispanic or Latinx				
White	20,464 (12.0)	934 (7.3)	4,397 (24.4)	5,133 (10.8)
Black or African American	4,565 (13.7)	238 (7.1)	1,248 (26.9)	3,078 (12.2)
AIAN	188 (12.0)	19 (11.1)	45 (20.8)	124 (10.5)
NHOPI	116 (10.6)	*	*	86 (10.3)
Asian	703 (4.4)	26 (2.0)	259 (12.4)	417 (3.3)
Two or More Races	1,049 (19.7)	77 (8.3)	266 (28.3)	706 (20.5)
Hispanic or Latinx	4,521 (9.5)	531 (8.6)	1,515 (19.8)	2,475 (7.4)

Source: Based on Substance Abuse and Mental Health Services Administration.[15]
Note: AIAN = American Indian or Alaska Native, NHOPI = Native Hawaiian or Other Pacific Islander.
*Indicates low precision.

Approximately 31.6 million Americans age 12 and above (11.5%) used cannabis in the past month, and 13.8 million (5%) used it daily or near daily.[15] In terms of demographics, most cannabis users are White and male. A slightly higher percentage of Black Americans use cannabis, and a slightly lower percentage of Hispanic/Latinx Americans. Use is concentrated in the 18- to 25-year-old age group, where nearly one in four males and one in five females reported using cannabis in the past month (Table 1-2).

TRENDS IN CANNABIS USE, 2002–2019

The survey methods for the NSDUH changed substantially in 2002, so it is best to look at trends starting in that year. From 2002 to 2014, overall prevalence of past-month cannabis use among persons age 12 or older increased by 35% (from 6.2% in 2002 to 8.4% in 2014); however, it did not increase for the 12- to 17-year-old age group.[18] Since then, the national trend in all age groups has been upward, with the slowest increase occurring among 12- to 17-year-olds, and the greatest increase among persons 26 and older (see Figure 1-1 for 2016–2019 data).[15] The 2019 NSDUH data show increases in past-month cannabis use for all age groups, including a statistically significant increase from 2018 to 2019 (from 8.6% to 10.2%) for those 26 or older, whose past-year daily or near-daily use also rose from 2.8% to 3.4%.[15]

More people are starting to use cannabis as well. According to NSDUH, in 2002 there were 2.2 million new users; by 2019 this number had risen to 3.5 million people, with the

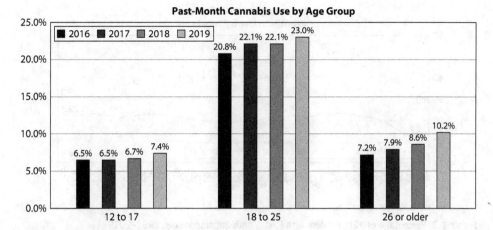

Source: Based on Substance Abuse and Mental Health Services Administration.[15]

Figure 1-1. Past-Month Cannabis Use for All Age Groups

largest increase coming in the 26 and older age group, as shown in Figure 1-2. Initiation among young people stayed consistent throughout the time period, at close to 1.4 million new users ages 12–17 every year.

Because NSDUH is conducted in the home, often with parents present, these youth numbers may be an undercount. In contrast, Monitoring the Future (MTF) has been conducting surveys in schools since 1975. As Figure 1-3 illustrates, over the past three decades there has been a significant decrease in past-month alcohol and tobacco use by 12th graders, while their 30-day prevalence of cannabis use has increased.[19]

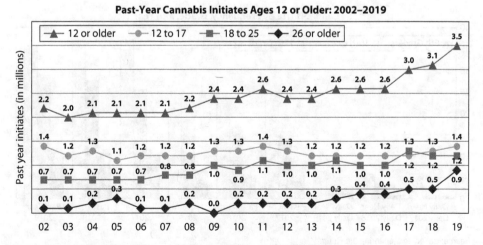

Source: Adapted from Substance Abuse and Mental Health Services Administration.[15]

Figure 1-2. Past-Year Cannabis Initiation Among Individuals Ages 12 or Older: 2002–2019

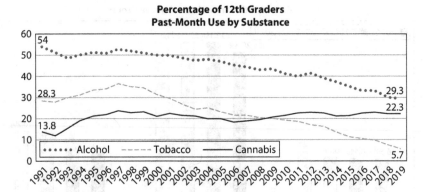

**Percentage of 12th Graders
Past-Month Use by Substance**

Source: Based on Monitoring the Future.[19]

Figure 1-3. Percentage of 12th Graders with Past-Month Substance Use: 1991-2019

Results for the past three years (Figure 1-4) show that past-year and past-month cannabis use has remained relatively stable or even slightly decreased for 12th graders, with roughly one in five students using in the past month. These rates have been climbing for 8th graders and 10th graders, and daily or near-daily use has gone up in all three grades, with statistically significant increases from 2018 to 2019 for 8th graders and 10th graders. For 12th graders, grade of onset of cannabis use has remained steady at 9th grade over 30 years; however, cannabis is increasingly displacing alcohol and cigarettes as the first substance used among adolescents who use multiple substances.[20]

A third source, the Youth Risk Behavior Surveillance System, sponsored in schools nationally by the Centers for Disease Control and Prevention, shows that past-month

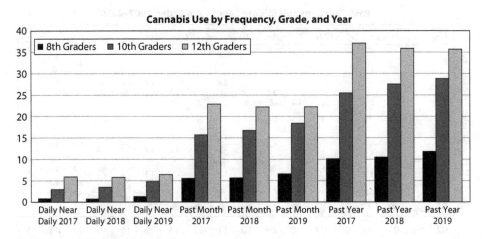

Cannabis Use by Frequency, Grade, and Year

Source: Based on Monitoring the Future.[19]

Figure 1-4. Cannabis Use by Frequency, Grade, and Year

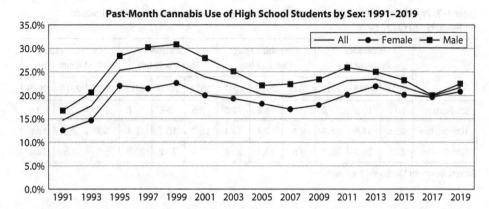

Past-Month Cannabis Use of High School Students by Sex: 1991–2019

— All ⬤ Female ■ Male

Source: Based on Centers for Disease Control and Prevention.[21]

Figure 1-5. Past-Month Cannabis Use of High School Students by Sex, 1991–2019

cannabis use among 9th to 12th graders peaked at roughly one in four students in 1997 and then fell to one in five in 2005, where it has remained stable, with 21.7% reporting past-month use in 2019. The male-female difference in past-month cannabis use narrowed to just 1.7 percentage points in 2019 (22.5% of boys and 20.8% of girls) among high school students (Figure 1-5).[21]

Black youth compared with White adolescents have historically had lower rates of cannabis use,[22] but according to MTF, use among Black 10th and 12th graders increased over the past decade, and as of 2019, their rates were higher than those of White adolescents of the same age.[23] Latinx and multiracial 12th graders have also increased their cannabis use.[24]

Vaping cannabis (discussed in more detail in Chapter 3) has caught on quickly among youth: 12th graders in the 2019 MTF survey reported the second largest single-year increase ever observed for any drug since that survey began in 1975 (the first being past-month nicotine vaping for 12th graders from the 2017–2018 survey). As of 2019, 14% of 12th graders, 12.6% of 10th graders, and 3.9% of 8th graders reported vaping cannabis in the past month (Table 1-3). For the first time, in its 2019 survey MTF asked about daily or near-daily cannabis vaping: 0.8% of 8th graders, 3% of 10th graders, and 3.5% of 12th graders reported this behavior.[19]

Use is rising among pregnant women as well. From 2002 to 2017, past-month cannabis use by pregnant women (ages 12 to 44) increased from 3.4% to 7%.[25] In 2019, 112,000 pregnant women (or 5.8% of pregnant women*) reported past-month cannabis use.[15]

---

*The Volkow study controlled for age, race/ethnicity, and family income in calculating their adjusted prevalence rates for 2002 to 2017. The 2019 percentage reported here is unadjusted.

Table 1-3. Prevalence of Cannabis Use and Cannabis Vaping for 8th, 10th, and 12th Graders (in Percent): 2017–2019

	Cannabis Past-Year Use			Cannabis Vaping Past-Year Use			Cannabis Past-Month Use			Cannabis Vaping Past-Month Use		
	2017	2018	2019	2017	2018	2019	2017	2018	2019	2017	2018	2019
8th Graders	10.1	10.5	11.8	3.0	4.4	7.0	5.5	5.6	6.6	1.6	2.6	3.9
10th Graders	25.5	27.5	28.8	8.1	12.4	19.4	15.7	16.7	18.4	4.3	7.0	12.6
12th Graders	37.1	35.9	35.7	9.5	13.1	20.8	22.9	22.2	22.3	5.0	7.5	14.0

Source: Based on Monitoring the Future.[19]

TRENDS IN PERCEPTIONS OF RISK

These increases in prevalence of use have corresponded with decreases in perceived risks to health and well-being. Perception of low harm from cannabis use is a risk factor that prospectively predicts more cannabis use, including during the important transition period from mid- to late adolescence.[26] Analysis of MTF data from 1991 through 2016 found youth prevalence averaging 31 percentage points higher for adolescents who perceived moderate versus great risk and 23 percentage points higher for youth who perceived no/slight versus moderate risk.[27] In addition, low perceived risks of harm may contribute to consuming multiple substances on one occasion: young adults (18 and older) who perceived simultaneous alcohol and cannabis use as less risky were more likely to use cannabis on days when they had more drinks compared to peers anticipating greater risk from simultaneous use.[28]

While national surveys have not yet measured perceived risks regarding the various forms of cannabis use (e.g., vaping, dabbing, edibles—see Chapter 3 for more detail), overall prevalence of perceiving great risk from smoking cannabis once or twice a week fell from 51.3% in 2002 to 36.3% in 2015 and then to 29.2% in 2019 in the general population age 12 and older. This downward trend occurred in all age groups and was significantly lower than perceived great risks for alcohol, tobacco, or illicit drug use during this time period.[15,18]

The MTF survey has found similarly that the percentage of 12th graders perceiving great risk of harm from regular cannabis use decreased by almost 23 percentage points since 2002, reaching 30.3% by 2019.[19]

SHARE OF USE BY FREQUENCY

Because the number of daily or near-daily users has increased sevenfold since 1992,[29] these frequent users account for a growing share of cannabis consumption. An analysis of three online surveys (conducted in 2013, 2018, and 2019) coupled with NSDUH data found that those using cannabis 21 or more days per month account for 80% of consumption and 71% of the days of use. In contrast, the nearly half (48%) of past-month users who report using 10 or fewer days per month consume less than 10% of the cannabis.[30] An earlier analysis of data between 2012 and 2013 found that frequent cannabis users purchased approximately 75% of cannabis grams bought and spent almost 60% of the dollars.

The same analysis showed that less-educated and lower-income individuals consume cannabis at disproportionately high rates. This raises significant equity issues. Daily or near-daily users over 21 years old without college degrees (approximately 3.5 million people) spent on average close to 9% of their household income on cannabis purchases compared with college graduates with no abuse or dependence who spent approximately 2% of their income buying cannabis.[29] As summarized in a recent news article, "The most frequent marijuana users aren't college-educated hipsters, but rather people without any college education, suggesting the changes in pot policy can have the largest impact on economically vulnerable populations."[31]

CANNABIS USE AFTER STATE-LEVEL LEGALIZATION

As of November 2020, 35 states plus the District of Columbia, Puerto Rico, and the US Virgin Islands had approved comprehensive, publicly available medical marijuana/cannabis programs, while 15 states, the District of Columbia, Guam, and the Northern Mariana Islands had legalized cannabis for adult nonmedical use. Major news outlets have increasingly communicated a more positive message about cannabis use than is warranted by the scientific evidence (see Chapter 2).[32] Abundant research literature in the alcohol and tobacco fields has documented that increased availability of these substances is associated with increases in use and related problems.[33,34] However, every state that has medicalized and/or legalized cannabis use for adults has done so differently, greatly complicating efforts to evaluate the effects of broader legal cannabis availability on patterns of cannabis consumption. Researchers estimate it will take at least a generation of experience with these laws and policies before their full effects on consumption-related benefits or harms will be known.[2]

Specific to medical cannabis laws, a systematic review and meta-analysis of 11 studies of the impact of medical cannabis laws, using data from four large national surveys, found no significant increases in adolescent cannabis use associated with medical cannabis laws through 2014.[35] A report by the European Monitoring Centre for Drugs and Drug Addiction summarized the peer-reviewed studies that have examined the effects of legalization of cannabis for nonmedical use on the prevalence of cannabis use. The authors note that although the results are mixed, studies focused on adults are more likely to find an increase compared with studies examining younger populations.[36] However, many variables could be affecting the results, including co-occurring binge drinking and proximity to a cannabis retail outlet, as well as different approaches states have taken to legalizing nonmedical use, and different methods used to collect survey data from young people.

A 2019 meta-analysis of six studies (identified as having a very low or low risk of bias) on cannabis legalization for nonmedical use in the United States found that legalization may be associated with a small increase in cannabis use among youth.[37] A 2019 study published after the meta-analysis found that while past-month use and past-month frequent use did not increase among youth, there was a 25% higher increase in risk for cannabis use disorder (CUD) among youth ages 12 to 17 (see Chapter 2 for more information on CUD) in states that legalized cannabis for nonmedical use compared with states that have not. However, a sensitivity analysis found that this increase may have been attributable to unmeasured confounders. The finding among adults 26 years and older was more robust: use and CUD increased for this age group in states that legalized cannabis for nonmedical use.[38]

CONCLUSION

This chapter sets the scene in data for the rest of the book. Cannabis policies need to reflect the most current knowledge of who is using cannabis, how much they are using, how prevalent heavy use is, and how much use is occurring in particular groups such as young people, poor people, racial/ethnic minority populations, and pregnant women.

From the research available thus far in this large natural experiment, it is fairly clear that legalization will increase adult use; the outcomes for youth are less clear. The health implications of these changes in consumption will depend on whether the potential health benefits of cannabis use outweigh the evidence of its possible harms. Accordingly, the next chapter summarizes the growing but still incomplete body of knowledge regarding the effects of cannabis—beneficial and harmful—on human health and safety.

REFERENCES

1. Upton R, Craker L, ElSohly M, et al. *Cannabis inflorescence: Cannabis spp.: Standards of Identity, Analysis, and Quality Control.* Scotts Valley, CA: American Herbal Pharmacopoeia; 2014.

2. Caulkins JP, Kilmer B, Kleinman MAR. *Marijuana Legalization: What Everyone Needs to Know.* 2nd ed. New York: Oxford University Press; 2016.

3. Pollio A. The name of cannabis: a short guide for nonbotanists. *Cannabis Cannabinoid Res.* 2016;1(1):234–238.

4. Holland K. Sativa vs. indica: what to expect across cannabis types and strains. 2019. Available at: https://healthline.com/health/sativa-vs-indica. Accessed March 22, 2020.

5. Raber JC, Elzinga S, Kaplan C. Understanding dabs: contamination concerns of cannabis concentrates and cannabinoid transfer during the act of dabbing. *J Toxicol Sci.* 2015;40(6):797–803.

6. Loflin M, Earleywine M. A new method of cannabis ingestion: the dangers of dabs? *Addict Behav.* 2014;39(10):1430–1433.

7. Solowij N, Broyd S, Greenwood LM, et al. A randomised controlled trial of vaporised Delta(9)-tetrahydrocannabinol and cannabidiol alone and in combination in frequent and infrequent cannabis users: acute intoxication effects. *Eur Arch Psychiatry Clin Neurosci.* 2019;269(1):17–35.

8. Englund A, Freeman TP, Murray RM, McGuire P. Can we make cannabis safer? *Lancet Psychiatry.* 2017;4(8):643–648.

9. Mechoulam R, Parker L. Towards a better cannabis drug. *Br J Pharmacol.* 2013;170(7): 1363–1364.

10. Pisanti S, Malfitano AM, Ciaglia E, et al. Cannabidiol: state of the art and new challenges for therapeutic applications. *Pharmacol Ther.* 2017;175:133–150.

11. Levinsohn EA, Hill KP. Clinical uses of cannabis and cannabinoids in the United States. *J Neurol Sci.* 2020;411:116717.

12. Hudak J. The Farm Bill, hemp legalization and the status of CBD: an explainer. Brookings Institution. *FIXGOV* blog, December 14, 2018. Available at: https://www.brookings.edu/blog/fixgov/2018/12/14/the-farm-bill-hemp-and-cbd-explainer. Accessed March 22, 2021.

13. Abernethy A. *Testimony Before the United States Senate: Hemp Production and the 2018 Farm Bill by Amy Abernethy, MD, PhD, Principal Deputy Commissioner, Food and Drug Administration.* US Food and Drug Administration, Dept of Health and Human Services; 2019.

14. Schauer GL, Njai R, Grant-Lenzy AM. Modes of marijuana use—smoking, vaping, eating, and dabbing: results from the 2016 BRFSS in 12 states. *Drug Alcohol Depend.* 2020;209:107900.

15. Substance Abuse and Mental Health Services Administration. *Key Substance Use and Mental Health Indicators in the United States: Results from the 2019 National Survey on Drug Use and Health.* HHS publication PEP20–07-01-001. NSDUH series H-55. Rockville, MD: Center for Behavioral Health Statistics and Quality, Substance Abuse and Mental Health Services Administration; 2020.

16. Greenfield TK, Kerr WC. Alcohol measurement methodology in epidemiology: recent advances and opportunities. *Addiction.* 2008;103(7):1082–1099.

17. Krumpal I. Determinants of social desirability in sensitive surveys: a literature review. *Quality & Quantity.* 2013;47(4):2025–2047.

18. Azofeifa A, Mattson ME, Schauer G, McAfee T, Grant A, Lyerla R. National estimates of marijuana use and related indicators—National Survey on Drug Use and Health, United States, 2002–2014. *MMWR Surveill Summ.* 2016;65(SS-11):1–25.

19. Monitoring the Future. *National Adolescent Drug Trends in 2019: Findings Released;* 2019. Available at: http://monitoringthefuture.org/pressreleases/19drugpr.pdf. Accessed August 23, 2021.

20. Keyes KM, Rutherford C, Miech R. Historical trends in the grade of onset and sequence of cigarette, alcohol, and marijuana use among adolescents from 1976–2016: implications for "Gateway" patterns in adolescence. *Drug Alcohol Depend.* 2019;194:51–58.

21. Centers for Disease Control and Prevention. Youth Risk Behavior Surveillance System (YRBSS) results: youth online high school results. 2020. Available at: https://www.cdc.gov/healthyyouth/data/yrbs/results.htm?s_cid=hy-YRBS-2020-1. Accessed March 25, 2021.

22. Miech R, Terry-McElrath YM, O'Malley PM, Johnston LD. Increasing marijuana use for black adolescents in the United States: a test of competing explanations. *Addict Behav.* 2019;93:59–64.

23. Miech RA, Johnston LD, O'Malley PM, Bachman JG, Schulenberg JE, Patrick ME. *Monitoring the Future National Survey Results on Drug Use, 1975–2019. Volume I: Secondary School Students.* Ann Arbor, MI: Institute for Social Research, University of Michigan; 2020.

24. Keyes KM, Wall M, Feng T, Cerdá M, Hasin DS. Race/ethnicity and marijuana use in the United States: diminishing differences in the prevalence of use, 2006–2015. *Drug Alcohol Depend.* 2017;179:379–386.

25. Volkow ND, Han B, Compton WM, McCance-Katz EF. Self-reported medical and nonmedical cannabis use among pregnant women in the United States. *JAMA.* 2019;322(2):167–169.

26. Cambron C, Kosterman R, Rhew IC, Catalano RF, Guttmannova K, Hawkins JD. Neighborhood structural factors and proximal risk for youth substance use. *Prev Sci.* 2020;21(4):508–518.

27. Terry-McElrath YM, O'Malley PM, Patrick ME, Miech RA. Risk is still relevant: Time-varying associations between perceived risk and marijuana use among US 12th grade students from 1991 to 2016. *Addict Behav.* 2017;74:13–19.

28. Yeomans-Maldonado G, Patrick ME. The effect of perceived risk on the combined use of alcohol and marijuana: results from daily surveys. *Addict Behav Rep.* 2015;2:33–36.

29. Davenport SS, Caulkins JP. Evolution of the United States marijuana market in the decade of liberalization before full legalization. *J Drug Issues.* 2016;46(4):411–427.

30. Caulkins JP, Pardo B, Kilmer B. Intensity of cannabis use: findings from three online surveys. *Int J Drug Policy.* 2020;79:102740.

31. Lopez G. Who uses the most marijuana—and what it means for legalization. *Vox.* March 13, 2015.

32. Abraham A, Zhang AJ, Ahn R, Woodbridge A, Korenstein D, Keyhani S. Media content analysis of marijuana's health effects in news coverage. *J Gen Intern Med.* 2018;33(9):1438–1440.

33. Babor T, Caetano R, Casswell S, et al. *Alcohol: No Ordinary Commodity: Research and Public Policy.* 2nd ed. New York: Oxford University Press; 2010.

34. Ashe M, Jernigan D, Kline R, Galaz R. Land use planning and the control of alcohol, tobacco, firearms, and fast food restaurants. *Am J Public Health.* 2003;93(9):1404–1408.

35. Sarvet AL, Wall MM, Fink DS, et al. Medical marijuana laws and adolescent marijuana use in the United States: a systematic review and meta-analysis. *Addiction.* 2018;113(6):1003–1016.

36. European Monitoring Centre for Drugs and Drug Addiction. *Monitoring and Evaluating Changes in Cannabis Policies: Insights From the Americas.* Luxembourg European Monitoring Centre for Drugs and Drug Addiction; 2020.

37. Melchior M, Nakamura A, Bolze C, et al. Does liberalisation of cannabis policy influence levels of use in adolescents and young adults? a systematic review and meta-analysis. *BMJ Open.* 2019;9.

38. Cerda M, Mauro C, Hamilton A, et al. Association between recreational marijuana legalization in the United States and changes in marijuana use and cannabis use disorder from 2008 to 2016. *JAMA Psychiatry.* 2019;77(2).

2

Therapeutic Effects and Harms From Cannabis and Cannabinoids

SUMMARY AND INTRODUCTION

- Substantial research supports the finding that cannabis and cannabinoid use can reduce chemotherapy-induced nausea, symptoms of chronic pain, multiple sclerosis–related spasticity, and seizure frequency in two rare forms of epilepsy. The majority of these therapeutic effects are from cannabis and cannabinoid-related medicines.
- Harms associated with cannabis use include increased risk of motor vehicle crashes, development of schizophrenia and other psychoses, respiratory symptoms (coughing, wheezing, phlegm), and lower birth weight of offspring.
- Cannabis use harms tend to increase with frequency, quantity, and potency of use.
- Cannabis use during adolescence is associated with greater risk of poor educational outcomes, cannabis dependence, depression, psychotic symptoms, anxiety, and suicide attempts.
- Whether cannabis complements or substitutes use of drugs other than tobacco remains unresolved, and there is no evidence that cannabinoids are effective in achieving abstinence from other drugs.

In November 2020, a search for "cannabis health benefits" on Google News yielded 74.6 million hits. The equivalent search for "cannabis health harms"? A mere 2.1 million results. Searches for "marijuana health benefits/harms" and "weed health benefits/harms" yielded similarly large gaps. Health benefits of the cannabis plant seem to be constantly in the news as cannabidiol (CBD) products proliferate throughout the country.

For drug products entering the marketplace legally, the federal Food and Drug Administration (FDA) requires an extensive application and testing process. To date, one drug derived directly from the cannabis plant (Epidiolex, see the following section on epilepsy) has successfully completed that process and come into the prescription drug marketplace, along with three synthetically derived medicines, dronabinols Marinol and Syndros, and nabilone Cesamet.[1] State-level medicalization and legalization of cannabis has permitted scores of products making health claims and containing CBD or THC or some combination of the two to come into the legal market. At the same time, there has been no federal agency systematically examining the evidence behind these claims; the FDA reviews such evidence only when submitted in the context of a new drug marketing application.

Research on benefits and harms of cannabis and cannabinoids is a rapidly developing field. It was beyond the scope of this book to conduct systematic reviews of the evidence in this area; this chapter instead relies heavily on systematic reviews and meta-analyses conducted by others. Chief among these is the 2017 report from the National Academies of Sciences, Engineering, and Medicine (NASEM), the nation's leading scientific advisory body, titled *The Health Effects of Cannabis and Cannabinoids: The Current State of Evidence and Recommendations for Research.*[2] This chapter summarizes the NASEM report's key findings and supplements them with findings from systematic reviews or meta-analyses published since the NASEM report's release and available through October 2020.[*]

The NASEM committee gave each outcome—beneficial or harmful—an evidence rating: conclusive (strong evidence from randomized controlled trials), substantial (strong evidence), moderate (some evidence), limited (weak evidence), and no or insufficient evidence to support the association. The particular focus of this chapter is on the NASEM findings with conclusive or substantial evidence. As emphasized in their report, more research is clearly needed; in many cases, their findings were tentative and will be subject to revision as more evidence is gathered. Appendix 1 describes in more detail the different levels of evidence used by the NASEM committee and lists its findings and conclusions by strength of evidence level, as not all of their findings are summarized here. In many of the US studies of cannabis use covered in the NASEM and other reviews, the cannabis product was provided by the National Institute on Drug Abuse, through the University of Mississippi, and is not considered similar to products currently sold in states where medical or nonmedical cannabis is available, because both the potency and the product types (see Chapter 3) are not comparable.[3-5]

The structure of this chapter is as follows: first, a discussion of evidence supporting therapeutic uses of cannabis and cannabinoids; second, a summary of the major health harms that have been shown to be associated with cannabis use; and finally, findings thus far from research into the impact of widening cannabis availability on health. While we include research on the therapeutic benefits from cannabis and cannabinoids, the use of the term *cannabis* throughout refers primarily to cannabis in its intoxicating forms.

THERAPEUTIC BENEFITS FROM CANNABIS AND CANNABINOIDS

The NASEM committee analyzed hundreds of potential or claimed therapeutic benefits of cannabis and cannabinoid use. The report's findings are far more limited than the myriad medical conditions that various state medical cannabis programs list as approved indications for cannabis use.[6,7] The report found substantial or conclusive evidence for

---

[*]We conducted searches for "cannabis" OR "marijuana" AND "health benefits" OR "health harms" AND "systematic reviews" OR "meta-analyses" from June 2016 (when the NASEM search time frame ended) through October 2020. In some topic areas where we found few or no systematic reviews or meta-analyses, we conducted a scoping review for relevant studies, prioritizing high quality studies published in the past five years.

treatment of three conditions: chemotherapy-induced nausea and vomiting, chronic pain, and multiple sclerosis spasticity symptoms.[2] In the majority of the studies showing effectiveness for these symptoms, the outcomes were tied not to use of cannabis itself but rather to cannabis-related medicines developed either as synthetic cannabinoids (nabilone and dronabinol) or as standardized extracts of THC (nabiximols).

Chemotherapy-Induced Nausea and Vomiting. On the strength of three systematic reviews, the NASEM report found conclusive evidence that cannabis or cannabinoids are effective as antiemetics in the treatment of chemotherapy-induced nausea and vomiting, primarily through the FDA-approved oral THC medicines nabilone and dronabinol. While there have been many anecdotal reports of the benefits of plant cannabis, either inhaled or ingested, as an effective treatment for chemotherapy-induced nausea and vomiting, the NASEM committee found no randomized trials of good quality to evaluate these options.[2]

Chronic Pain. The NASEM committee found five systematic reviews of good to fair quality showing that adults with chronic pain treated with cannabis or cannabinoids were more likely to experience a clinically significant reduction in pain symptoms. The majority of the studies evaluated the use of nabiximols (a specific cannabis extract, trade name Sativex), produced by a UK biotech firm dedicated to work on cannabinoids. These studies were performed outside the United States, as use of nabiximols has not been approved by the FDA. Five systematic reviews/meta-analyses published after the NASEM report found small effects for cannabis and cannabinoids in alleviating various types of pain.[8-12]

Multiple Sclerosis Spasticity Symptoms. The NASEM report also concluded, based on evidence from randomized control trials included in systematic reviews, that orally administered THC and nabiximols are "probably effective for reducing patient-reported spasticity scores in patients with MS." The effect appears to be modest, as reflected by an average reduction of 0.76 units on a 0-to-10 scale.[2]

Epilepsy. While the NASEM report found insufficient evidence regarding cannabinoids as an effective treatment for epilepsy, in 2018 the FDA approved Epidiolex, a CBD oral solution, for the treatment of seizures associated with two rare forms of epilepsy.[1] A 2018 systematic review found that pharmaceutical-grade CBD may reduce seizure frequency in some forms of pediatric epilepsy,[13] and a 2020 review concluded that "medical practitioners can be confident prescribing this medicine [Epidiolex]" in two populations of patients with drug-resistant epilepsy.[14]

Other Therapeutic Effects. The NASEM committee found some evidence (moderate, in their terms) that cannabinoids are an effective treatment to improve short-term sleep outcomes in individuals with obstructive sleep apnea syndrome, fibromyalgia, chronic pain, and multiple sclerosis. A subsequent 2019 review of sleep outcomes from clinical trials concluded that while participants often report a subjective improvement in their sleep quality, objective data are lacking, and clinical ramifications are unclear.[15]

There was weak (limited) evidence that cannabis or oral cannabinoids could increase appetite and decrease weight loss associated with HIV/AIDS; improve symptoms of

Tourette syndrome; improve anxiety symptoms as assessed by a public speaking test for individuals with social anxiety disorder; improve outcomes after a traumatic brain injury or intracranial hemorrhage; or improve symptoms of post-traumatic stress disorder (PTSD; a single, small trial). A systematic review published in 2017 found insufficient evidence to draw conclusions about either benefits or harms from cannabis use among patients with PTSD but noted that several studies were underway.[16] Two recent systematic reviews found that while cannabis and cannabinoids may have potential therapeutic effects for improving PTSD symptoms, there is not enough evidence regarding their safety and efficacy.[17,18]

Finally, the committee concluded that cannabinoids are an *ineffective* treatment for improving symptoms associated with dementia or intraocular pressure associated with glaucoma or reducing depressive symptoms in individuals with chronic pain or multiple sclerosis.[2]

A subsequent systematic review and meta-analysis published in 2019 reviewed 83 studies of whether use of cannabinoids could assist with mental disorders. The authors concluded that "there is scarce evidence to suggest that cannabinoids improve depressive disorders and symptoms, anxiety disorders, attention-deficit hyperactivity disorder, Tourette syndrome, post-traumatic stress disorder, or psychosis" and that "there remains insufficient evidence to provide guidance on the use of cannabinoids for treating mental disorders within a regulatory framework."[19] A systematic review published in 2020 concluded that while there was no convincing evidentiary support for the use of cannabinoids for use in any mental health application, there was "tentative support" for CBD's ability to reduce social anxiety and mixed evidence for adjunctive use in schizophrenia.[18]

Finally, one of the NASEM report's conclusions regarding chronic pain could readily apply to other areas of potential benefit: "While the use of cannabis for the treatment of pain is supported by well-controlled clinical trials . . . very little is known about the efficacy, dose, routes of administration, or side effects of commonly used and commercially available cannabis products in the United States."[2]

CANNABIS HARMS

While there is definitive evidence of fewer therapeutic benefits from cannabis than many may assume,[20] there may be more harms related to cannabis use than the general public understands or hears about from media stories on the health effects of cannabis.[21] It is also important to note at the outset that, as we discuss in Chapter 3, the potency of cannabis has been increasing over time, and older studies may thus have used weaker forms of the drug than those in current use. Similar to the research on therapeutic harms, a systematic review of health-related harms published in 2020 confirmed that there are little data on the "dose dependency" of these effects, which is essential in defining what constitutes risky use of cannabis.[22]

Cannabis Harms to Youth

As of 2018, about a half million adolescents between the ages of 12 and 17 and two million young adults ages 18 to 25 had a cannabis use disorder.[23] Researchers believe that "the fact that the endocannabinoid system is dynamically altered during adolescence in brain areas central to reward, decision-making, and motivation suggests that cannabis exposure during this critical developmental phase may have long-term influence on behaviors linked to the mesocorticolimbic system,"[24] that is, the area of the brain thought to play an important role in rewards, motivation, learning, memory, and movement.

Early initiation of cannabis use is associated with a host of health concerns, including more intensive cannabis use, impaired cognitive functioning and school performance, and increased risk of dropping out of school.[25] In Australia and New Zealand, a meta-analysis of three longitudinal studies estimated that the elimination of cannabis use before age 18 would reduce the high school noncompletion rate by 17%.[26]

Frequent cannabis use in adolescence, as well as high-potency cannabis use, is associated with greater risk of poor educational outcomes, cannabis dependence, depression, psychotic symptoms, anxiety, and suicide attempts.[27,28] Evidence indicates that adolescents are not particularly adept at adjusting dosage based on the strength of the product.[28] A case-control study of 901 first-episode psychosis patients compared with 1,237 controls from 11 mental health clinics in five European countries found not only that those who started using cannabis at 15 years of age or younger were at greater odds of developing a psychotic disorder but that those who began using high-potency cannabis (10% THC or more) by 15 years of age had twice the risk compared with those who initiated at older ages.[29]

Cannabis and Mental Health

A recent systematic review and meta-analysis of studies on cannabis and mental health concluded that "cannabis consumption in adolescence is associated with increased risk of developing major depression in young adulthood and suicidality, especially suicidal ideation." According to the study, while the increased risk is moderate, given monthly use rates (and daily or near-daily use rates) by US adolescents, this risk translates to "413,326 adolescent cases of depression potentially attributable to cannabis exposure."[30]

Cannabis use likely increases the risk of developing schizophrenia and other psychoses; the higher the use, the greater the risk.[2] In the European case-control study cited above, odds of psychotic disorder among daily users were 3.2 times higher than for individuals who had never used cannabis; high-potency cannabis users had 1.6 times higher odds. The authors concluded that "the strongest independent predictors of whether any given individual would have a psychotic disorder or not were daily use of cannabis and use of high-potency cannabis."[29] A systematic review of studies from the previous five years published in 2020 confirmed the longitudinal data supporting a causal link between cannabis and psychosis. It concluded as well that THC has an exacerbating effect on schizophrenia symptoms.[31]

Transition from substance-induced psychoses to an enduring psychotic disorder like schizophrenia is higher following cannabis-induced psychosis (34%) than psychoses stemming from use of other substances, including amphetamines (22%) and hallucinogens (26%).[32] A meta-analysis of 20 cannabis studies found no difference in severity of negative schizophrenia symptoms (e.g., inability to show emotion, difficulty talking, and withdrawal from social situations) between cannabis users and nonusers, and small increases among cannabis users in positive symptoms, such as hallucinations and delusions.[33]

Cannabis-Impaired Driving

Driving under the influence of cannabis is remarkably common in the United States. Among adults, a National Roadside Survey found that 8.6% of weekend nighttime drivers tested positive for THC in 2007, and that rose to 12.6% in 2013–2014, a 48% increase in the prevalence of drivers testing positive for cannabis in just seven years.[34] According to self-reports recorded in the National Survey of Drug Use and Health (NSDUH), in 2018 12 million US residents aged 16 and older (or 4.7% of this population) reported driving under the influence of cannabis in the past 12 months.[*] Driving under the influence of cannabis was more prevalent among males and persons between the ages of 16 and 34 years of age, with the highest prevalence (12.4%) among 21- to 25-year-olds, followed closely by 16- to 20-year-olds (9.2%).[35]

While close to half (48%) of cannabis users in a recent survey believe it is safe to drive while under the influence of cannabis,[36] research suggests otherwise. In both simulated and real driving, driving stability appears significantly impaired after THC consumption.[37] Cannabis use is associated with poorer driving performance, longer response times, and slower driving speeds.[38] Effects on performance are rapid: recent smoking and/or blood THC concentrations of 2 to 5 mg/mL (roughly what occurs with smoking just a portion of one joint [39]) are associated with considerable driving impairment, particularly in occasional cannabis smokers.[40] These effects increase with the quantity of cannabis consumed,[38,40] although the effects may be less pronounced in chronic cannabis users.[41]

The level of THC detected in blood tends to be higher when THC is consumed with alcohol,[42,43] and compared with alcohol or cannabis use alone, co-use of cannabis and alcohol, even at low levels, increases the risk for driving impairment.[42] An analysis of national Fatality Analysis Reporting System (FARS) data from 2011 through 2016 found that compared with drivers testing negative for cannabis, those testing positive were 50% more likely to test positive for alcohol as well.[44]

---

[*]For a point of comparison, in 2018, 20.5 million, or 8%, of the population, reported driving under the influence of alcohol in the past 12 months.

However, measurement issues abound when it comes to assessing driving under the influence of cannabis (see Chapter 9 for more detail). That said, authoritative reviews of the evidence have found significant associations between cannabis use and impaired driving: a 2016 meta-analysis concluded that driving under the influence of cannabis was associated with 20 to 30% higher odds of a motor vehicle crash.[45] The NASEM committee found "substantial evidence" of a statistical association between cannabis use and increased risk of motor vehicle crashes (their second-strongest category).[2] Studies of cannabis-impaired driving after expansions in cannabis availability, for instance through legalization, also suggest that greater cannabis use is associated with more motor vehicle crashes; those will be discussed below along with other health effects of wider cannabis availability.

Cannabis and Homicide Victims

Multiple studies have documented associations between cannabis use and homicide victims. A 2009 meta-analysis of eight studies (one each from Sweden and Canada, the rest from the United States) found that on average, 6% of homicide victims tested positive for cannabis and that the proportion of victims testing positive was increasing over time.[46] An analysis published in 2020 of toxicological data from 12,639 homicide victims from nine states* between 2004 and 2016 found cannabis in 22.3% in 2004, which rose to 42.1% by 2016. At the same time, there was a slight decline in presence of alcohol (Figure 2-1). Young, male, and Black victims were more likely to test positive for cannabis use.[47]

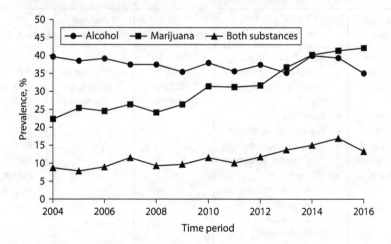

Source: Reprinted with permission from Nazarov and Li.[47]

Figure 2-1. Prevalence of Alcohol and Marijuana Detected in Homicide Victims by Calendar Year in Nine States

*The states included in this study were Colorado, Georgia, Massachusetts, New Jersey, Oregon, Rhode Island, South Carolina, Virginia, and Wisconsin.

The authors noted that "the prevalence of marijuana detected in homicide victims is about three times the prevalence of self-reported past-year marijuana use in the general population and has increased more rapidly than in the general population."[47] Unlike alcohol,[48] there is no clear causal pathway between cannabis use and homicide, but the increase in the percentage of victims testing positive for cannabis and the increasing rates over time raise concerns and merit more attention and research.

Another review of international studies on the toxicology of homicide victims and offenders found four studies with cannabis data on offenders. These studies found that anywhere from 5% to 32% of offenders tested positive for cannabis.[49] However, there is again no clear causal pathway.

Problem Cannabis Use

While problematic or harmful use of alcohol has been clearly defined,[50] no equivalent official diagnostic category for problem cannabis use exists.[51] The 2017 NASEM report construed problem cannabis use broadly to encompass various hazardous or potentially harmful use patterns, including those related to cannabis use disorder (CUD; see below), dependence, and abuse. Table 2-1 summarizes the report's findings regarding risk factors for the development of problem cannabis use.[2]

Table 2-1. Summary of Evidence Regarding Risk Factors for Development of Problem Cannabis Use

Risk Factors			Not Risk Factors	
Substantial Evidence	Moderate Evidence	Limited Evidence	Substantial Evidence	Moderate Evidence

• Frequency of cannabis use
• Being male *and* smoking cigarettes
• Early age of initiation into cannabis use
	• Use of three or more drugs (including tobacco or alcohol) prior to cannabis initiation
	• Being male
	• Major depressive disorder
	• During adolescence:
	  ○ Frequency of cannabis use
	  ○ Oppositional behaviors
	  ○ A younger age of first alcohol use
	  ○ Nicotine use
	  ○ Parental substance use
	  ○ Poor school performance
	  ○ Antisocial behaviors
	  ○ Childhood sexual abuse
		• Childhood anxiety
		• Childhood depression
			• Stimulant treatment for ADHD during adolescence	• Anxiety
				• Personality disorders
				• Bipolar disorders
				• Adolescent ADHD
				• Alcohol or nicotine dependence alone

Source: Based on NASEM.[2]

Box 2-1. Cannabis Use Disorder

According to the *Diagnostic and Statistical Manual of Mental Disorders, Fifth Edition*, the criteria for a diagnosis of cannabis use disorder is a problematic pattern of cannabis use leading to clinically significant impairment or distress, as manifested by at least two of the following, occurring within a 12-month period:

1. Cannabis is often taken in larger amounts or over a longer period than was intended.
2. There is a persistent desire or unsuccessful efforts to cut down or control cannabis use.
3. A great deal of time is spent in activities necessary to obtain cannabis, use cannabis, or recover from its effects.
4. Craving, or a strong desire or urge to use cannabis.
5. Recurrent cannabis resulting in a failure to fulfill major role obligations at work, school, or home.
6. Continued cannabis use despite having persistent or recurrent social or interpersonal problems caused or exacerbated by the effects of cannabis.
7. Important social, occupational, or recreational activities are given up or reduced because of cannabis use.
8. Recurrent cannabis use in situations in which it is physically hazardous.
9. Cannabis use is continued despite knowledge of having a persistent or recurrent physical or psychological problem likely to have been caused or exacerbated by cannabis.
10. Tolerance, as defined by either of the following:
    a. A need for markedly increased amounts of cannabis to achieve intoxication or desired effect.
    b. Markedly diminished effect with continued use of the same amount of cannabis.
11. Withdrawal, as manifested by either of the following:
    a. The characteristic withdrawal syndrome for cannabis
    b. Cannabis (or a closely related substance) is taken to relieve or avoid withdrawal symptoms.

Source: Reprinted with permission from *Diagnostic and Statistical Manual of Mental Disorders, Fifth Edition.*[52]

Cannabis Use Disorder

Unlike problem cannabis use, CUD is a diagnosable psychiatric condition defined as a problematic pattern of cannabis use leading to clinically significant personal, social, physical, and/or psychological distress or impairment. Box 2-1 lays out the 11 CUD symptoms identified by the American Psychiatric Association; the severity of the condition worsens (mild, medium, or severe) as the number of symptoms increases.[52]

Approximately 22% of cannabis users will develop a CUD and 13% will have cannabis dependence; the likelihood of developing cannabis dependence increases to one in three among those who use cannabis on a weekly or daily basis.[53] Black Americans (2.4% in 2013), Native Americans (4.15%), and mixed-race adults (3.5%) have a higher prevalence of cannabis abuse or dependence compared with White Americans (1.3%).[54]

Cannabis and Other Substances

Do cannabis users substitute cannabis for other drugs (e.g., heroin, alcohol, or tobacco), and thus could one benefit of cannabis use be a reduction in overall harms from drug use? Or does cannabis use more commonly complement use of other drugs, thereby increasing overall drug use? The NASEM committee concluded there was moderate evidence of a statistical association between cannabis use and the development of substance dependence or a substance use disorder for other substances, including alcohol, tobacco, and other illegal drugs.[2] The relationship between cannabis and other drug use, including tobacco, is complex and sometimes the opposite of popular belief.

Tobacco. The NASEM committee found limited (weak) evidence that cannabis users are more likely to start smoking.[2] However, e-cigarette users may be more likely to use cannabis: a recent systematic review and meta-analysis of 21 studies found that youth with a history of e-cigarette use had significantly higher odds of cannabis use.[55] This confirmed the finding of an earlier systematic review that tobacco use among youth is strongly and independently associated with current and subsequent use of cannabis.[56] What is not clear is the direction of the association—that is, whether e-cigarette or tobacco use leads to cannabis use or the reverse.

Opioids. Cannabis use is clearly associated with polydrug use. Analysis of NSDUH data from 2015 found that medical cannabis users (those who responded yes when asked if any of their cannabis use was recommended by a doctor or other health care professional) were more likely to use prescription pain relievers both medically and nonmedically.[57] Toxicological testing data from two national samples of drivers (FARS from 2011 through 2016 and the 2013–2014 National Roadside Survey) showed that drivers who test positive for cannabis are significantly more likely to test positive for prescription opioids compared with drivers testing negative for cannabis.[44]

However, the NASEM committee found no evidence to support or refute the hypothesis that cannabinoids are an effective treatment for achieving abstinence in the use of addictive substances.[2] A subsequent systematic review and meta-analysis found no consensus among studies that cannabis use is associated with reduced opioid use or longer treatment retention when used during methadone therapy by patients with opioid use disorder.[58] A 2020 review concluded that there were conflicting results and no strong data to support anecdotal and correlational reports of a benefit of cannabis in reducing opioid overdoses.[59] And, in the only data set able to look longitudinally, analysis of data from the National Epidemiologic Survey on Alcohol and Related Conditions (NESARC) from 2001–2002 and 2004–2005 showed that cannabis use appeared to increase rather than decrease risk of nonmedical prescription opioid use and opioid use disorder. These results remained robust after controlling for potentially confounding effects of several demographic and clinical covariates strongly associated with cannabis use. The authors speculated that "if cannabis use tends to increase opioid use, it is possible that the recent increase in cannabis use may have worsened the opioid crisis."[60]

Other Health Harms

Both the NASEM committee (substantial evidence) and a recent systematic review and meta-analysis concluded that long-term cannabis smoking is associated with respiratory symptoms such as chronic cough, phlegm, wheezing, sputum production, shortness of breath, and more frequent chronic bronchitis[2,61]; however, evidence is weaker regarding progression to obstructive lung disease, emphysema, or lung cancer, compared with the clear evidence in these areas for chronic tobacco smokers.[62-65]

There is emerging evidence that secondhand cannabis smoke can put nonusers at risk. Because this area of research is relatively new, the evidence comes primarily from single studies as opposed to systematic reviews or meta-analyses. Exposure to rats impaired their cardiovascular functioning considerably longer than exposure to tobacco smoke,[66] while chemical analysis has found cannabis smoke to contain multiple carcinogenic components in common with tobacco smoke.[67] National Survey on Drug Use and Health data from 2002 to 2015 showed that past-month cannabis use among parents with children in the home increased from 4.9% to 6.8%. In 2015, an estimated 5.3 million to 9 million children in the United States lived with a parent who currently used cannabis.[68] In one study, researchers placed air particle monitors in 298 homes in San Diego, California. Homes where parents reported smoking cannabis had seven-day average air particle concentrations at levels similar to homes of tobacco-smoking parents. Children living in homes with indoor cannabis use had 83% higher odds of adverse health outcomes compared with children in homes with no indoor cannabis smoking. While not statistically significant, these findings suggest the need to monitor and research the impact on children of secondhand cannabis smoke.[69]

The NASEM committee also found substantial evidence that smoking cannabis during pregnancy is associated with lower birth weight.[2] While there is limited research that THC is detectable in human milk,[70] the American Academy of Pediatrics concluded in a 2018 review that there was insufficient evidence to determine the safety or harm of cannabis use during breastfeeding.[71]

While the NASEM report found limited evidence of an association between cannabis use and ischemic strokes or the triggering of acute myocardial infarctions (heart attacks),[2] a systematic review published in 2017 found an association between exposure to cannabis-based products and cardiovascular disease, with the strongest evidence in relation to ischemic strokes.[72] The American Heart Association issued a scientific statement in September 2020 that stated that the evidence is still inconclusive for cannabis use and adverse cardiovascular outcomes.[73]

Appendix 1 provides the complete list of findings of the NASEM committee—nearly 100 conclusions regarding health effects of cannabis and cannabinoids, which the appendix categorizes by strength of research evidence. Building upon the NASEM findings, recent systematic reviews confirm that cannabis use is associated with higher risks of psychosis, motor vehicle crashes, respiratory problems, testicular cancer, and low birth weight.[22,61,65,74]

CANNABIS HARMS AND THE CHANGING LEGAL CONTEXT

Ideally, research into the experiments that states and countries are undertaking regarding cannabis legalization would provide additional insight into the degree to which cannabis use helps or harms human health. However, states and countries have gone about making cannabis more widely available in very different ways, making comparison of "legalized" versus "medicalized" versus other states a complex endeavor. With that caveat in mind, we summarize what research has found thus far on health effects of widening cannabis availability.

Cannabis Use Disorders

One of the most pressing questions regarding legalization is whether it increases use among young people. Chapter 1 already presented the very mixed findings in response to this question. Regarding harms among youth, the first national study to examine the association of state legalization of cannabis for nonmedical use with prevalence of CUD appeared in 2019. It found a 25% greater increase of past-year CUD—a rise from 2.18% to 2.72%—among 12- to 17-year-olds after enactment of laws legalizing cannabis for nonmedical use, compared with states that did not enact these laws; however, a sensitivity analysis indicated that unmeasured confounders may explain the association. As pointed out in Chapter 1, this problem appeared not to affect the increase found in past-year CUD in the 26 and older age group, from 0.9% to 1.23%.[75]

Multiple studies have found that medical marijuana laws have been associated with higher adult treatment admissions for cannabis use disorders,[76] particularly in states that have allowed dispensaries.[77,78] According to one study, between 1992 and 2012 an additional 500,000 cases of CUD among adults may have been attributable to the implementation of medical cannabis laws.[79] However, it is difficult to credit effects of this size to medical marijuana laws alone. As Smart and Pacula have cautioned, national surveys indicate that medical cannabis users represent less than 10% of past-year cannabis users, and as such, "medical cannabis laws target a group that is far too small to drive the effects we are seeing in many of these population studies."[80]

Cannabis-Impaired Driving

Multiple studies have found that as legal availability increases, whether through medicalization or full legalization, more drivers test positive for cannabis; however, research is still mixed regarding whether legalization results in more cannabis-involved fatal crashes, or even more fatal traffic crashes overall, since measurement of cannabis involvement is so challenging. Research is also needed to ascertain whether drivers may be substituting cannabis for alcohol. The following bullets summarize key findings thus far:

- Analysis of data from FARS (the principal federal source for data on highway safety) on fatal car crashes in six states from 1999 to 2010 found that the presence of cannabis (or cannabinol, a metabolite of THC) in drivers increased from 4.2% to 12.2%.[81] However, FARS data come to the federal government from the states and territories, and their validity is limited by the lack of consistent drug-testing policies and procedures among states and how the states report these to the federal government.[82]

- From 2007 to 2010 in California, a period in which the state permitted medical cannabis use, drivers testing positive for cannabis significantly increased; by 2010, 8.5% of weekend nighttime drivers tested positive for THC, and medical cannabis permit holders were more likely than non–permit holders to test positive for THC.[83]

- Colorado permitted medical use of cannabis in 2000 but greatly loosened restrictions on it in 2009. Analysis of FARS data from Colorado from 1994 to 2011, compared with data from 34 nonmedical cannabis states, found a decline in marijuana-positive drivers in the medicalization period prior to 2009, followed by a rapid increase: by the end of 2011, 10% of drivers were testing positive for cannabis use.[84]

- FARS data analyzed from 2009 to 2015 found that three years after Colorado and Washington State legalized cannabis for nonmedical use, changes in motor vehicle crash fatality rates were not statistically different from those in similar states that had not legalized cannabis for medical or nonmedical use.[85] However, note that commercial sales in these states did not begin until 2014.

- Another study that examined Colorado and Washington data from 2000 to 2016 used synthetic controls (i.e., control groups created to emulate certain variables in the experimental states) and found similar changes in cannabis-related, alcohol-related, and overall traffic fatality rates between the control groups and the two states, suggesting legalization did not affect these rates.[86]

- Roadside surveys in Washington immediately before legalization of cannabis sales in 2014, and six months and one year after implementation, found an increase in the percentage of drivers who tested positive for THC, from 14.6% prior to legal cannabis sales to 21.4% one year later, but the change was not statistically significant.[87]

- A more recent study in the same state found that the proportion of cannabis-positive drivers involved in fatal crashes had doubled since legalization; by 2017, 21% of all drivers involved in fatal crashes were THC-positive.[88]

- An ecological study that examined changes in traffic fatalities in Colorado and Washington since the opening of retail cannabis stores (with FARS data from 2014 to 2017 compared with data from 2005 through 2013 and using synthetic controls) found legalizing cannabis for nonmedical use associated with an increase in traffic fatalities in Colorado but not in Washington. The authors speculate that changes in how the laws were implemented (e.g., density of retail cannabis stores), out-of-state cannabis tourism, and local factors may explain the different results.[89]

- A 2020 study that looked at data from Alaska, Colorado, Oregon, and Washington with two years of data after the opening of retail stores found that legalizing cannabis for nonmedical use was associated with increased traffic fatality rates. Applying these rates to the nation (should national legalization occur) would yield an estimate of 6,800 excess traffic fatalities each year.[90]

The fact that studies with more data since commercialization find greater effects than earlier work underscores the need for continued surveillance and study and points toward the possibility that effects will be greater with full implementation of legalization (e.g., opening and outlet density of retail cannabis stores). The majority of studies conducted to date have focused on traffic fatalities, and it is possible that cannabis impairment may be more associated with nonfatal traffic crashes, but analyses of these data are even more difficult because of challenges with reporting and data availability.[86] Finally, measurement problems abound in the assessment of cannabis use and intoxication in conjunction with driving, a topic covered in greater detail in Chapter 9.

Cannabis and Hospitalizations

Several studies have looked at hospital data from Colorado to evaluate the impact of legalization on health. One retrospective study compared data from three Colorado trauma centers with three trauma centers in states without "permissive marijuana laws" from 2012 to 2015. Rates for cannabis-related traumatic injury (e.g., from a motor vehicle crash, fall, sports, gunshot wound) serious enough for the full trauma team to be activated increased in the Colorado centers specifically after retail cannabis sales began in 2014, but not in the other states.[91] Hospitalizations with cannabis-related codes increased by 70% between 2013 and 2015 in Colorado, pre-legislation and post-legalization. Cannabis-related emergency department visits increased by 19% between 2013 and 2014, with a disproportionate increase among tourists, but decreased 27% between 2014 and 2015, to a rate lower than in 2013.[92,93]

Finally, a retrospective study of nearly 10,000 emergency department visits to a single Colorado hospital between 2012 and 2016 found that approximately a quarter (25.7%) were at least partially attributable to cannabis, with more than a third of these—9.3%—related to edible cannabis. Edible products accounted for 10.7% of cannabis-attributable visits between 2014 and 2016, at a time when sales of edibles represented only 0.32% of total cannabis sales (as measured by kilograms of THC) in Colorado.[94]

Cannabis and Poisonings

Analysis of cannabis exposures reported to the US National Poison Data System from 2010 to 2017, comparing the 10 states permitting legal sale of cannabis to states that did not, and taking into account when sales were fully legalized, revealed that the start of nonmedical cannabis commercialization was associated with 5.06–5.80 more exposures per 1,000,000 population per quarter, which was a 67%–77% increase relative to the prelegalization average.[95]

CONCLUSION

There are four conditions for which the evidence is substantial that cannabis and cannabinoid use may be beneficial, and there is a longer list of probable harms. As the data from both hospitalizations and poisonings post-legalization show, the forms in which cannabis is made available and the legal structures surrounding that availability both play an important role in determining how much harm cannabis use can cause. The next two chapters focus on these two important topics: the rapidly evolving nature of cannabis as a product and the options for creating broad regulatory systems to govern its availability should states decide to loosen prohibitions or restrictions on cannabis use and/or sales.

REFERENCES

1. US Food and Drug Administration. FDA regulation of cannabis and cannabis-derived products: questions and answers. 2019. Available at: https://www.fda.gov/newsevents/publichealthfocus/ucm421168.htm. Accessed March 23, 2021.

2. National Academies of Sciences, Engineering, and Medicine. *The Health Effects of Cannabis and Cannabinoids: The Current State of Evidence and Recommendations for Research.* Washington, DC: National Academies Press; 2017.

3. Marijuana plant material available from the NIDA Drug Supply Program. 2016. Available at: https://www.drugabuse.gov/research/research-data-measures-resources/nida-drug-supply-program-dsp/nida-drug-supply-program-dsp-ordering-guidelines/marijuana-plant-material-available. Accessed March 23, 2021.

4. Stith SS, Vigil JM. Federal barriers to *Cannabis* research. *Science.* 2016;352(6290):1182.

5. Vergara D, Bidwell LC, Gaudino R, et al. Compromised external validity: federally produced cannabis does not reflect legal markets. *Sci Rep.* 2017;7(46528).

6. Levinsohn EA, Hill KP. Clinical uses of cannabis and cannabinoids in the United States. *J Neurol Sci.* 2020;411:116717.

7. Klieger SB, Gutman A, Allen L, Pacula RL, Ibrahim JK, Burris S. Mapping medical marijuana: state laws regulating patients, product safety, supply chains and dispensaries, 2017. *Addiction.* 2017;112(12):2206–2216.

8. Stockings E, Campbell G, Hall WD, et al. Cannabis and cannabinoids for the treatment of people with chronic noncancer pain conditions: a systematic review and meta-analysis of controlled and observational studies. *Pain.* 2018;159(10):1932–1954.

9. Mücke M, Phillips T, Radbruch L, Petzke F, Häuser W. Cannabis-based medicines for chronic neuropathic pain in adults. *Cochrane Database Syst Rev.* 2018;3(3):CD012182.

10. Nugent SM, Morasco BJ, O'Neil ME, et al. The effects of cannabis among adults with chronic pain and an overview of general harms: a systematic review. *Ann Intern Med.* 2017;167(5): 319–331.

11. Fisher E, Moore RA, Fogarty AE, et al. Cannabinoids, cannabis, and cannabis-based medicine for pain management: a systematic review of randomised controlled trials. *Pain.* 2020.

12. Moore RA, Fisher E, Finn DP, et al. Cannabinoids, cannabis, and cannabis-based medicines for pain management: an overview of systematic reviews. *Pain.* 2020.

13. Stockings E, Zagic D, Campbell G, et al. Evidence for cannabis and cannabinoids for epilepsy: a systematic review of controlled and observational evidence. *J Neurol Neurosurg Psychiatry.* 2018;89(7):741–753.

14. Braithwaite I, Bhagavan C, Doppen M, Kung S, Oldfield K, Newton-Howes G. Medicinal applications of cannabis/cannabinoids. *Curr Opin Psychol.* 2020;38:1–10.

15. Kuhathasan N, Dufort A, MacKillop J, Gottschalk R, Minuzzi L, Frey BN. The use of cannabinoids for sleep: a critical review on clinical trials. *Exp Clin Psychopharmacol.* 2019;27(4): 383–401.

16. O'Neil ME, Nugent SM, Morasco BJ, et al. Benefits and harms of plant-based cannabis for posttraumatic stress disorder: a systematic review. *Ann Intern Med.* 2017;167(5):332–340.

17. Orsolini L, Chiappini S, Volpe U, et al. Use of medicinal cannabis and synthetic cannabinoids in post-traumatic stress disorder (PTSD): a systematic review. *Medicina (Kaunas).* 2019;55(9):525.

18. Sarris J, Sinclair J, Karamacoska D, Davidson M, Firth J. Medicinal cannabis for psychiatric disorders: a clinically-focused systematic review. *BMC Psychiatry.* 2020;20(1):24.

19. Black N, Stockings E, Campbell G, et al. Cannabinoids for the treatment of mental disorders and symptoms of mental disorders: a systematic review and meta-analysis. *Lancet Psychiatry.* 2019;6(12):995–1010.

20. Keyhani S, Steigerwald S, Ishida J, et al. Risks and benefits of marijuana use: a national survey of US adults. *Ann Intern Med.* 2018;169(5):282–290.

21. Abraham A, Zhang AJ, Ahn R, Woodbridge A, Korenstein D, Keyhani S. Media content analysis of marijuana's health effects in news coverage. *J Gen Intern Med.* 2018;33(9):1438–1440.

22. Campeny E, Lopez-Pelayo H, Nutt D, et al. The blind men and the elephant: systematic review of systematic reviews of cannabis use related health harms. *Eur Neuropsychopharmacol.* 2020;33:1–35.

23. Substance Abuse and Mental Health Services Administration. *Key Substance Use and Mental Health Indicators in the United States: Results from the 2018 National Survey on Drug Use and Health.* Rockville, MD: Center for Behavioral Health Statistics and Quality, Substance Abuse and Mental Health Services Administration; 2019. HHS Publication No. PEP19-5068. NSDUH Series H-54.

24. Hurd YL, Michaelides M, Miller ML, Jutras-Aswad D. Trajectory of adolescent cannabis use on addiction vulnerability. *Neuropharmacology.* 2014;76(pt B):416–424.

25. Volkow ND, Baler RD, Compton WM, Weiss SR. Adverse health effects of marijuana use. *N Engl J Med.* 2014;371(9):879.

26. Horwood LJ, Fergusson DM, Hayatbakhsh MR, et al. Cannabis use and educational achievement: findings from three Australasian cohort studies. *Drug Alcohol Depend.* 2010;110(3):247–253.

27. Silins E, Horwood LJ, Patton GC, et al. Young adult sequelae of adolescent cannabis use: an integrative analysis. *Lancet Psychiatry.* 2014;1(4):286–293.

28. Wilson J, Freeman TP, Mackie CJ. Effects of increasing cannabis potency on adolescent health. *Lancet Child Adolesc Health.* 2019;3(2):121–128.

29. Di Forti M, Quattrone D, Freeman TP, et al. The contribution of cannabis use to variation in the incidence of psychotic disorder across Europe (EU-GEI): a multicentre case-control study. *Lancet Psychiatry.* 2019;6(5):427–436.

30. Gobbi G, Atkin T, Zytynski T, et al. Association of cannabis use in adolescence and risk of depression, anxiety, and suicidality in young adulthood: a systematic review and meta-analysis. *JAMA Psychiatry.* 2019;76(4):426–434.

31. Patel S, Khan S, M S, Hamid P. The association between cannabis use and schizophrenia: causative or curative? a systematic review. *Cureus.* 2020;12(7):e9309.

32. Murrie B, Lappin J, Large M, Sara G. Transition of substance-induced, brief, and atypical psychoses to schizophrenia: a systematic review and meta-analysis. *Schizophr Bull.* 2020;46(3):505–516.

33. Sabe M, Zhao N, Kaiser S. Cannabis, nicotine and the negative symptoms of schizophrenia: systematic review and meta-analysis of observational studies. *Neurosci Biobehav Rev.* 2020;116:415–425.

34. Berning A, Compton R, Wochinger K. *Results of the 2013–2014 National Roadside Survey of Alcohol and Drug Use by Drivers.* Washington, DC: National Highway Traffic Safety Administration; 2015.

35. Azofeifa A, Rexach-Guzman BD, Hagemeyer AN, Rudd RA, Sauber-Schatz EK. Driving under the influence of marijuana and illicit drugs among persons aged >/=16 years— United States, 2018. *MMWR Morb Mortal Wkly Rep.* 2019;68(50):1153–1157.

36. Holden D. Half of marijuana users in the US think they're fine to drive stoned. *BuzzFeed News*. April 23, 2019. Available at: https://www.buzzfeednews.com/article/dominicholden/half-marijuana-users-us-safe-drive-while-high. Accessed March 23, 2021.

37. Micallef J, Dupouey J, Jouve E, et al. Cannabis smoking impairs driving performance on the simulator and real driving: a randomized, double-blind, placebo-controlled, crossover trial. *Fundam Clin Pharmacol*. 2018;32(5):558–570.

38. Ronen A, Gershon P, Drobiner H, et al. Effects of THC on driving performance, physiological state and subjective feelings relative to alcohol. *Accid Anal Prev*. 2008;40(3):926–934.

39. Huestis MA. Human cannabinoid pharmacokinetics. *Chem Biodivers*. 2007;4(8):1770–1804.

40. Hartman RL, Huestis MA. Cannabis effects on driving skills. *Clin Chem*. 2013;59(3):478–492.

41. Schwope DM, Bosker WM, Ramaekers JG, Gorelick DA, Huestis MA. Psychomotor performance, subjective and physiological effects and whole blood Delta(9)-tetrahydrocannabinol concentrations in heavy, chronic cannabis smokers following acute smoked cannabis. *J Anal Toxicol*. 2012;36(6):405–412.

42. Downey LA, King R, Papafotiou K, et al. The effects of cannabis and alcohol on simulated driving: Influences of dose and experience. *Accid Anal Prev*. 2013;50:879–886.

43. Lukas SE, Orozco S. Ethanol increases plasma Delta(9)-tetrahydrocannabinol (THC) levels and subjective effects after marihuana smoking in human volunteers. *Drug Alcohol Depend*. 2001;64(2):143–149.

44. Li G, Chihuri S. Is marijuana use associated with decreased use of prescription opioids? toxicological findings from two US national samples of drivers. *Subst Abuse Treat Prev Policy*. 2020;15(1):12.

45. Rogeberg O, Elvik R. The effects of cannabis intoxication on motor vehicle collision revisited and revised. *Addiction*. 2016;111(8):1348–1359.

46. Kuhns JB, Wilson DB, Maguire ER, Ainsworth SA, Clodfelter TA. A meta-analysis of marijuana, cocaine and opiate toxicology study findings among homicide victims. *Addiction*. 2009;104(7):1122–1131.

47. Nazarov O, Li G. Trends in alcohol and marijuana detected in homicide victims in 9 US states: 2004–2016. *Inj Epidemiol*. 2020;7(1):2.

48. Naimi TS, Xuan Z, Cooper SE, et al. Alcohol involvement in homicide victimization in the United States. *Alcohol Clin Exp Res*. 2016;40(12):2614–2621.

49. Darke S. The toxicology of homicide offenders and victims: a review. *Drug Alcohol Rev*. 2010;29(2):202–215.

50. National Institute on Alcohol Abuse and Alcoholism. Drinking levels defined. National Institutes of Health. 2020. Available at: https://www.niaaa.nih.gov/alcohol-health/overview-alcohol-consumption/moderate-binge-drinking. Accessed March 23, 2021.

51. Casajuana C, Lopez-Pelayo H, Balcells MM, Miquel L, Colom J, Gual A. definitions of risky and problematic cannabis use: a systematic review. *Subst Use Misuse.* 2016;51(13):1760–1770.

52. American Psychiatric Association. *The Diagnostic and Statistical Manual of Mental Disorders, 5th Edition.* 2013.

53. Leung J, Chan GCK, Hides L, Hall WD. What is the prevalence and risk of cannabis use disorders among people who use cannabis? a systematic review and meta-analysis. *Addict Behav.* 2020;109:106479.

54. Wu L-T, Zhu H, Swartz MS. Trends in cannabis use disorders among racial/ethnic population groups in the United States. *Drug Alcohol Depend.* 2016;165:181–190.

55. Chadi N, Schroeder R, Jensen JW, Levy S. Association between electronic cigarette use and marijuana use among adolescents and young adults: a systematic review and meta-analysis. *JAMA Pediatr.* 2019;173(10):e192574.

56. Ramo DE, Liu H, Prochaska JJ. Tobacco and marijuana use among adolescents and young adults: a systematic review of their co-use. *Clin Psychol Rev.* 2012;32(2):105–121.

57. Caputi TL, Humphreys K. Medical marijuana users are more likely to use prescription drugs medically and nonmedically. *J Addict Med.* 2018;12(4):295–299.

58. McBrien H, Luo C, Sanger N, et al. Cannabis use during methadone maintenance treatment for opioid use disorder: a systematic review and meta-analysis. *CMAJ Open.* 2019;7(4):E665–E673.

59. Babalonis S, Walsh SL. Therapeutic potential of opioid/cannabinoid combinations in humans: review of the evidence. *Eur Neuropsychopharmacol.* 2020;36:206–216.

60. Olfson M, Wall MM, Liu S-M, Blanco C. Cannabis use and risk of prescription opioid use disorder in the United States. *Am J Psychiatry.* 2018;175(1):47–53.

61. Ghasemiesfe M, Ravi D, Vali M, et al. Marijuana use, respiratory symptoms, and pulmonary function: a systematic review and meta-analysis. *Ann Intern Med.* 2018;169(2):106–115.

62. Tashkin DP, Roth MD. Pulmonary effects of inhaled cannabis smoke. *Am J Drug Alcohol Abuse.* 2019;45(6):596–609.

63. Ribeiro L, Ind PW. Marijuana and the lung: hysteria or cause for concern? *Breathe (Sheff).* 2018;14(3):196–205.

64. Martinasek MP, McGrogan JB, Maysonet A. A systematic review of the respiratory effects of inhalational marijuana. *Respir Care.* 2016;61(11):1543–1551.

65. Ghasemiesfe M, Barrow B, Leonard S, Keyhani S, Korenstein D. Association between marijuana use and risk of cancer: a systematic review and meta-analysis. *JAMA Netw Open.* 2019;2(11):e1916318.

66. Wang X, Derakhshandeh R, Liu J, et al. One minute of marijuana secondhand smoke exposure substantially impairs vascular endothelial function. *J Am Heart Assoc.* 2016;5(8):e003858.

67. Moir D, Rickert WS, Levasseur G, et al. A comparison of mainstream and sidestream marijuana and tobacco cigarette smoke produced under two machine smoking conditions. *Chem Res Toxicol.* 2008;21(2):494–502.

68. Goodwin RD, Cheslack-Postava K, Santoscoy S, et al. Trends in cannabis and cigarette use among parents with children at home: 2002 to 2015. *Pediatrics.* 2018;141(6):e20173506.

69. Posis A, Bellettiere J, Liles S, et al. Indoor cannabis smoke and children's health. *Prev Med Rep.* 2019;14:100853.

70. Bertrand KA, Hanan NJ, Honerkamp-Smith G, Best BM, Chambers CD. Marijuana use by breastfeeding mothers and cannabinoid concentrations in breast milk. *Pediatrics.* 2018;142(3):e20181076.

71. Ryan SA, Ammerman SD, O'Connor ME, Committee on Substance Use and Prevention, Section on Breastfeeding. Marijuana use during pregnancy and breastfeeding: implications for neonatal and childhood outcomes. *Pediatrics.* 2018;142(3):e20181889.

72. Jouanjus E, Raymond V, Lapeyre-Mestre M, Wolff V. What is the current knowledge about the cardiovascular risk for users of cannabis-based products? a systematic review. *Curr Atheroscler Rep.* 2017;19(6):26.

73. Page RL 2nd, Allen LA, Kloner RA, et al. Medical marijuana, recreational cannabis, and cardiovascular health: a scientific statement from the American Heart Association. *Circulation.* 2020;142(10):e131–e152.

74. Mohiuddin M, Blyth FM, Degenhardt L, et al. General risks of harm with cannabinoids, cannabis, and cannabis-based medicine possibly relevant to patients receiving these for pain management: an overview of systematic reviews. *Pain.* 2020.

75. Cerda M, Mauro C, Hamilton A, et al. Association between recreational marijuana legalization in the United States and changes in marijuana use and cannabis use disorder from 2008 to 2016. *JAMA Psychiatry.* 2020;77(2):165–171.

76. Chu YW. The effects of medical marijuana laws on illegal marijuana use. *J Health Econ.* 2014;38:43–61.

77. Pacula RL, Powell D, Heaton P, Sevigny EL. Assessing the effects of medical marijuana laws on marijuana use: the devil is in the details. *J Policy Anal Manage.* 2015;34(1):7–31.

78. Wen H, Hockenberry JM, Cummings JR. The effect of medical marijuana laws on adolescent and adult use of marijuana, alcohol, and other substances. *J Health Econ.* 2015;42:64–80.

79. Hasin DS, Sarvet AL, Cerda M, et al. US adult illicit cannabis use, cannabis use disorder, and medical marijuana laws: 1991–1992 to 2012–2013. *JAMA Psychiatry.* 2017;74(6):579–588.

80. Smart R, Pacula RL. Early evidence of the impact of cannabis legalization on cannabis use, cannabis use disorder, and the use of other substances: findings from state policy evaluations. *Am J Drug Alcohol Abuse.* 2019;45(6):644–663.

81. Brady JE, Li G. Trends in alcohol and other drugs detected in fatally injured drivers in the United States, 1999–2010. *Am J Epidemiol.* 2014;179(6):692–699.

82. Berning A, Smither DD. Understanding the limitations of drug test information, reporting, and testing practices in fatal crashes. National Highway Traffic Safety Administration; 2014. Traffic Safety Facts Research Note. DOT HS 812 072. Available at: https://crashstats.nhtsa.dot.gov/Api/Public/ViewPublication/812072. Accessed March 24, 2021.

83. Johnson MB, Kelley-Baker T, Voas RB, Lacey JH. The prevalence of cannabis-involved driving in California. *Drug Alcohol Depend.* 2012;123(1–3):105–109.

84. Salomonsen-Sautel S, Min SJ, Sakai JT, Thurstone C, Hopfer C. Trends in fatal motor vehicle crashes before and after marijuana commercialization in Colorado. *Drug Alcohol Depend.* 2014;140:137–144.

85. Aydelotte JD, Brown LH, Luftman KM, et al. Crash fatality rates after recreational marijuana legalization in Washington and Colorado. *Am J Public Health.* 2017;107(8):1329–1331.

86. Hansen B, Miller K, Weber C. Early evidence on recreational marijuana legalization and traffic fatalities. *Econ Inquiry.* 2020;58(2):547–568.

87. Ramirez A, Berning A, Carr K, et al. *Marijuana, Other Drugs, and Alcohol Use by Drivers in Washington State.* Washington, DC: National Highway Traffic Safety Administration; 2016. DOT HS 812 299.

88. Tefft BC, Arnold LS. *Cannabis Use Among Drivers in Fatal Crashes in Washington State Before and After Legalization.* Washington, DC: AAA Foundation for Traffic Safety; 2020.

89. Santaella-Tenorio J, Wheeler-Martin K, DiMaggio CJ, et al. Association of recreational cannabis laws in Colorado and Washington State with changes in traffic fatalities, 2005–2017. *JAMA Intern Med.* 2020;180(8):1061–1068.

90. Kamer RS, Warshafsky S, Kamer GC. Change in traffic fatality rates in the first 4 states to legalize recreational marijuana. *JAMA Intern Med.* 2020;180(8):1119–1120.

91. Chung C, Salottolo K, Tanner A 2nd, et al. The impact of recreational marijuana commercialization on traumatic injury. *Inj Epidemiol.* 2019;6(1):3.

92. Ghosh TS, Vigil DI, Maffey A, et al. Lessons learned after three years of legalized, recreational marijuana: the Colorado experience. *Prev Med.* 2017;104:4–6.

93. Kim HS, Hall KE, Genco EK, Van Dyke M, Barker E, Monte AA. Marijuana tourism and emergency department visits in Colorado. *N Engl J Med.* 2016;374(8):797–798.

94. Monte AA, Shelton SK, Mills E, et al. Acute illness associated with cannabis use, by route of exposure: an observational study. *Ann Internl Med.* 2019;170(8):531–537.

95. Shi Y, Liang D. The association between recreational cannabis commercialization and cannabis exposures reported to the US National Poison Data System. *Addiction.* 2020;115(10):1890–1899.

3

The Changing Cannabis Product Mix and Environmental Health and Quality Concerns

SUMMARY AND INTRODUCTION

- Health effects and outcomes of cannabis use vary based on the component of the plant, its THC content, how it was processed, and the route of ingestion, all of which need to be considered when creating regulations.
- Both potency and route of ingestion are changing, and while smoking continues to be the most common method, there are significant increases in vaping, dabbing, and consuming edibles.
- Federal regulation and research sponsorship have been limited because the federal Controlled Substances Act classifies cannabis as a Schedule I substance with no medical use.
- Thus far, states have been responsible for establishing quality standards, testing for THC content, determining what if any chemicals and pesticides are permitted, and overseeing and regulating the laboratories charged with these responsibilities.
- With rapid product-related changes occurring, states need to establish and continually reevaluate regulatory environments as new products and health data emerge.

Cannabis is a complex substance for would-be regulators. As described in Chapter 1, the cannabis plant has multiple components, only some of which are intoxicating. The plant's intoxicants come in multiple strengths and can be made even stronger through various processing methods. As an agricultural product, cannabis is subject to environmental contaminants that can threaten the health of its users. Cannabis can also be ingested or experienced in a variety of ways, and how users are taking it in is changing over time. This chapter defines and discusses trends in both the range of products available and the modes of their use. It then outlines the challenges governments face in ensuring the safety and quality of these products.

PRODUCTS AND DELIVERY METHODS

Users have access to a changing panoply of products made from cannabis plants, and they consume these products in different ways. Products include concentrates, extracts, and edibles. Delivery methods include smoking or inhaling from cigarettes (joints), pipes (bowls), water pipes (bongs, hookahs), and blunts (cigars filled with cannabis); eating or drinking cannabis-infused food products and beverages; and vaporizing or dabbing the product. Lesser known THC delivery methods include tinctures, strips, sprays, lozenges (all applied orally); transdermal topicals such as lotions, balms, and oils; and intravenous and rectal routes.[1-3] Descriptions of the most common product types and delivery methods follow.

Concentrates and Extracts

Legalization for nonmedical use appears to be driving increased emphasis on THC content, exemplified in the rising use of cannabis concentrates processed to maximize THC while removing excess plant material and other impurities. Concentrates can have THC levels as high as 70 to 90%,[4,5] posing specific and serious health risks.

Extracts are a type of concentrate that use solvents to draw out desired substances from the plant. The primary difference between a concentrate and an extract is how trichomes (the tiny and THC-rich hair- or crystal-like stalks on the surface of the plant) are collected. To produce an extract, a solvent (alcohol, carbon dioxide, butane, propane, etc.) is used to "wash" the trichomes off the cannabis plant.

Butane hash oil (BHO) and carbon dioxide wax (CO_2) are examples of extracts; each of these comes in varying textures such as shatter, badder, budder, and crumble.[6] Rosin and dry sift or "kief" are examples of concentrates made without using solvents.[7] THC crystals now exist as a type of concentrate and can be up to 100% THC (see Figure 3-1 for examples of concentrates).[8,9]

High THC levels in concentrates may have serious health and safety consequences. A study of college students in a state that allowed cannabis use only for medical purposes

Piece of cannabis oil concentrate (shatter)

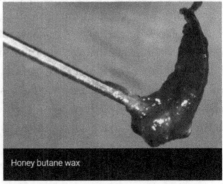
Honey butane wax

Source: Photos reprinted from US Drug Enforcement Administration.[9]

Figure 3-1. Examples of Concentrates

found more frequent use of BHO associated with higher levels of physical dependence, impaired control, cannabis-related academic/occupational problems, poor self-care, and cannabis-related risk behavior. After accounting for potential confounders, BHO use was still associated with higher levels of physical dependence on cannabis, but the study could not determine whether BHO use was leading to physical dependence or if dependent students were more likely to use BHO.[10] Another study found concentrate users at a higher risk of continued and frequent cannabis use. A study of adolescent cannabis use in a cohort of California high school students with no history of heavy cannabis use found that students who used concentrates one or two days a month at baseline had progressed a year later to an average of 9.4 days a month. Users of combustible cannabis increased to about 2.8 days a month, and there were no significant increases among users of blunts, vapor, or edible cannabis.[11]

Beyond the potential harms of high THC content, the process for producing extracts and concentrates can be dangerous as well. A Colorado study of patients admitted for burns associated with BHO extraction found no such cases from January 2008 to September 2009, in that state a period prior to legalization of both commercial production and distribution for medical use, compared with 31 cases from October 2009 to August 2014. (As of January 2014 both medical and nonmedical cannabis were legal in Colorado.) Nearly all the cases were flash burns from explosions within an enclosed space.[12] A similar retrospective chart review of patients in a Northern California burn center between January 2007 and December 2014 (when only medical cannabis was legal in California) found 101 patients burned during the production of BHO, including three who died from their injuries. Five patients were between the ages of 2 and 17. Study authors noted a dramatic increase in patients presenting with such burns, particularly from 2012 to 2014.[13]

Smoking (Combusted Cannabis Materials)

Inhalation is still the most common method of consumption, at least nationally. THC levels can range from less than 1% to approximately 30% in most cannabis materials (e.g., dried buds) used for smoking,[14-17] with average THC levels between 9% and 20%.[17-19] As detailed in Chapter 2, cannabis smoking is associated with a variety of acute and chronic health harms.[1]

Vaping

Vaporizing or "vaping" cannabis has grown in popularity along with nicotine vaping and uses a delivery device known as a vaporizer. These devices heat a liquid and deliver cannabinoids via vapor; they include e-cigarettes, vape pens, and vape mods, which are larger than vape pens and known for higher vapor production. While first-generation vape pens heated oil cartridges to the point of vaporization, newer ones offer more options for vaporizing a variety of products, including dried cannabis buds or leaves and various forms of concentrates, and offer better temperature control and portability.[1,20]

Vaporizers emit minimal odor, rendering public cannabis use less detectable. Vaping cartridges lack standardized levels of THC potency, which can leave consumers confused and result in unintended intoxicating effects. A non-peer-reviewed analysis of 19 samples from 13 popular cartridge brands found that THC content (measured in milligrams per milliliter of concentrate) ranged from 14% to 71%.[21]

Dabbing

"Dabbing" cannabis has become more prevalent as advanced methods of extraction have made available a wider range of cannabis concentrates. Traditionally, dabbing occurs when a user places a cannabis concentrate on a heated water-pipe attachment (known as a nail); the concentrate vaporizes and the user immediately inhales the vapor through a water-pipe device known as a dab rig.[5] BHO is one common form of dabbing concentrate, produced by extracting THC from cannabis plant material using butane as a solvent. BHOs have average THC concentrations of more than 50% to 60% and can go as high as 80%.[18,22,23]

Dabbing draws its popularity from the efficiency with which it can deliver a "high." According to an online convenience sample study of hash oil users (n=357) published in 2014, the most common reasons users preferred dabs to other cannabis products were that they required fewer hits to achieve the desired effects, their effects were stronger, and the "high" had a different effect. A majority of the sample (58%) had used vaporizers before, and of those, 32% preferred dabs to vaporizers. This sample of dab users also self-reported on average an increase in both withdrawal and tolerance compared with when they used flower cannabis.[4]

Edibles

Cannabis-infused edibles, increasingly common in states with nonmedical cannabis markets, may resemble popular candies, sweets, and beverages. Critics have decried their youth appeal and their potential for increasing risk of early initiation and accidental ingestion by very young children unaware that they are consuming a cannabis-infused product.[24-28]

Research suggests that users face at least three barriers to determining appropriate dosages for edibles. The first involves serving size and number of servings. Many products contain multiple servings: For example, a cookie may be labeled as containing multiple servings but be packaged and marketed as if it were a single serving. A chocolate bar may offer 100 mg of THC but not be divided into individually packaged 10 mg pieces. Such ambiguities render users vulnerable to mistakenly consuming multiple doses at once.[29]

Second, edible products may have unequal amounts of THC concentration within a particular product and the concentration may be mislabeled. Tests conducted in 2014 (prior to legalization of cannabis for nonmedical use) of retail products selected from dispensaries in cities in California and Washington State showed that of 75 products tested, 17% were accurately labeled, 23% contained more than the stated dose, and 60% contained less than the stated dose.[30] There are also food-safety hazards: since production of cannabis-infused edibles or beverages involves many steps, from cultivation to processing the cannabis to manufacturing the food and infusing the cannabis, at each step contamination or other safety issues may occur.[31]

Third, as shown in Table 3-1, intoxication from edibles occurs more slowly than with other delivery methods, making consumers vulnerable to believing that they have consumed less than intended.[32] When consumed orally, the THC in cannabis travels through the gastrointestinal tract to the bloodstream and next to the liver, where it converts to a more potent form that then crosses the blood-brain barrier. Smoked or vaped cannabis, in contrast, reaches the brain within minutes, causing a stronger peak effect but a briefer "high." The result is that consumers of edibles experience slower but longer-lasting intoxication.[33]

Tinctures

Cannabis tinctures are alcohol-based cannabis extracts that are normally placed under the tongue or directly in the mouth. Tinctures can also be blended with food and beverages.

Delivery Methods and Intoxicating Effects

Table 3-1 summarizes cannabis's intoxicating effects, including onset, intensity, and duration, based on the most common delivery methods. Smoking, vaping, and dabbing rapidly deliver THC from the lungs to the brain, while oral ingestion results in slower and more delayed peak THC concentration.[2] Other individual-level factors that may influence the effects of cannabis include amount consumed, the consumer's weight, and the consumer's metabolism and excretion rates.

As described in Chapter 1, a systematic review of studies examining how cannabidiol (CBD) influences the effects of THC in humans concluded that when cannabis contains

Table 3-1. Routes of Administration and Time Frames for THC Intoxication

Route of Administration	Time Until "High"	Intensity and Length of "High"
Smoking/Vaping	Seconds to minutes	1 to 3.5 hours
Dabbing	Seconds to minutes	Reported stronger intoxicating effect than smoking/vaping
Edibles	30 minutes to 2 hours	5 to 8 hours

Source: Based on NASEM.[3]

a combination of THC and CBD, CBD may reduce the effects of THC. Results have been mixed, however, as various studies considered different dosage levels, routes of administration, and THC-to-CBD ratios.[34,35] Nevertheless, the Lower-Risk Cannabis Use Guidelines, developed based on existing science by an international group of public health experts, include a recommendation that users choose products with a balanced THC-to-CBD ratio.[36]

TRENDS IN MODES OF USE

The limited data available suggest that both youth and adults are changing their modes of consumption as cannabis becomes more legally available,[33] with a higher percentage of users dabbing, vaping, and consuming edibles.

Adults

In 2014, data from a national consumer panel survey of adults found that the overwhelming majority of cannabis users were smoking it. Just 16.1% consumed edibles, 7.6% reported vaping, and prevalence of dabbing was so low that it was included in an "other" category.[37] Just two years later, 6,000 participants age 18 and older from 12 states answered an optional marijuana module in the Behavioral Risk Factor Surveillance System from the Centers for Disease Control and Prevention (CDC). In this sample

- The prevalence of past-month cannabis use was 9.1%, and the most commonly reported mode of use was smoking (90.7%); and
- Almost 25% reported consuming edibles, 19.5% reporting vaping, 14.6% reported dabbing, and nearly a third used multiple modes to consume cannabis.[38]

From 2016 to 2017 in Colorado, the number of adults reporting multiple use methods rose from 43.1% to 50%. By 2017, while smoking was still the most common method (84.3%), eating or drinking had risen to 40.4%, vaping to 29.1%, and dabbing to 21.1%. The increases in all three methods of use were significant compared with 2016 data.[39] In Washington State, vaporizable concentrate sales increased by 770% from the 2014–15 to the 2015–16 fiscal year.[40]

Youth

Adolescent modes of cannabis consumption appear to be shifting toward more potent products and delivery methods, which may pose more significant harms.[1] An analysis of Monitoring the Future data gathered by the National Institute on Drug Abuse from 2015 to 2018 found that among 12th-grade past-year cannabis users, smoking prevalence was decreasing and vaping and edible use was on the rise.[41] (See Box 3-1 on EVALI.) Nationally, a 2016 sample (n=2,630) of adolescents recruited through online advertisements found that while 99% of cannabis users smoked cannabis, 61% consumed edibles and 44% reported vaping cannabis.[50] In Colorado in 2015, 40% of high school students who had used cannabis in the past month reported multiple modes of use, including 28% who dabbed and 21.8% who vaped.[51] From 2015 to 2017, among Colorado high school students cannabis smoking decreased from 86.8% to 77.8% and vaping fell from 5.1% to 4.0%. At the same time, the number of users ingesting rose from 2.1% to 9.8% and dabbers grew from 4.3% to 7.6%.[52]

In California, a survey of 5,390 high school students in one school district (conducted prior to legalization of cannabis for nonmedical use) found that 33% had used cannabis in their lifetime. Half of these reported using cannabis in the past 30 days, and 72% of lifetime and 82% of past-month users reported using edibles in their lifetimes.[53] Young edible users consumed cannabis more frequently in the past 30 days, were more likely to do so on school property, first used it at a younger age, and made more attempts to stop using than nonedible cannabis users.[53] In youth focus groups conducted in the San Francisco Bay Area, teens reported consuming edibles primarily to reduce the likelihood of getting caught with a cannabis product.[54] These findings point to the need to put in place additional protections to reduce youth access to edibles and high-potency products.

Box 3-1. E-cigarette, or Vaping, Product Use–Associated Lung Injury

A well-publicized outbreak of severe pulmonary disease among vapers in 2019 turned out to be attributable primarily to the use not of e-cigarettes but of THC-containing vaping products.[42] As of February 2020, the Centers for Disease Control and Prevention (CDC) reported 2,807 hospitalizations with 68 deaths related to e-cigarette or vaping product use-associated lung injury (EVALI). Of 2,022 hospitalized patients who had provided data on substance use by January 2020, 82% reported using THC-containing products and 33% reported exclusive use of THC-containing products.[43] Eighty percent of those hospitalized used THC vaping products, with a median patient age of 24 years; 16% of those hospitalized were under 18.[44] These vaping products came primarily from informal rather than commercial sources: of the 809 patients who named a source for their THC products, 78% acquired them solely from informal and therefore likely unregulated sources (i.e., friends, family, dealers, or other sources) and 16% used only commercial sources; the remaining 6% used products from both sources.[45] Laboratory studies found vitamin E acetate, used as a thickening agent in vaping products containing THC, strongly linked to the EVALI outbreak,[46,47] but it is possible that other chemicals contributed as well.[48] The CDC has recommended against adding vitamin E acetate to any e-cigarette or vaping product[43]; however, as of December 2019, only a few states had passed laws banning the use of vitamin E acetate in vaping products.[49]

TRENDS IN POTENCY

Even before the advent of the newer extraction methods described above, there was evidence of a trend toward stronger cannabis products. A 2016 primer on cannabis legalization observed that "counting extracts, today's material is perhaps five times as potent, on average, as the material the baby boomers started smoking in the 1960s".[55]

The authors identified four key factors in cannabis cultivation and preparation for market that have led to this dramatic change in potency:

- Change in the market from selling leaves to selling flowers;
- Shift away from pollinated plants to sinsemilla produced by unpollinated female plants;
- Advanced growing techniques (controlled environments with regard to lighting, fertilizer, and soil); and
- Selective breeding.[55]

Several sources confirm this trend. Average potency of cannabis products seized by the Drug Enforcement Administration (DEA) rose from approximately 4% in 1995 to 12% in 2014, while the CBD content fell from approximately 0.28% to less than 0.15%. This amounts to a change in THC-to-CBD ratio from 14:1 in 1995 to 80:1 in 2014.[22] By 2017, the average THC concentration of seized DEA products rose to 17.1% and the mean CBD concentration dropped to 0.14%, continuing upward trends in THC potency levels and THC-to-CBD ratios.[17]

In Europe, resin (hashish or hash) potency increased from an average of 8.14% THC in 2006 to 17.22% in 2016, while herbal cannabis potency rose from 5% to 10.22% THC.[56] A systematic review and meta-analysis of studies from seven countries published between 1970 and 2017 found THC concentrations in herbal cannabis up by 0.29% each year, THC concentrations in resin increasing by 0.57% each year, and no evidence of changes in CBD levels in either herbal cannabis or resin.[15]

In Washington State, from July 2014 to September 2016 cannabis flowers accounted for two-thirds of total expenditures, but their market share declined over time, as cannabis extracts grew to more than 21% of expenditures. Among flower products, strains with greater than 15% THC grew from less than 60 to 92.5% of sales, with mean THC potency at 20.6% across the study period. Cost per unit fell as potency increased,[18] suggesting that simple economics may be a key driver of this trend. The wax/shatter/resin/dab segment was both the largest and fastest-growing product category: the average number of transactions per store per day in this category rose from 5 in June 2015 to 17 a year later.[14]

There are at least three health concerns related to higher-potency products on the market. First, the limited research available suggests that users are likely to consume higher doses of THC, sometimes unintentionally, when using higher-potency products.[57,58] Second, these products appear to appeal to heavy users seeking high levels of intoxication, potentially increasing both the frequency and the intensity of use by this high-risk cohort. (See Box 3-2 on Titration and Tolerance.) Third, higher-potency products may be particularly dangerous for young or inexperienced users. These consequences may in turn lead to more dependence and harms, including emergency room visits and motor vehicle crash fatalities.[36,63,64]

Box 3-2. Titration and Tolerance

Some studies have demonstrated that people may partially titrate their THC consumption by changing their smoking behavior, given varying THC concentrations. One study from the United Kingdom found that cannabis users titrate the amount of cannabis they roll in joints according to THC concentrations (but not by CBD concentrations) and that these decisions are not influenced by frequency of use or cannabis type.[59] Another study, from the Netherlands, found that users who prefer higher THC concentrations added more cannabis to their joints as THC concentrations increased, but then they tended to inhale lower volumes; however, this behavior did not compensate for the higher THC concentrations, resulting in only partial titration.[57]

Titration efforts may vary based on user age and frequency of cannabis use as well as THC-to-CBD ratios. An early study in the Netherlands found that younger frequent cannabis users tended to seek maximum levels of intoxication and showed less evidence of titration.[60] One of the first studies of intoxication and impairment effects of products from the legalized Colorado markets (with groups consuming either flower with 16% or 24% THC or concentrates with 70% or 90% THC) found that while the concentrate users displayed higher THC levels across all time frames, they did not show greater short-term subjective, cognitive, or balance impairment, suggesting that users may self-titrate to achieve similar THC levels as the potency of their cannabis increases or that higher-potency users may have developed a tolerance.[61] A systematic review published in 2018 on cannabis use and the development of tolerance found that acute effects of cannabis use are less prominent in regular cannabis users compared with nonregular users, with cognitive function showing the highest degree of tolerance and acute intoxicating and cardiac effects of THC lessened with regular exposure. There was limited evidence of partial tolerance in other behavioral, physiological, and neural effects.[62] While the science on titration and tolerance continues to evolve, the fact that concentrate users displayed high THC levels is concerning for long-term health outcomes.

ENVIRONMENTAL HEALTH AND QUALITY CONCERNS

As a cultivated plant, cannabis also raises environmental health and quality issues for regulators. Without federal oversight, states must grapple with evidence-based standards and protections around pesticides and organic growing techniques, harmful exposures to workers and consumers, and laboratory testing standards to determine the safety and quality of cannabis products.

Typically, regulation of all of this would lie at the federal level. The absence of regulations from the Environmental Protection Agency (EPA), the Food and Drug Administration, and the Occupational Health and Safety Administration/National Institute for Occupational Safety and Health has created a scientific and regulatory vacuum. Additionally, federal statutory limitations on most cannabis research have made states' and scientists' efforts to design evidence-based environmental health and quality regulations for cannabis even more difficult.

Worker and Consumer Safety Issues

Cannabis plants are susceptible to multiple pests during cultivation. However, because of the illegal federal status of cannabis, national regulations regarding pesticides for agricultural use do not apply to these plants.[65] Organic farming techniques are available and widely used among small cannabis growers but are difficult to take to larger scale, especially in indoor operations where pests and mildew can be more prevalent.[66] The industry itself has developed voluntary standards and certifications for organic or "clean" cannabis, which for some certifications go beyond existing state-level standards.

The nongovernmental, nonprofit American Herbal Pharmacopoeia published a list of pesticides most likely to be used on cannabis, developed by testing samples from the University of Mississippi—the only sanctioned federal source of cannabis for research purposes—and from DEA over the past 30 years.[67] However, this limited sampling makes the list a poor substitute for more systematic monitoring of possible contaminants in the cannabis supply. Requiring organic farming techniques may be one way to encourage small as opposed to large producers, the regulatory advantages of which are discussed in Chapter 4.

Cannabis industry workers and consumers risk exposure to contaminants of several types, including pesticides, microbial agents, solvents, and metals. Pests and fungal diseases can cause economic damage to cannabis crops, but residues from pesticides and other microbes used to combat these threats can put both cannabis workers and consumers at risk. For example, a study of employees in an indoor grow facility in Washington State found that 71% of employees reported one or more work-related symptoms, with 65% reporting respiratory symptoms, and lab tests found a high proportion of employees with probable work-related asthma.[68] However, 97% of the employees included in the survey were cannabis users, with 81% smoking cannabis multiple times a day, confounding research outcomes yet mirroring findings from a qualitative study of Washington's cannabis industry in which 84% of employees were cannabis users and 55% smoked every day. Many of these employees "acknowledged their willingness to withstand occupational hazards or challenges due to their passion for cannabis and desire to work in this industry."[69]

Normally, EPA would develop and publish tolerance levels setting the legal maximum amount for pesticide residue on a raw agricultural product. Residue tolerances approved for tobacco are not adequate measures for cannabis, as tobacco is considered a nonfood crop and is processed, consumed, and stored differently than cannabis.[65] As a leading toxicologist pointed out, "Cannabis would likely have significant data needs [in relation to approved pesticide use] compared with other recognized crops, as it is smoked, ingested in a variety of edible forms and applied directly to the skin in numerous formulations."[65]

Pesticidal residues are clearly a problem: a 2013 study found them in 60.3 to 69.5% of samples from handheld glass pipes, 42.2 to 59.9% from unfiltered water pipes, and between 0.08% and 10.9% from filtered water pipes.[70] In this scientific and regulatory vacuum, most states have developed lists of pesticides that may be used on cannabis and in what amounts.[71-79] Massachusetts has taken a different approach and has banned the use of all pesticides (apart from some minimum-risk products) on cannabis.[80]

Microbial contamination from molds or bacteria can also occur during cannabis growing, handling, or processing. These contaminants may be especially harmful for medical cannabis users who are already immunocompromised.[81] Cannabis plants can also take up into their flowers high levels of metals from soil or growing mediums, posing a further health risk. Additional metals exposure may come from use of vaping devices reliant on heated metal coils.[81]

Separate from concerns about pesticides and other chemicals used on the plants themselves are the risks inherent in producing cannabis concentrates, given the solvents used to extract them. Analysis of 57 concentrate samples from the California medical cannabis market found that more than 80% were contaminated in some form by chemicals, including residual solvents (83%) and pesticides (33%).[5] Again, some of these risks could be mitigated by requiring organic and pesticide-free cultivation.

Cannabis-infused food and beverage products raise food-safety issues. The National Environmental Health Association suggests that states set and implement standards for safe storage and sanitation of these products to decrease chances of contamination from pesticides and microbials and put in place food safety plans, including plans for recall of contaminated products.[82]

Toxicological research, exposure modeling, and risk assessment analyses looking at the different routes of exposure (e.g., inhalation, ingestion, topical/dermal application) are needed and required for a full assessment of the potential risks that environmental and occupational exposures pose to cannabis workers and consumers.[83]

Environmental Health and Climate Change Concerns

Several environmental concerns arise related to cannabis cultivation. One study has concluded that cannabis terpenes—the organic compounds in the cannabis plant that give it a distinctive odor and flavor—can result in increases in ozone concentration, which is detrimental to air quality.[84] Cannabis cultivation can also bring with it waste products such as organic pollutants and agrochemicals and requires high levels of water and energy for certain types of production.[85,86]

For example, cannabis growers in the Northern California coastal region apply an estimated 22 liters or more of water per plant per day during the June–October growing season; researchers estimate that this totals approximately three billion liters per square kilometer of greenhouse-grown cannabis each growing season.[87] This is concerning, as between 2012 and 2016 the number of cannabis plants in Northern California increased by 183% and the total area under cultivation grew by 91%. Some of these expansions took place in areas of high environmental sensitivity, including near habitats of endangered species.[88] Thus, some organizations have created recommendations in relation to cannabis and sustainable development.[89] In Denver, for example, the Department of Public Health and the Environment created an *Environmental Management Best Practices Guide*.[90]

Again, the lack of a robust and standardized national laboratory testing system for cannabis leaves states on their own. California, with a sophisticated Department of Pesticide Regulation already in place, is widely seen as a national leader both in the stringency of its cannabis regulations regarding pesticides and in its use of third-party laboratories for testing.[83] As another leading example, Canada requires in its pesticide regulations testing for 96 compounds and sets residue limits that are mostly lower than those of California.[83] In addition, each year Canadian regulators conduct multiple unannounced inspections at each licensed producer. Pesticides commonly used on other agricultural products may have very different effects on cannabis. Health Canada's testing led to a voluntary recall by two Canadian cannabis producers that had used myclobutanil, a mildew-killing pesticide that when burned—as will happen if it is used on cannabis or tobacco—produces toxic gases such as hydrogen cyanide.[91]

Testing at various stages of the product life (e.g., flower, concentrate, final product), using third-party laboratories with standardized and uniform methods for testing and validation, and establishing protocols for handling products that fail testing standards are important considerations.

A substantial agenda of research is needed to comprehensively address environmental health and quality concerns about cannabis products:

- Research into plant growth cycles to best minimize water, fertilizer, fungicide, and pesticide application;
- Analysis of wastewater streams to evaluate and reduce pollutant concentrations and reduce solvent use;
- Measurement of outdoor and indoor air quality to discern the emission rates of volatile compounds at all phases of the growing process and reduce emissions, and to identify and quantify risks to workers and the environment in grow operations; and
- Creation and standardization of laboratory testing for cannabis products.[85]

Chapter 9 returns to these concerns in the context of ongoing monitoring, surveillance, and enforcement needs.

CONCLUSION

The present wild west nature of the cannabis market is perhaps nowhere more evident than when it comes to the products themselves. While more research and testing are clearly needed, states have not waited and cannot wait for research outcomes. Whether by ballot initiative or legislation, legalization has moved far ahead of science-based knowledge of the plant itself. With cannabis use rising in many populations and health benefits as well as health harms attendant on that use, states are having to create systems and regulations that on the one hand satisfy the desires of their voting publics to end cannabis prohibition and on the other protect their populations, both cannabis users and nonusers, from negative effects of broader cannabis availability.

The following chapters of this book are devoted to helping states thread that needle. Drawing on research and experience both in cannabis and in alcohol and tobacco regulation, the book seeks to provide a one-stop shop for state regulators charged with regulating a product about which much is still unknown. As outlined in the Introduction, the next two chapters focus first on the large-scale systems issues involved in creating a state-level cannabis regulatory apparatus and then on the social justice ramifications of past and current cannabis policies. At the beginning of a series of chapters delving into more specific regulatory issues, Chapter 6 returns to cannabis products and specific recommendations regarding them as part of a larger discussion of best practices for regulating cannabis marketing.

REFERENCES

1. Russell C, Rueda S, Room R, Tyndall M, Fischer B. Routes of administration for cannabis use—basic prevalence and related health outcomes: a scoping review and synthesis. *Int J Drug Policy.* 2018;52:87-96.

2. Huestis MA. Human cannabinoid pharmacokinetics. *Chem Biodivers.* 2007;4(8):1770–1804.

3. National Academies of Sciences, Engineering, and Medicine. *The Health Effects of Cannabis and Cannabinoids: The Current State of Evidence and Recommendations for Research.* Washington, DC: National Academies Press; 2017.

4. Loflin M, Earleywine M. A new method of cannabis ingestion: the dangers of dabs? *Addict Behav.* 2014;39(10):1430–1433.

5. Raber JC, Elzinga S, Kaplan C. Understanding dabs: contamination concerns of cannabis concentrates and cannabinoid transfer during the act of dabbing. *J Toxicol Sci.* 2015;40(6):797–803.

6. Spindle TR, Bonn-Miller MO, Vandrey R. Changing landscape of cannabis: novel products, formulations, and methods of administration. *Curr Opin Psychol.* 2019;30:98–102.

7. Weedmaps. What are cannabis concentrates and how do you consume them? 2019. Available at: https://weedmaps.com/learn/products-and-how-to-consume/cannabis-concentrates. Accessed March 24, 2021.

8. Black L. The world's strongest pot product is for sale in Seattle, and it looks almost like crystal meth. *The Stranger.* November 22, 2017. Available at: https://www.thestranger.com/weed/2017/11/08/25572732/the-worlds-strongest-pot-product-is-for-sale-in-seattle-and-it-looks-almost-like-crystal-meth. Accessed July 29. 2021.

9. US Drug Enforcement Administration. What you should know about marijuana concentrates/honey butane oil. Get Smart About Drugs. 2020. Available at: https://www.getsmartaboutdrugs.gov/content/what-you-should-know-about-marijuana-concentrates-honey-butane-oil#cannabisextractphotos. Accessed July 29, 2021.

10. Meier MH. Associations between butane hash oil use and cannabis-related problems. *Drug Alcohol Depend.* 2017;179:25–31.

11. Barrington-Trimis JL, Cho J, Ewusi-Boisvert E, et al. Risk of persistence and progression of use of 5 cannabis products after experimentation among adolescents. *JAMA Netw Open.* 2020;3(1):e1919792.

12. Bell C, Slim J, Flaten HK, Lindberg G, Arek W, Monte AA. Butane hash oil burns associated with marijuana liberalization in Colorado. *J Med Toxicol.* 2015;11(4):422–425.

13. Romanowski KS, Barsun A, Kwan P, et al. Butane hash oil burns: a 7-year perspective on a growing problem. *J Burn Care Res.* 2017;38(1):e165–e171.

14. Caulkins JP, Bao Y, Davenport S, et al. Big data on a big new market: insights from Washington State's legal cannabis market. *Int J Drug Policy.* 2018;57:86–94.

15. Freeman TP, Craft S, Wilson J, et al. Changes in delta-9-tetrahydrocannabinol (THC) and cannabidiol (CBD) concentrations in cannabis over time: systematic review and meta-analysis. *Addiction.* 2020;forthcoming.

16. Hammond D, Goodman S. Knowledge of tetrahydrocannabinol and cannabidiol levels among cannabis consumers in the United States and Canada. *Cannabis Cannabinoid Res.* 2020; forthcoming.

17. Chandra S, Radwan MM, Majumdar CG, Church JC, Freeman TP, ElSohly MA. New trends in cannabis potency in USA and Europe during the last decade (2008–2017). *Eur Arch Psychiatry Clin Neurosci.* 2019;269(1):5–15.

18. Smart R, Caulkins JP, Kilmer B, Davenport S, Midgette G. Variation in cannabis potency and prices in a newly legal market: evidence from 30 million cannabis sales in Washington State. *Addiction.* 2017;112(12):2167–2177.

19. Okey SA, Meier MH. A within-person comparison of the subjective effects of higher vs. lower-potency cannabis. *Drug Alcohol Depend.* 2020;216:108225.

20. Giroud C, de Cesare M, Berthet A, Varlet V, Concha-Lozano N, Favrat B. e-cigarettes: a review of new trends in cannabis use. *Int J Environ Res Public Health.* 2015;12(8):9988–10008.

21. O'Shaughnessy's. All vape pen oils are not created equal. Available at: https://beyondthc.com/all-vape-pens-are-not-created-equal. Accessed March 24, 2021.

22. ElSohly MA, Mehmedic Z, Foster S, Gon C, Chandra S, Church JC. Changes in cannabis potency over the last 2 decades (1995–2014): analysis of current data in the United States. *Biol Psychiatry.* 2016;79(7):613–619.

23. Stogner JM, Miller BL. Assessing the dangers of "dabbing": mere marijuana or harmful new trend? *Pediatrics.* 2015;136(1):1–3.

24. Richards JR, Smith NE, Moulin AK. Unintentional cannabis Iingestion in children: a systematic review. *J Pediatr.* 2017;190:142–152.

25. Wang GS, Roosevelt G, Le Lait MC, et al. Association of unintentional pediatric exposures with decriminalization of marijuana in the United States. *Ann Emerg Med.* 2014;63(6): 684–689.

26. Wang GS, Le Lait MC, Deakyne SJ, Bronstein AC, Bajaj L, Roosevelt G. Unintentional pediatric exposures to marijuana in Colorado, 2009–2015. *JAMA Pediatr.* 2016;170(9):e160971.

27. Wang GS, Hoyte C, Roosevelt G, Heard K. The continued impact of marijuana legalization on unintentional pediatric exposures in Colorado. *Clin Pediatr (Phila).* 2019;58(1): 114–116.

28. Whitehall JM, Harrington C, Lang CJ, Chary M, Bhutta WA, Burns MM. Incidence of pediatric cannabis exposure among children and teenagers aged 0 to 19 years before and after medical marijuana legalization in Massachusetts. *JAMA Network Open.* 2019;2(8).

29. MacCoun RJ, Mello MM. Half-baked—the retail promotion of marijuana edibles. *N Engl J Med.* 2015;372(11):989–991.

30. Vandrey R, Raber JC, Raber ME, Douglass B, Miller C, Bonn-Miller MO. Cannabinoid dose and label accuracy in edible medical cannabis products. *JAMA.* 2015;313(24):2491–2493.

31. White AE, Van Tubbergen C, Raymes B, Contreras AE, Scallan Walter EJ. Cannabis-infused edible products in Colorado: food safety and public health implications. *Am J Public Health.* 2020;110(6):790–795.

32. Volkow ND, Baler R. Emergency department visits from edible versus inhalable cannabis. *Ann Intern Med.* 2019;170(8):569–570.

33. Barrus DG, Capogrossi KL, Cates SC, et al. Tasty THC: promises and challenges of cannabis edibles. *Methods Rep RTI Press.* 2016:10.3768.

34. Freeman AM, Petrilli K, Lees R, et al. How does cannabidiol (CBD) influence the acute effects of delta-9-tetrahydrocannabinol (THC) in humans? a systematic review. *Neurosci Biobehav Rev.* 2019;107:696–712.

35. Mongeau-Perusse V, Jutras-Aswad D. Challenging CBD protective effect against THC-related outcomes: a call for robust clinical trials. *Addiction.* 2021;116(1):207–2080.

36. Fischer B, Russell C, Sabioni P, et al. Lower-risk cannabis use guidelines: a comprehensive update of evidence and recommendations. *Am J Public Health.* 2017;107(8):e1–e12.

37. Schauer GL, King BA, Bunnell RE, Promoff G, McAfee TA. Toking, vaping, and eating for health or fun: marijuana use patterns in adults, US, 2014. *Am J Prev Med.* 2016;50(1):1–8.

38. Schauer GL, Njai R, Grant-Lenzy AM. Modes of marijuana use—smoking, vaping, eating, and dabbing: results from the 2016 BRFSS in 12 states. *Drug Alcohol Depend.* 2020;209:107900.

39. Colorado Department of Public Health and Environment. Monitoring health concerns related to marijuana in Colorado: 2018 summary. 2018. Available at: https://marijuanahealthinfo. colorado.gov. Accessed April 5, 2021.

40. Carlini BH, Garrett SB, Harwick RM. Beyond joints and brownies: marijuana concentrates in the legal landscape of WA State. *Int J Drug Policy.* 2017;42:26–29.

41. Patrick ME, Miech RA, Kloska DD, Wagner AC, Johnston LD. Trends in marijuana vaping and edible consumption from 2015 to 2018 among adolescents in the US. *JAMA Pediatr.* 2020;174(9):900–902.

42. Centers for Disease Control and Prevention. CDC, FDA, states continue to investigate severe pulmonary disease among people who use e-cigarettes. Media statement. August 21, 2019. Available at: https://www.cdc.gov/media/releases/2019/s0821-cdc-fda-states-e-cigarettes.html. Accessed August 2, 2021.

43. Centers for Disease Control and Prevention. Outbreak of lung injury associated with the use of e-cigarette, or vaping, products. 2020. Available at: https://www.cdc.gov/tobacco/basic_information/e-cigarettes/severe-lung-disease.html#key-facts-vit-e. Accessed March 24, 2021.

44. Lozier MJ, Wallace B, Anderson K, et al. Update: demographic, product, and substance-use characteristics of hospitalized patients in a nationwide outbreak of e-cigarette, or vaping, product use–associated lung injuries—United States, December 2019. *MMWR Morb Mortal Wkly Rep.* 2019;68(49):1142–1148.

45. Ellington S, Salvatore PP, Ko J, et al. Update: product, substance-use, and demographic characteristics of hospitalized patients in a nationwide outbreak of e-cigarette, or vaping, product use–associated lung injury—United States, August 2019–January 2020. *MMWR Morb Mortal Wkly Rep.* 2020;69(2):44–49.

46. Duffy B, Li L, Lu S, et al. Analysis of cannabinoid-containing fluids in illicit vaping cartridges recovered from pulmonaryIinjury patients: identification of vitamin E acetate as a major diluent. *Toxics.* 2020;8(1):8.

47. Blount BC, Karwowski MP, Shields PG, et al. Vitamin E acetate in bronchoalveolar-lavage fluid associated with EVALI. *N Engl J Med.* 2020;382(8):697–705.

48. King BA, Jones CM, Baldwin GT, Briss PA. The EVALI and youth vaping epidemics—implications for public health. *N Engl J Med.* 2020;382(8):689–691.

49. Boudi FB, Patel S, Boudi A, Chan C. Vitamin E Acetate as a plausible cause of acute vaping-related illness. *Cureus.* 2019;11(12):e6350.

50. Knapp AA, Lee DC, Borodovsky JT, Auty SG, Gabrielli J, Budney AJ. Emerging trends in cannabis administration among adolescent cannabis users. *J Adolesc Health.* 2019;64(4):487–493.

51. Tormohlen KN, Brooks-Russell A, Ma M, Schneider KE, Levinson AH, Johnson RM. Modes of marijuana consumption among Colorado high school students before and after the initiation of retail marijuana sales for adults. *J Stud Alcohol Drugs.* 2019;80(1):46–55.

52. Tormohlen KN, Schneider KE, Johnson RM, Ma M, Levinson AH, Brooks-Russell A. Changes in prevalence of marijuana consumption modes among Colorado high school students from 2015 to 2017. *JAMA Pediatr.* 2019 173(10):988–989.

53. Friese B, Slater MD, Battle RS. Use of marijuana edibles by adolescents in California. *J Prim Prev.* 2017;38(3):279–294.

54. Friese B, Slater MD, Annechino R, Battle RS. Teen use of marijuana edibles: a focus group study of an emerging issue. *J Prim Prev.* 2016;37(3):303–309.

55. Caulkins JP, Kilmer B, Kleinman MAR. *Marijuana Legalization: What Everyone Needs to Know.* 2nd ed. New York, NY: Oxford University Press; 2016.

56. Freeman TP, Groshkova T, Cunningham A, Sedefov R, Griffiths P, Lynskey MT. Increasing potency and price of cannabis in Europe, 2006–16. *Addiction.* 2019;114(6):1015–1023.

57. van der Pol P, Liebregts N, Brunt T, et al. Cross-sectional and prospective relation of cannabis potency, dosing and smoking behaviour with cannabis dependence: an ecological study. *Addiction.* 2014;109(7):1101–1109.

58. Freeman TP, Winstock AR. Examining the profile of high-potency cannabis and its association with severity of cannabis dependence. *Psychol Med.* 2015;45(15):3181–3189.

59. Freeman TP, Morgan CJ, Hindocha C, Schafer G, Das RK, Curran HV. Just say 'know': how do cannabinoid concentrations influence users' estimates of cannabis potency and the amount they roll in joints? *Addiction.* 2014;109(10):1686–1694.

60. Korf DJ, Benschop A, Wouters M. Differential responses to cannabis potency: a typology of users based on self-reported consumption behaviour. *Int J Drug Policy.* 2007;18(3):168–176.

61. Bidwell LC, Ellingson JM, Karoly HC, et al. Association of naturalistic administration of cannabis flower and concentrates with intoxication and impairment. *JAMA Psychiatry.* 2020;77(8):787–796.

62. Colizzi M, Bhattacharyya S. Cannabis use and the development of tolerance: a systematic review of human evidence. *Neurosci Biobehav Rev.* 2018;93:1–25.

63. Englund A, Freeman TP, Murray RM, McGuire P. Can we make cannabis safer? *Lancet Psychiatry.* 2017;4(8):643–648.

64. Volkow ND, Baler RD, Compton WM, Weiss SR. Adverse health effects of marijuana use. *N Engl J Med.* 2014;371(9):879.

65. Stone D. Cannabis, pesticides and conflicting laws: the dilemma for legalized states and implications for public health. *Regul Toxicol Pharmacol.* 2014;69(3):284–288.

66. Seltenrich N. As legal cannabis spreads, growers go organic—and beyond. *Environmental Health News.* June 12, 2019. Available at: https://www.ehn.org/as-legal-cannabis-spreads-growers-go-organic-and-beyond-2638712724.html. Accessed August 2, 2021.

67. American Herbal Pharmacopoeia. *Cannabis inflorescence: Cannabis spp.: Standards of Identity, Analysis, and Quality Control.* Scotts Valley, CA: American Herbal Pharmacopoeia; 2014.

68. Sack C, Ghodsian N, Jansen K, Silvey B, Simpson CD. Allergic and respiratory symptoms in employees of indoor cannabis grow facilities. *Ann Work Expo Health.* 2020;64(7):754–764.

69. Ehrlich T, Simpson C, Busch Isaksen T. Sociopolitical externalities impacting worker health in Washington State's cannabis Industry. *Ann Work Expo Health.* 2020;64(7):683–692.

70. Sullivan N, Elzinga S, Raber JC. Determination of pesticide residues in cannabis smoke. *J Toxicol.* 2013;2013:378168.

71. California Department of Pesticide Regulation. Cannabis, hemp, and pesticides. 2020. Available at: https://www.cdpr.ca.gov/docs/cannabis/index.htm. Accessed March 24, 2021.

72. Oregon Department of Agriculture. Cannabis and pesticides. 2020. Available at: https://www.oregon.gov/ODA/programs/Pesticides/Pages/CannabisPesticides.aspx. Accessed March 24, 2021.

73. Washington State Department of Agriculture. Pesticide and fertilizer use for the production of marijuana in Washington. 2020. Available at: https://agr.wa.gov/departments/marijuana/pesticide-use. Accessed March 24, 2021.

74. Colorado Department of Agriculture. Pesticide use in cannabis production information. 2020. Available at: https://www.colorado.gov/pacific/agplants/pesticide-use-cannabis-production-information. Accessed March 24, 2021.

75. Alaska Department of Environmental Conservation. Cannabis and pesticides. 2021. Available at: https://dec.alaska.gov/eh/pest/cannabis/. Accessed April 27, 2021.

76. Illinois Secretary of State. 2020 Illinois Register rules of governmental agencies. In: Index Department ACD, ed. *Title 8, Illinois Administrative Code, Part 1300.* Springfield, IL: 2020.

77. Maine Department of Administrative and Financial Services. Rules for the certification of marijuana testing facilities. In: Services MDoAaF, ed. *Code of Maine Rules 18-691, Chapter 5.* Augusta, ME: 2019.

78. Michigan Marijuana Regulatory Agency. Department banned chemical active ingredients—updated. October 2019. Available at: https://www.michigan.gov/documents/lara/Department_Banned_Pesticide_Active_Ingredient_List_620039_7.pdf. Accessed March 26, 2021.

79. Nevada Department of Agriculture. Pesticide use on marijuana. 2019. Available at: http://agri.nv.gov/Plant/Environmental_Services/Pesticide_Use_on_Medical_Marijuana. Accessed March 24, 2021.

80. Lebeaux J. Pesticide use on cannabis advisory. September 2018. Available at: https://www.mass.gov/doc/pesticide-use-on-cannabis-advisory/download. Accessed August 2, 2021.

81. Seltenrich N. Cannabis contaminants: regulating solvents, microbes, and metals in legal weed. *Environ Health Perspect.* 2019;127(8):82001.

82. National Environmental Health Association. *Food Safety Guidance for Cannabis-Infused Products.* Denver, CO: National Environmental Health Association; 2019.

83. Seltenrich N. Into the weeds: regulating pesticides in cannabis. *Environ Health Perspect.* 2019;127(4):42001.

84. Wang C, Wiedinmyer C, Ashworth K, et al. Potential regional air quality impacts of cultivation facilities in Denver, Colorado. *Atmos Chem Phys.* 2019;19(22):13973–13987.

85. Ashworth K, Vizuete W. High time to assess the environmental impacts of cannabis cultivation. *Environ Sci Technol.* 2017;51(5):2531–2533.

86. Mills E. The carbon footprint of indoor *Cannabis* production. *Energy Policy.* 2012;46:58–67.

87. Carah JK, Howard JK, Thompson SE, et al. High time for conservation: adding the environment to the debate on marijuana liberalization. *Bioscience.* 2015;65(8):822–829.

88. Butsic V, Carah JK, Baumann M, Stephens C, Brenner JC. The emergence of cannabis agricultural frontiers as environmental threats *Environ Res Letters.* 2018;13(12):124017.

89. Riboulet-Zemouli K, Anderfuhren-Biget S, Días Velásquez M, Krawitz M. *Cannabis and Sustainable Development: Paving the Way for the Next Decade in Cannabis and Hemp Policies.* Vienna: FAAAT think & do tank; 2019. License: CC BY-NC-SA 3.0 IGO. Available at: https://faaat.net/publications/9791097087340. Accessed March 24, 2021.

90. Denver Department of Public Health and the Environment. *Cannabis Enviornmental Best Management Practices Guide.* Denver, CO: Denver Dept of Public Health and the Environment; 2019.

91. Government of Canada. Clarification from Health Canada on myclobutanil and cannabis. 2017. Available at: https://www.canada.ca/en/health-canada/news/2017/03/clarification_fromhealthcanadaonmyclobutanilandcannabis.html. Accessed March 24, 2021.

II. REGULATING NONMEDICAL CANNABIS

Product regulation is complex and comes in many forms. Most product regulation in the United States emanates from the federal level. This facilitates open markets among the 50 states, with some assurance that products purchased from Maine to Hawaii meet the same minimal quality and safety standards. Federal regulation has been particularly crucial when it comes to food and drugs. The thalidomide tragedies of the early 1960s brought about amendments to the Food, Drug, and Cosmetic Act requiring, for the first time, that drug manufacturers provide proof of drug safety and effectiveness before being permitted to place their products in interstate commerce.

As an illegal drug at the federal level, however, cannabis has never had to meet this test. States are left on their own, not only to establish standards for quality but also to design full regulatory systems that cover every aspect of a legal marketplace. To satisfy the political will of legislators and/or voting publics, state regulators face a daunting array of tasks, including replacing the illegal market with an orderly legal one, rectifying some of the injustices attributed to cannabis prohibition, ensuring both collection of revenue (in which many states have great interest) and safe and consistent products, and protecting against false claims and predatory marketing, all while making cannabis more widely available.

Evidence regarding and options for building a system that meets these needs and that incorporates a public health perspective is the subject of Chapters 4 and 5. Presentation and evaluation of regulatory models and experience precedes a full discussion of the need for, experiments in, and lessons learned regarding the infusion of social justice principles into cannabis regulation.

Following these two chapters, the book more deeply explores the key areas of product regulation. The alcohol policy field has developed a useful taxonomy of regulation in market societies.[1,2] The basic elements of marketing may be summarized by the "four P's" of marketing: product, promotion, price, and place (distribution or physical availability). This book uses that taxonomy to outline regulatory tasks and policy options and evidence of their effectiveness for each of these four areas. A penultimate chapter explores the surveillance and monitoring systems needed to evaluate the effectiveness of cannabis regulation, and the final chapter summarizes the policy recommendations and offers a vision for the future.

REFERENCES

1. Mosher JF. Alcohol policy and the nation's youth. *J Public Health Policy*. 1985;6(3):295–299.

2. Greisen C, Grossman ER, Siegel M, Sager M. Public health and the four P's of marketing: alcohol as a fundamental example. *J Law, Med Ethics*. 2019;47(suppl 2):51–54.

4

Cannabis Regulatory Systems

We have come to the conclusion that the most satisfactory solution of the problem of alcohol requires elimination of the private profit motive in the retail sale of liquor. This cannot conceivably be accomplished under a license system, however rigid and well enforced. . . . There is in the licensing of the private selling of liquor an irreconcilable and permanent conflict with social control.

–Fosdick and Scott[1]

SUMMARY AND INTRODUCTION

- Cannabis regulatory system options range from allowing home production only to fully commercializing cannabis production and supply.
- Decades of cannabis prohibition have left in place significant illegal markets, and new and regulated legal markets will not replace these overnight.
- Cannabis control systems can learn from regulators' experience with alcohol and tobacco in establishing independent regulated tiers, enabling local control, keeping businesses small and diverse, and taking steps to prevent industry influence.
- Systems that start more conservatively, giving public health concerns as much weight as economic interests, can always expand or liberalize in the future; going in the opposite direction will likely be much more difficult, since commercial operators are likely to oppose market restrictions.
- Monopolies, public authorities, and public health-focused licensing regulatory systems are three systems that provide greater control over the distribution, sales, and promotion of the product.

REGULATORY SYSTEMS: A PUBLIC HEALTH PERSPECTIVE

As stated in the introduction, a public health approach to cannabis regulation will prioritize five goals:

- Preventing youth cannabis use;
- Controlling the prevalence, frequency, and intensity of cannabis use;

- Reducing cannabis-related harms to individuals and communities;
- Ensuring accurate information about the risks of cannabis use; and
- Minimizing the influence of the cannabis industry and the profit motive in setting cannabis policies.

These goals could as easily apply to alcohol or tobacco, the other two major addictive substances readily available nationwide. Indeed, states that have legalized nonmedical cannabis use have, by and large, chosen regulatory systems and controls modeled after profit-driven alcohol-licensing systems. Numerous researchers have concluded that this alcohol model has been ineffective in addressing alcohol-related problems such as excessive consumption and underage drinking, as well as in protecting public health and safety more generally.[2-6] Evidence that alcohol-related emergency room visits and mortality have increased dramatically in recent years underscores this failure.[7,8] The pillars of the alcohol approach—high taxes, controlled availability, and limited advertising and marketing—have eroded steadily over time.[9] With alcohol as the fourth leading actual cause of death in the United States,[10] and with those deaths continuing to rise,[8] this increasingly seems a poor model to emulate.

Options put forward by researchers and advocates for drug policy reform range from full prohibition to a completely open and free market.[11-13] This chapter focuses on approaches between these two extremes, describing the strengths and weaknesses of each from a public health perspective, as well as legal concerns about their feasibility in light of current federal law. This chapter includes models that have been implemented in other countries and for products other than cannabis.

LESSONS FROM ALCOHOL AND TOBACCO REGULATORY SYSTEMS

Throughout history, authorities at all levels—tribal, regional, federal, state, and local—have imposed restrictions and product design requirements on substances, including alcohol, tobacco, pharmaceuticals, food products, and many other goods potentially hazardous to consumers, as a means to protect the public from harm. Regulating access to products to protect public health and safety and prevent social disorder has been a basic function of nearly all human societies to date.

Legalization of cannabis for nonmedical use follows two grand experiments with regulatory systems for intoxicating and/or addictive commodities: alcohol and tobacco. Regulation of these two products has gone in generally opposite directions over the past 100 years. Alcohol regulation was highly restrictive at the repeal of national prohibition and has become progressively less so over time. Tobacco was marketed widely and with few restrictions until the 1964 surgeon general's report. Following that report, federal regulation increased, but often in ways that preempted stronger state action or in other ways that benefited the tobacco industry.[14]

Beginning in the 1990s, and particularly in the wake of the 1998 Master Settlement Agreement, tobacco regulation at every level—federal, state, and local—has become more stringent, but it still has significant limitations.[15] For instance, advocates have worked tirelessly to enact smoke-free policies that are associated with decreases in secondhand smoke exposure, tobacco use among young people and adults, and adverse health effects, yet barriers to adoption and implementation are common, and smoke-free laws are not as widespread as they could be.[16] As another example, while the surgeon general has found that licensing retailers is an evidence-based tobacco control measure to reduce tobacco use,[17] 12 states still do not have license requirements for tobacco retailers.[18] Public health advocates have worked for decades to prevent tobacco-related harms and have achieved great success in passing local, federal, and international policies to reduce tobacco use and protect the public's health. However, tobacco use remains the leading cause of preventable death in the United States and globally, prematurely killing 480,000 people in this country each year.[19]

The United States has experimented with outright prohibitions of various substances at various times, including tobacco in some states during the nineteenth century, but the most prominent example of this regulatory extreme was the national prohibition on alcohol manufacturing and sales, in the name of public safety, imposed on alcohol in the United States between 1920 and 1933. When alcohol prohibition ended, the federal government charged states with setting up systems to control the distribution and sales of alcohol in a manner that would best protect their citizens. Fosdick and Scott, in their 1933 seminal analysis *Toward Liquor Control*, offered a menu of types of systems and legislation that states could implement. The authors reflected, "It can be a wise blend of accepted principle and courageous experiment, a judicious balance between the tradition and experience of the past and the adventure and promise of the future."[1] In other words, effective regulation should fuse science ("accepted principle") and innovation ("courageous experiment").

States largely began their alcohol regulatory efforts with two main goals: (1) to eliminate the illegal alcohol market and (2) to avoid encouraging alcohol consumption.

They also sought to infuse their regulatory systems with other principles, such as protecting youth from the alcohol trade and preventing the alcohol industry from aggressively setting community norms and practices. At the same time, states acknowledged that many citizens wanted to be able to consume alcohol legally.[1] Since the initial policies were adopted in the 1930s, there has been something of a collective amnesia about the reasons they were put in place. At the same time, the size and concentration of power within the US alcohol industry has grown significantly. The 10 largest companies in each sector—beer, distilled spirits, and wine—sell more than two-thirds of the alcohol produced in that sector. Anheuser-Busch, the largest beer producer, has also become the largest beer distributor in the United States, despite regulations put in place following Prohibition to keep wholesalers separate from producers. The companies' political efforts match their size. In 2017, federal lobbying expenditures by alcohol producers approached $32 million; companies spent an additional $11.8 million lobbying state legislatures in that year.[20]

The steady flow of lobbying dollars has been a factor in alcohol policies becoming steadily more liberal over time. In the wake of the COVID-19 pandemic, many states declared alcohol sales an essential service and removed limits on home delivery and carryout cocktails. Some state regulators would have difficulty justifying current state alcohol control systems in the light of the principles set early on. Unfortunately, 104,000 individuals still die from alcohol-related causes in the United States each year.[21]

Nearly 100 years after the "noble experiment" of national alcohol prohibition, many state governments find themselves in a similar situation in relation to cannabis, with one key difference: there is no national mandate, as the federal government has yet to task the states with regulating cannabis as it did with alcohol through the 21st Amendment.

SELECTING A REGULATORY SYSTEM: THE NEED FOR A CAUTIOUS APPROACH

The first message for would-be cannabis regulators is to proceed with caution, for at least two reasons. First, legalization will expand cannabis access and availability, and, as discussed in Chapter 7, expanded availability is linked to increases in the kinds of public health and safety problems described in Chapter 2. Second, the continued status of cannabis as an illegal Schedule I drug under federal law creates substantial legal uncertainty for states choosing to legalize cannabis for nonmedical use. Currently, the federal government has taken an informal, hands-off approach to state legalization, but it could reverse that decision, rendering state legalization laws null and void and shutting down commercial operations.

The 2013 Cole memorandum (see Box 4-1) set priority enforcement areas for the federal government,[22] and states that have legalized nonmedical cannabis appear to have set up systems that attempt to ensure they will not be in violation of these priorities. However, the 2018 Sessions memorandum rescinded these guidelines,[23] underscoring the ambiguity in how the federal government will proceed over the long run.

In addition to incorporating a public health perspective, states can and should try to anticipate new federal laws and regulations that could have dramatic effects on how they may structure regulatory systems for cannabis.[24]

RAND's Drug Policy Research Center sponsored a meeting of alcohol, tobacco, and illegal-drug-policy researchers in February 2013 to foster discussions about "developing public health regulations for marijuana: lessons from alcohol and tobacco" and summarized conclusions from that meeting in a journal article.[25] The authors laid out more

Box 4-1. The Cole Memorandum

In August 2013, Deputy Attorney General James M. Cole issued a memorandum for all US attorneys stating that the Department of Justice, while recognizing the continued prohibition of cannabis/marijuana under the Controlled Substances Act, is "committed to using its limited investigative and prosecutorial resources to address the most significant threats in the most effective, consistent, and rational way." As such, Cole outlines the following enforcement priorities as particularly important to the federal government:

- Preventing the distribution of marijuana to minors;
- Preventing revenue from the sale of marijuana from going to criminal enterprises, gangs, and cartels;
- Preventing the diversion of marijuana from states where it is legal under state law in some form to other states;
- Preventing state-authorized marijuana activity from being used as a cover or pretext for the trafficking of other illegal drugs or other illegal activity;
- Preventing violence and the use of firearms in the cultivation and distribution of marijuana;
- Preventing drugged driving and the exacerbation of other adverse public health consequences associated with marijuana use;
- Preventing the growing of marijuana on public lands and the attendant public safety and environmental dangers posed by marijuana production on public lands; and
- Preventing marijuana possession or use on federal property.[22]

Source: Adapted from US Department of Justice.[22]

specific objectives in the legalization of nonmedical cannabis that flow from the broader goals articulated above:

- Minimize access, availability, and use by youth;
- Minimize drugged driving;
- Minimize dependence and addiction;
- Minimize consumption of cannabis products with unwanted contaminants and uncertain potency; and
- Minimize concurrent use of cannabis and alcohol, particularly in public settings.

Note the absence of increasing revenue as a goal in this list. As is the case with alcohol, control systems that seek increased revenue for the state set up a conflict of interest between public safety and various public goods, including raising funds for government services and other laudable activities, encouraging small businesses, and rectifying past social injustices.[26] An overarching goal of establishing an orderly, crime-free legalization system, with or without a profit motive, can complement the public health goals and objectives listed above.

Given the uncertain legal climate and potential health and safety risks, starting with a more restrictive government-controlled system may be more effective as an experiment in cannabis control. States can modulate their regulatory systems over time as they gather data on the effectiveness of their structures in meeting public health goals. Experience with alcohol and tobacco control suggests that implementing a more restrictive system is much more difficult once a liberal one is in place.[27]

Before going into the details of specific regulatory models, it is important to note the general tasks that any regulatory system must accomplish to protect public health. These include limiting the concentration and influence of private industry, delineating segments or tiers of the industry in part to accomplish this, protecting and promoting citizen input through allowing localities within a state a voice in shaping cannabis availability within their borders, and planning for and funding enforcement.

CREATING AND REGULATING AN INDUSTRY

Industry Influence: Profitability, Industry Concentration, and Lobbying

Regulatory systems must address the role of the cannabis industry and manage the profitability of the cannabis market if states choose to permit a legal market. Interest in profits can dictate practices such as bulk discounting, targeted marketing, and introductory pricing (i.e., setting prices below cost to encourage new users), all of which can undermine public health goals. Experience from the alcohol and tobacco fields has demonstrated that for-profit businesses have a vested interest in increasing the number of consumers and encouraging heavier use, two goals directly in opposition to public health.

Worldwide spending in legal (medical and nonmedical) cannabis markets grew to $14.9 billion in 2019, with $12.4 billion in the United States alone.[28] As discussed in Chapter 1, the heaviest users (those who consume daily or near daily—37% of past-month cannabis users) account for about 80% of consumption.[29] Thus, like the alcohol market, where 10% of drinkers consume nearly 60% of the alcohol sold,[30] a relatively small percentage of cannabis users make up the majority of the cannabis market.

Dependence of the private for-profit cannabis industry on the heaviest users creates incentives to increase their numbers. A public-health-first regulatory system will need to be a strong counterweight to these incentives. To achieve this, it will have to limit businesses' ability to shape public policies solely or predominantly in their own financial interest. Thus, regulators should give serious consideration to limiting industry profitability in a cannabis regulatory system or to creating a legalized system that doesn't include a for-profit private industry. Limiting or prohibiting the involvement of for-profit businesses in the market may come through the creation of government entities (as is the case currently with wholesale alcohol in 17 states) or nonprofit organizations. The sections below on monopolies and public health licensing systems describe these options in more detail.

According to an expert in alcohol regulatory systems, regulators should also put measures in place to keep industry players small and diverse: "Small businesses are more likely to be responsive to the community, more easily regulated at the local level, and less likely to engage in sophisticated mass marketing strategies and lobbying campaigns."[31]

In contrast, vertically integrated systems, which permit single operators to own or control production, processing, distribution, and/or retailing, can tilt the competitive scales in favor of larger operators, who then benefit from economies of scale. This in turn may result in lower prices as well as concentration of the market in the hands of a small number of companies (as has happened in the US beer industry).[20]

An effective regulatory model will limit the level of influence that industry members may have. As leading public health researchers have warned, "Once the laws are in place, private economic interests participate in an ongoing dance with officials that often tests the integrity of individuals and institutions. The outcome is too often what political scientists call 'regulatory capture,' in which the regulated industry gets control of the regulatory machinery for its own private ends."[2] This problem can be exacerbated if the industry becomes more concentrated, leaving a small number of companies controlling most of the market.

At a minimum, any regulatory system should restrict industry members from serving on any government body, committee, or advisory group. Numerous studies have documented harmful industry influences in the creation and implementation of alcohol and tobacco policies and systems, so much so that the World Health Organization embedded the principle of excluding the tobacco industry from policy discussions in its global tobacco treaty, the Framework Convention on Tobacco Control.[5,32] To date, however, many of the US states that have legalized cannabis for nonmedical use lack such conflict-of-interest restrictions.[5]

In the same vein, states should consider separating administrative authority—the power to grant licenses, for example—from enforcement of restrictions regarding those licenses in order to minimize the risk of regulatory capture.[33] Decoupling enforcement budgets from funding of the regulatory agency can also prevent conflicts of interest for regulators between generating revenues and controlling the trade.

Regulating the Four Tiers of the Industry

Following alcohol prohibition, the federal government mandated the creation of three industry tiers—production, wholesaling, and retail—and mandated separations between the tiers to prevent vertical integration as one means of keeping alcohol companies small. However, as of 2016, just two companies produced two-thirds of the beer sold in the United States.[20] The resulting political power they wield led one former alcohol regulator to point out that the alcohol control system envisioned at the end of Prohibition looks very different from the alcohol regulatory environment today. Over time, alcohol companies and their allies have eroded many of the protective policies initially adopted.[34,35]

Unlike alcohol, the cannabis market has four distinct industry tiers: production/ cultivation, product processing/packaging, wholesaling/distribution, and retailing.

Each of the regulatory systems described in this chapter may be applied to one or more of the tiers, and states may mix and match them across tiers. For example, states may license cultivators with few restrictions, create a state monopoly system for distribution, and permit retail distribution only through social clubs. States may maintain a strictly tiered system, like that in place for alcohol after Prohibition, or they may permit some degree of vertical integration, allowing businesses to operate across tiers.

Options for restricting the growth of cannabis companies vary across the tiers. In production, state and local authorities can cap the size of cannabis-growing facilities to keep large producers from controlling the market and to help prevent a surplus of cannabis, which could lead to lower retail prices or end up in the illegal market. Washington State created three levels of plant canopy licenses, with the largest capped at 30,000 square feet. A recent report on licensed cannabis canopy spaces in that state found that cannabis cultivators were using less than half their allotted licensed canopy,[36] suggesting that maximum canopy sizes could be reduced. In contrast, Oregon currently faces a surplus of cannabis supply, which some attribute to low license fees and large permitted canopy sizes.[37]

In the retail tier, states can limit the size and number of cannabis distributors selling directly to the public, as well as the amount of cannabis an individual retailer may sell in a given time frame. Prohibiting the accumulation of licenses by single individuals or entities within a tier (horizontal integration) and prohibiting individuals or entities from owning or controlling companies in more than one tier (vertical integration) can also help to diversify business interests.

States have taken divergent approaches both to delineation of the tiers of the cannabis industry and to restrictions on integration across tier lines. In Washington State, a licensee may hold both a cultivator/producer and a processor license, but neither a cultivator nor a processor may hold a retail license.[38] Other states, such as California, Colorado, and Oregon, allow vertical integration for nonmedical cannabis.[39] Massachusetts, while requiring different licenses for each tier, allows an individual or entity to own at most three licenses in each tier, essentially permitting vertical integration while attempting to avoid the creation of large companies with oligopoly or monopoly power.

In addition to limiting the size of cannabis enterprises, a ban on vertical integration can help to distance and protect retailers from undue pressures from producers regarding sales and advertising practices. An independent wholesale tier can facilitate tax collection and minimum-pricing compliance by providing fewer points of tax collection and price enforcement. Clear separation of the tiers can facilitate more effective regulatory monitoring, as different tiers become the locus of enforcement regarding quality control, packaging requirements, environmental practices, production limits, pricing policies, and sales to minors.[31]

Setting limits on the size of cannabis producers and retailers can help smaller players enter the cannabis business while preventing large corporations from taking over the market. Reasonable licensing fees offer another avenue for allowing and encouraging small entities to participate.

Local Control

While the main focus of this chapter is on state-level regulatory frameworks, states need also to structure their systems to preserve and encourage local authority and input. For instance, local input was crucial to the scuttling of a proposal in California to allow police officers to become licensed owners of cannabis businesses, which would have created a conflict of interest between licensing and enforcement.[40] The authors of *Toward Liquor Control* highlighted this as an important recommendation following the repeal of alcohol prohibition: "In recognizing the diversity of sentiment that exists within the state, in trying to adapt the law to the opinion of the community so as to gain its support, local option marked a wise and shrewdly conceived development."[1] Alaska, California, Colorado, Massachusetts, and Washington State all permit local authorities to "opt in" to the location of cannabis stores within their jurisdictions. Oregon, in contrast, only permits local governments to opt out of sales or use through general election referenda.[27]

If a locality decides to allow commercial cannabis businesses, it should also have the regulatory authority to make decisions regarding the time, place, and manner of these businesses, as is the case with alcohol and tobacco licensing in many jurisdictions, so long as the local regulations are at least as restrictive as state law and do not conflict with state requirements. It is critical that states not preempt local jurisdictions from adopting stricter regulations than those in place at the state level. Preemption is a consistent problem regarding tobacco and alcohol as well as other health problems. Alcohol licensing is a patchwork of preemption across states, with some cities having the power to vote a single precinct dry while others have little or no control over locations and practices of alcohol outlets.[41] In tobacco control, smoke-free laws have been a significant preemption battleground between states and cities.[42]

Thus far in cannabis regulation, states may require both a state and a local license to operate, and local jurisdictions may impose additional restrictions on hours of sale; signage; distance from other outlets, schools, recovery homes, and other sensitive land uses; product delivery; and so on. In Washington State, 125 cities and 30 counties have passed local ordinances to address retail cannabis sales. These include zoning policies, limits on business hours, and distance requirements.[43] Nevada authorizes local jurisdictions to regulate cannabis operations by imposing additional time, place, and manner restrictions through local zoning regulations.[44] Public health experts have created public health–oriented model ordinances that California jurisdictions can use to regulate cannabis outlets.[45,46] There are also examples of local governments running their own retail operations in Alaska, Maryland, Minnesota, North Carolina, and South Dakota for alcohol, and in the town of Stevenson, Washington, for cannabis.[47]

Enforcement and Compliance

Effective and consistent enforcement and compliance are essential to any regulatory system in order to maintain a stable marketplace and public safety. Studies have shown that enforcement of alcohol regulations is woefully under-resourced, but enforcement of alcohol laws has been found to improve public safety, at least in relation to preventing youth access to alcohol and reducing alcohol-impaired driving.[48,49] Businesses in industries like this with the potential to cause public health harms require governments that consistently monitor their compliance with regulations, and that levy increasing administrative sanctions for successive violations, including fines, suspensions, and license revocations when necessary.

Chapter 9 explores these needs in greater depth. In this chapter on requirements of a regulatory system, it suffices to point out that as cannabis moves from a largely unregulated and illegal market to a regulated one, states will need to ensure adequate resources and expertise for enforcement. The level and type of enforcement required depend on the regulatory system. Monopolies and public authorities may require fewer enforcement resources than commercial regulatory systems, as the profit motive may be less and the opportunities for corruption fewer. Any regulatory system will require the development of clear enforcement guidance and protocols to ensure fair and consistent enforcement, as well as careful consideration about where to put that function, whether in some existing agency or in a new entity.

ADDRESSING THE ILLEGAL MARKET

Another key regulatory task is dealing with the illegal market. Decades of cannabis prohibition have left in place significant illegal distribution systems, and new and regulated legal markets will not immediately replace these. RAND researchers estimate that three years following Washington State's creation of a new regulatory system, residents were obtaining between 40% and 60% of their THC from licensed outlets.[50] Oregon reported gaining approximately 55% of the cannabis market through its new regulatory system,[51] and recent estimates for Colorado indicate that 82% of Colorado's cannabis consumer market is now in the legal market (see Chapter 8 for more information).[52]

Converting an illegal market to a legal regulatory framework will take time and active enforcement. Each regulatory system affects the illegal market differently, depending on how regulators set policy and go about implementation in such critical areas as taxation and pricing, product restrictions, physical availability, and marketing. For example, allowing home cultivation may increase product supply in the illegal market; a commercial licensing regulatory system with an abundance of retail outlets may reduce sales of illegal products but exacerbate public health problems associated with cannabis (as described in Chapter 7).

Cannabis prohibition has also exacerbated existing social injustices, with particularly harsh consequences for Black and Latinx communities. Chapter 5 discusses these in greater detail. Replacing the illegal market with a legal cannabis marketplace and at the same time rectifying past injustices greatly complicates the regulatory task and may lead to significant unintended consequences from both a public health and a social justice perspective. However, there are ways for jurisdictions to address social inequality and historic injustice without relying on the route taken to date by most states—namely, putting achievement of these goals in the hands of a private, for-profit cannabis market.

MODELS OF REGULATORY SYSTEMS

The issues described above should all be taken into consideration in developing a cannabis regulatory system. While later chapters go more deeply into policies under each of the four P's of marketing, a key test of any overall regulatory system is how well it facilitates state action in these four areas and how it handles industry influence throughout. Below are six regulatory system options with an analysis of the strengths and weaknesses of each system in relation to facilitating state action across the four P's and limiting industry influence. Box 4-2 describes the Dutch approach to cannabis sales, which is not included in the six regulation system options as it does not appear feasible in the United States.

Box 4-2. Retail Sales Only (the Netherlands)

While the Dutch approach is probably not feasible in the United States, it is summarized here because it has received sporadic attention from the US news media. In the Netherlands, cannabis production and distribution are illegal. However, in the mid-1970s, the Dutch effectively decriminalized personal possession and cannabis use among adults. While the sale of cannabis remained an offense, sale of small amounts was permitted in outlets known as "coffee shops."

These "coffee shops" operate under strict licensing conditions, with no one under 18 allowed on the premises, customers permitted to purchase no more than 5 grams per day, sales of other drugs (including alcohol) and public nuisance activities prohibited, and cannabis or other drug advertising strictly limited. In this way, the Dutch sought to separate cannabis sales from other, "harder" illegal drug markets. However, they have struggled with the "backdoor" problem: tacit acceptance of legal retail outlets engaging with illegal production and cultivation markets not subject to government regulation or control.[11,53-55] In 2020, the Dutch government began a four-year experiment in which up to 10 cultivators will be selected to legally provide cannabis to approximately 80 "coffee shops" in 10 municipalities.[56,57]

1. Home Cultivation Only

A regulatory system that permits home cultivation while continuing to prohibit commercial production, distribution, and sales allows jurisdictions to move toward decriminalization of personal use while possibly leading to a smaller increase in consumption and problems than is likely to accompany full commercialization. Home cultivation regulations generally impose specific limits on the number of plants an individual may grow (although a single plant may produce a lot of product); they may also include limits on potency, use of pesticides, gifting product to another without monetary exchange, and location of cultivation,[58] although these may be difficult to enforce in noncommercial (i.e., home) settings. Prior to allowing legal sales, Alaska passed a law in 1975 that treated cannabis possession as a civil offense, and the Alaska Supreme Court ruled shortly thereafter that the state's constitution protected the privacy of cannabis possession and use within the home.[59] Some jurisdictions, including the District of Columbia and Vermont, have allowed personal cultivators to share their crop with friends and family.

Systems permitting home cultivation only will minimize industry influence, as commercial interests are not allowed. They also eliminate the possibility for retail stores. However, such systems have tended to lack sufficient mechanisms for regulating product quality, including the use of pesticides or the safety of concentrates or edibles. It is also challenging under such systems for law enforcement to monitor compliance to ensure the prevention of illegal sales, enforce limits on the number of plants under cultivation, or prevent youth access.

2. Cannabis Collectives or Co-ops

Cannabis collectives, sometimes called cannabis social clubs (CSCs),* offer a regulatory option that permits cannabis consumers to cultivate, distribute, and consume cannabis while still banning commercial growth and distribution. These clubs are noncommercial organizations comprising adult cannabis users who work together to cultivate and distribute enough cannabis to meet their personal needs in a closed-circuit system.[60] California's and Washington State's medical cannabis systems allowed for collective and cooperative models prior to each state's legalization of cannabis for nonmedical use.[61,62]

These systems, operating under the gray area of being illegal at the federal level and loosely regulated by the states, proved challenging for law enforcement. It was difficult to distinguish medical from illegal grows (e.g., medical patients growing more than the authorized amount and selling product illegally), and the proliferation of dispensaries

---

*These collectives are not to be confused with social consumption locations, which involve granting licenses that allow individuals to purchase and consume cannabis on site.

supposedly set up to serve patients made it difficult to track and audit whether many of them were truly operating as nonprofits or conspiring with illegal grows. As one researcher concluded, "It is unlikely that California will serve as a model for other states [in relation to the medical cannabis system] because of its failure to distinguish between medical and recreational users."[63]

Uruguay developed a more complete regulatory process for cannabis social clubs for nonmedical use, including registering them as civil organizations and requiring documentation of club infrastructure, security, and operations. Uruguay also allows self-cultivation, as well as the sale of cannabis through pharmacies, but these three modes of access are mutually exclusive—individuals must choose among self-cultivating cannabis, being part of a CSC, or purchasing cannabis from pharmacies.[64] As of June 2020, Uruguay had 158 CSCs.[65] Limited to at least 15 and no more than 45 members, the CSCs must obtain prior approval to run a nonprofit organization and register with both the Ministry of Education and Culture and the Institute for Regulation and Control of Cannabis (IRCCA). IRCCA then conducts an on-site inspection to determine club operations, including days and times of activity, adjacent areas, advertising and promotions (not allowed on building facades), and crop plan and delivery systems. Inspectors also enforce a minimum 150-meter distance from any educational facilities for those age 18 and younger and/or addiction treatment centers.[64] Members may receive a maximum of 40 grams per month and may not sell their products to the public.[64]

In other countries, CSCs have evolved from laws decriminalizing cannabis possession. Activists have argued in these countries that their laws implicitly permit cultivation, distribution, and use among a specific membership group, with only the commercialization of the product remaining a criminal offense.[60] Activists set up CSCs in Spain in the early 1990s,[60] with other European countries, including France, the United Kingdom, and Belgium, following their lead by the 2000s.[66] A survey conducted in 2018–2019 found that CSCs were operating in 13 European countries.[67] These clubs also exist in Argentina, Colombia, and Chile.[64]

As of 2017 there were an estimated 800 to 1,000 CSCs in Spain and approximately 7 in Belgium.[60,68] As essentially unregulated clubs (although they do register as associations in their respective countries), they are self-regulating and self-enforcing entities. Many follow broad good practice codes developed by the European Coalition for Just and Effective Drug Policies (ENCOD; www.encod.org), with age restrictions for members, boards of directors, maximum sharing amounts per month or per exchange fair, and, at least in Belgium, some product quality control measures. In Spain and Belgium, CSCs do not limit the number of members, although most CSCs in Belgium have fewer than 100.[68] In Spain, this has led individuals to apply to more than one CSC and in some cases to explore selling outside the CSC or converting a CSC into a larger commercial enterprise.[60]

Advantages of CSCs include their ability to minimize private industry influence by prohibiting commercial interests. They allow members to share products and strains, and the CSCs theoretically help address any problems of overproduction by one individual. With regulations similar to those in Uruguay and sufficient enforcement resources, jurisdictions can regulate product quality, including use of pesticides and safety of concentrates or edibles. However, without consistent regulation and enforcement, collectives may lead to an increase of product in the illegal market or to criminal enterprises taking advantage of and turning them into de facto profit-making businesses.

3. Government Wholesale and/or Retail Monopolies

In a public cannabis wholesale and retail monopoly, a single government agency is the sole cannabis wholesaler/distributor and retailer. Nordic countries have at times included production in their government monopoly systems for alcohol; this option is less feasible for cannabis, given the ease and widespread nature of cannabis cultivation. Under this option, privately owned, government-licensed producers must sell to the government monopoly agency, and that agency controls all distribution and retail sales. (This is the cannabis equivalent of the current Swedish alcohol monopoly on sales of spirits, wine, and beer above 3.5% abv.) The government is thus the single buyer (technically, a monopsonist) and holds a monopoly on cannabis wholesaling of products offered by multiple producers. One variant of this is a wholesale-only monopoly where private retailers and not the government agency handle sales to the public. Borland has proposed a similar system, the "Regulated Market Model," for tobacco sales.[69]

In a public health–oriented monopoly system, a Cannabis Control Agency (CCA) would determine generic packaging, set wholesale and retail prices, define what promotions are permitted, and establish conditions for sale. Such conditions could include bans on high-potency products or incentives for less potent products or products with lower THC-to-CBD ratios. The CCA would decide which products may be sold at retail through its wholesale purchasing capability. As the sole buyer, it could choose not to list any products that appear dangerous, misleading, or harmful, as numerous US state alcohol monopolies have done for products such as powdered or extreme-strength alcohol.[70]

As the sole purchaser from cultivators, the agency would have virtually unlimited control over the types, quantity, quality, and strength of the product. The CCA could also use its price-setting powers to encourage or discourage use of particular products, as Scandinavian alcohol control systems have done for lower-strength alcoholic beverages. The CCA could also create rules governing maximum market share to ensure a diversity of cannabis producers in the marketplace. If a jurisdiction chose to be the sole retailer in addition to being the sole wholesaler, it could also set retail prices to consumers and restrict outlet density and hours and days of sale. Monopolies could also facilitate efficient collection and enforcement of taxes on cannabis.

The substantial public health advantages of state monopolies have to be weighed against the risks states would take in moving into doing business with a Schedule I drug. The National Alcohol Beverage Control Association represents state and local alcohol monopolies in the United States. Their vice president, Steve Schmidt, summarized the advantages of a government monopoly:

1. As the sole wholesaler, the agency decides what products will be sold in its jurisdiction. The agency can review a variety of factors including: marketing of the product, customer needs, and safety. The agency can also keep out of the marketplace those products deemed to be dangerous (e.g., high proof grain alcohol, alcohol mixed with "energy" ingredients such as caffeine or taurine, powdered alcohol).
2. All taxes imposed at the wholesale and retail level can be collected without the need for enforcement of private businesses, resulting in 100% tax collection.
3. The agency has enhanced authority regarding prices and marketing.
4. The agency can determine the number, type and location of retail outlets. (Steve Schmidt, MS, and Neal Insley, JD, National Alcohol Beverage Control Association, in person interview, July 15, 2019.)

In the United States, 17 states have implemented a wholesale and/or retail monopoly model for alcohol sales. Studies have repeatedly found, and the Task Force on Community Preventive Services has confirmed, an association between these alcohol control systems and better public health and public safety outcomes.[71] Cannabis control systems could employ many of the same structures, such as a ban on vertical integration or some degree of monopoly control over distribution and sale, in order to protect public health. The CCA would require independent and open governance under a charter that clearly spells out its objectives. The CCA board and staff would need to have expertise in a variety of fields and a clearly established separation from producers.

Since October 2018, when Canada legalized the production, distribution, sales, and possession of cannabis for nonmedical use, five Canadian provinces have adopted a wholesale government monopoly combined with a retail sales model in which all sales take place in government stores, while six have put in place a hybrid of government wholesale distribution and public and private stores. In all but Saskatchewan and Manitoba, the government controls online sales and delivery.[72] The national agency Health Canada issues the licenses for production/cultivation of cannabis.[73]

No US state has used a monopoly model for cannabis thus far. However, in her 2020 budget, then–Rhode Island governor Gina Raimondo proposed one. Under her proposal, the state government would operate adult-use cannabis shops, sourcing the product through private contractors. This could create legal jeopardy for employees at those stores. As long as cannabis remains illegal at the federal level, it would potentially put state employees in violation of federal law. However, anyone who accepts and deposits cannabis-related funds from members of the private cannabis industry to state officials is at similar risk of prosecution, since doing so is a federal offense.[74]

The Cole memorandum (see Box 4-1) has suspended such prosecutions for the time being, a key element in the progression toward legalization of nonmedical adult use at the state level.

4. Public Authority

Rather than a specific government agency, a public authority could serve the coordinating function in a monopoly model. Public authorities are agencies created by governments to engage directly in the economy for public purposes. They differ from standard government agencies in that they operate outside the administrative framework of state or local government.

Such an authority would have the same potential strengths and weaknesses as a government monopoly agency such as the CCA previously described. However, as a single, special-purpose entity distinct from direct state government, an authority could enter into contracts, make purchasing decisions, and in general operate more closely in line with commercial enterprises, with the result that industry members may find working with it easier than dealing with a government agency. Authorities normally have greater flexibility in setting policies in areas such as human resources and procurement, which can have distinct advantages when selling a product and hiring store employees. Effective January 1, 2019, the Virginia General Assembly converted Virginia's alcoholic beverage control (ABC) monopoly from an agency into an authority. The change was made to allow the Virginia ABC to "be more flexible and efficient as a retailer, wholesaler, and regulator of the sale of distilled spirits."[75]

A cannabis public authority might be able to respond more quickly to the ever-changing marketplace and institute policy changes should public health and safety harms arise. For as long as the cannabis trade is illegal under federal law, a public authority might provide a mechanism for state and local governments to set up a cannabis system without requiring direct state or local government employees to violate federal laws, particularly in the current laissez-faire environment of federal law enforcement. On the downside, while public authorities will have strengths similar to those of government monopolies at either the wholesale or retail level, their operations may be less transparent than in standard government agencies, and safeguards would be needed to prevent regulatory capture by the industry.

Just one US jurisdiction experimented with the public authority model for cannabis: the city of North Bonneville, Washington, opted to open a government-run retail store as a public development authority in 2015. The store later moved to the neighboring town of Stevenson. Its website stated, "We are unique in our industry in that our primary focus is public health and safety," with all profits used for the benefit of the community,[47] but as of December 2020, the website was not active and it is unclear whether the store was still part of a public authority or has become a commercial retail establishment.

5. Licensed Regulatory System

Under a licensed regulatory model, state and local authorities regulate a private industry and marketplace to ensure that cannabis businesses operate only within the boundaries of the law. Regulatory options for such a system can be public health oriented or commercially oriented, with possibly different goals and objectives depending on the structure and system created. Two different subsystems within the licensed regulatory framework are described below: first, a public health–focused licensing system; second, a more traditional commercial licensing system. No jurisdiction in the country has yet created a public health–focused licensing system; examples of the differences between the two systems help highlight the strengths and weaknesses of each approach.

Public Health–Focused Licensing System

A public health approach to licensing would likely place primary responsibility for cannabis regulation in the state's health department, in collaboration with public safety agencies, so that health promotion and protection remain the priority (rather than maintaining an efficient market or maximizing tax revenue).[76]

Under this model, states would require separate licenses for all parts of the supply chain, including producers (i.e., cultivators and processors), wholesalers/distributors, and retailers, and would prohibit vertical integration. Licensing processes can limit competition by restricting both the size and number of producers as well as the number of retail licenses given; this in turn can help keep prices high, facilitate effective tax collection, limit the location and density of retail outlets, and reduce the potential for diversion of the product into informal or illegal channels. Keeping the number of retail licenses small while setting licensing fees to offset the costs of regulating the industry also helps control regulatory costs and sufficiently supports enforcement and compliance without relying on tax revenues that tie regulators' interests to industry growth.

A public health–focused licensing system could also require that industry members be nonprofit organizations or collectives. This would eliminate much of the profit motive, reduce aggressive marketing, and somewhat limit the organization's ability to lobby. As part of medical cannabis systems, at least nine states required medical cannabis dispensaries to operate as nonprofit entities as of February 2017.[77] However, no state that has legalized nonmedical cannabis use has gone this route.

The state health department could create an advisory panel with enhanced authority to review and approve products, labeling, marketing, pricing, and so on, populated primarily by public health professionals. This advisory panel could also include representatives from affected areas such as agriculture, law enforcement, criminal justice, and environmental protection, and it could consult with experts from other government departments (a state agriculture department advising on pesticides, for example).

Industry members would be prohibited from serving on the advisory panels. While public health agencies may not be as experienced in business licensing as other government agencies, in consultation and partnership with other government agencies a strong advisory panel could help facilitate proper oversight and implementation of cannabis regulation.

Commercial Licensing System

States have most commonly implemented commercial licensing systems for production, distribution, and retail sale of nonmedical cannabis. The majority of US states (34 and the District of Columbia) rely exclusively on such a system for alcohol control. Colorado and Washington State were the first to do so for cannabis, in 2014; Alaska, California, Illinois, Massachusetts, Maine, Michigan, Nevada, Oregon, and Vermont followed, but with key variations in policies affecting such areas as taxation and marketing, product, and outlet restrictions. So far, all 11 states rely on private companies to control production, distribution, and retailing. It remains to be seen what type of system the four states that voted to legalize cannabis for nonmedical use in November 2020 (Arizona, Montana, New Jersey, and South Dakota) will create. Public health researchers have observed that "the approach to legalization now being adopted in U.S. states—commercialization on the alcohol model—is one of the worse [sic] versions, most likely to yield big increases in problem use because compulsive users are the most profitable customers."[2]

A state's cannabis licensing authority is likely to reflect the priorities of the agency that houses it. Treasury or other revenue-collecting agencies may have a greater interest in an orderly marketplace and reliable collection of duties and fees than, for instance, a body oriented toward public health or law enforcement.[11] No state has given a public health agency the lead in formulating nonmedical cannabis licensing and enforcement regulations. Three (Alaska, Oregon, and Washington) have turned over the issue to the state's alcohol regulatory agencies. Colorado and Nevada have housed their cannabis licensing and regulatory divisions in the departments of revenue and of taxation, respectively.

The lead regulatory agency may put controls in place regarding qualifications of licensees, age restrictions, location and density of outlets, taxes, product labeling, and so on. However, experience with alcohol suggests that such controls are more readily eased over time than strengthened.[35] Unchecked growth of large companies operating across multiple levels of the industry will likely harm the ability of smaller producers or retailers to remain in the market. The Cole memorandum's ban on transport of cannabis across state lines currently puts a damper on the growth and concentration of the industry; federal legalization may unleash market forces driving toward these, and states will need to be ready with measures governing size and ownership of cannabis firms.

Table 4-1 provides an overview of four key elements that differentiate these two systems: vertical integration, business sizes, profit motives, and industry conflicts of interest.

Table 4-1. Public Health-Focused vs. Commercial Licensing Models

Key Provisions	Public Health Approach	Commercial Approach
Vertical Integration	• Establishes a multi-tiered system with different license types for each tier. • Licensees may not own or control more than one type of license.	• May have separate licenses for each tier but allow for ownership of more than one tier or allow one license to encompass more than one tier.
Business Sizes	• Limits the number of licenses that one owner/investor can have. • Restricts the total number of licenses in any jurisdiction. • Specifies maximum size of any industry participant (e.g., acreage or number of plants for producers, inventory for wholesalers, retail sales or inventory for retailers) and sets limits to encourage small businesses.	• Sets few or no limits either on the size of cannabis businesses or on the number of licenses owners/investors may possess.
Profit Motives	• Requires industry members to be nonprofit organizations or collectives. • Prohibits lobbying and most forms of advertising. • Prohibits license transfers (selling licenses). • Establishes annual license fees that cover, at a minimum, the costs for regulating the industry.	• Permits for-profit corporations and businesses with little or no restrictions on lobbying activities. • Allows for selling of licenses. • License fees generally do not offset the costs of regulating the industry and of the public health-related harms from the product.
Industry Conflicts of Interest	• Establishes advisory panels with enhanced review authority and primarily populated by public health professionals. • Prohibits industry members from serving on advisory panels or as cannabis control commissioners.	• Permits industry members to serve on advisory panels and/or as commission members. • Allows industry lobbying of panel and commission members.

6. Hybrid Models

In practice, jurisdictions sometimes combine aspects of these regulatory models:

• Washington State does not allow home cultivation for nonmedical cannabis and follows some of the principles of the public health–focused licensing model by prohibiting vertical integration for the most part and limiting outlet density.
• California's Department of Public Health (CDPH) oversees manufacturing practices in that state, as well as manufacturer licensing and cannabis packaging and

labeling, while the California Department of Food and Agriculture (CDFA) monitors cultivation and the track-and-trace system used statewide to record the movement of cannabis products through the commercial supply chain. At the same time, the California Bureau of Cannabis Control (BCC) regulates retailers, distributors, testing labs, and microbusinesses.[78] Industry members have significant representation on California's Cannabis Advisory Committee, which has the power to advise the BCC, the CDPH, and the CDFA on the "development of regulations that help protect public health and safety and reduce the illegal market for cannabis."[79]

- The District of Columbia and all the states but Washington that now permit cannabis for nonmedical use allow in some way for home cultivation.
- Uruguay allows home cultivation, licenses cannabis clubs, and tightly controls where nonmedical cannabis can be sold. As of April 2019, just 17 pharmacies in all of Uruguay had a license to sell nonmedical cannabis, with only four strains of cannabis available in those pharmacies.[80]
- In Canada, many provinces have adopted a wholesale and/or retail monopoly model while also allowing individuals to cultivate cannabis plants at home for personal use.

Table 4-2 summarizes the strengths and weaknesses of each of the regulatory systems described above.

POLICY RECOMMENDATIONS

States increasingly face pressures to liberalize their cannabis laws and allow commercial sales. In 13 states so far, these pressures have taken the form of ballot initiatives that have legalized nonmedical adult use. While these may accurately express the will of the voting public, they go forward without the benefit of the deliberative and public debate and shaping that often accompanies legislative measures. Cannabis regulation is complex and can have far-reaching effects on population health and safety. If states choose to go the route of legalizing cannabis for adult nonmedical use, they will generally have greater ability to tailor cannabis regulation if it proceeds through normal legislative procedures, as has been the case in Illinois and Vermont.

In this chapter, dealing with the illegal cannabis market is identified as an essential regulatory task. Later chapters present evidence regarding what has happened to those illegal markets in states that have already legalized; here, simply note that illegal markets are disappearing more slowly than regulators may have anticipated. As discussed in Chapter 9, an effective regulatory system must provide sufficient funds for monitoring and enforcement, even if revenues accruing to state government from the legalized trade are lower than expected.

Table 4-2. Cannabis Regulatory System Options Strengths and Weaknesses

Cannabis Regulatory System	Strengths	Weaknesses	Examples of Jurisdictions Using This Model	Examples From Other Products
1. Home cultivation only: Adults may cultivate up to a maximum number of plants (and may in some cases give a certain amount to others).	**Physical availability:** no retail stores allowed **Industry influence:** minimized, as commercial interests are not allowed	**Product restrictions/controls:** generally no mechanisms to regulate/monitor product quality, use of pesticides, safety of concentrates or edibles	District of Columbia Vermont (but moving soon to licensed regulatory system)	Home brewing of beer permitted by the federal government (even during national prohibition) but in limited quantities
2. Cannabis collectives or co-ops: Individuals may cultivate up to a maximum number of plants and can share (either give or sell at cost) with other club members.	**Physical availability:** no retail stores allowed **Product restrictions:** state can include public health controls on potency, amount allowed to be shared, use of pesticides, etc. **Industry influence:** minimized, as commercial interests are not allowed.	**Product restrictions/controls:** generally no mechanisms to regulate/monitor product quality, use of pesticides, safety of concentrates or edibles	Spain (although not explicitly allowed by national laws, some local jurisdictions have regulations permitting these) Uruguay (hybrid; available in pharmacies as well)	Medical cannabis systems in California and Washington State prior to legalization of cannabis for nonmedical use
3. Government wholesale and/or retail monopolies: A single government agency is the sole wholesaler and/or retailer of cannabis products cultivated and/or processed by many producers.	**Pricing:** controls over prices at wholesale and/or retail can keep prices from falling too low; taxes on production are easier to collect and monitor **Physical availability:** controls over outlet density, hours and days of sale, etc., can limit physical availability **Product restrictions:** controls can limit the products on the market, their potency, serving size, and packaging; can mandate warning labels **Promotions/marketing:** agency can keep products generic, banning branding or labeling and thus eliminating most marketing and promotional opportunities	**Promotions:** if retail level is not part of the monopoly, private retailers may conduct extensive marketing that can promote excessive consumption and expand the market	**Wholesale and retail:** New Brunswick Northwest Territories Nova Scotia Prince Edward Island Quebec **Wholesale and retail hybrid:** Alberta British Columbia Newfoundland and Labrador Nunavut Ontario Yukon	**Wholesale and retail:** Distilled spirits in Alabama, Idaho, Montana, Montgomery County (Maryland), New Hampshire, North Carolina, Oregon, and Vermont Wine and distilled spirits in Pennsylvania and Utah **Wholesale only:** Distilled spirits in Iowa, Maine, Mississippi, West Virginia Wine and distilled spirits in Wyoming

(Continued)

Table 4-2. (Continued)

Cannabis Regulatory System	Strengths	Weaknesses	Examples of Jurisdictions Using This Model	Examples From Other Products
4. Public authority: Similar to a monopoly, but the state government creates a single, independent, special-purpose public authority that is the sole purchaser and distributor of cannabis. May include retail as well.	**Pricing:** controls over prices at wholesale and/or retail can keep prices from falling too low; taxes on production are easier to collect and monitor **Physical availability:** controls over outlet density, hours and days of sale, etc. can limit physical availability **Product restrictions:** controls can limit the products on the market, their potency, serving size, and packaging; can mandate warning labels **Promotions/marketing:** agency can keep products generic, banning branding or labeling and thus eliminating most marketing and promotional opportunities **Industry influence:** limited by controls on the membership of governing and advisory bodies; industry members may find it easier to work with a public authority than a monopoly, as a public authority operates more like a commercial enterprise	**Industry influence:** if retail level is not part of the authority, private retailers may conduct extensive marketing that can promote excessive consumption and expand the market	North Bonneville/ Stevenson Public Development Authority, Wash. (as of 2019)	Virginia Alcoholic Beverage Control Authority for distilled spirits

(Continued)

Table 4-2. (Continued)

Cannabis Regulatory System	Strengths	Weaknesses	Examples of Jurisdictions Using This Model	Examples From Other Products
5. Licensed regulatory system, public health–focused: Competitive private market, subject to laws and regulations, public health and safety goals set and regulated by state department of health.	**Pricing:** has authority to set prices through price controls, including minimum pricing levels and taxes **Physical availability:** can restrict licenses by size, number, and density to reduce availability and keep prices higher **Product restrictions:** strict controls can limit the products on the market, their potency, serving size, and packaging; can mandate warning labels **Industry influence:** managed through a prohibition on vertical integration, required licensing of all tiers, limits on number of licenses permitted to each owner; to reduce profit motive may require that licensees be nonprofit organizations or collectives; prohibits industry members from lobbying or serving on advisory panels	**Industry influence:** if not properly established, public health agencies inexperienced in business licensing and regulations may fall prey to industry capture	None	None

(Continued)

Table 4-2. (Continued)

Cannabis Regulatory System	Strengths	Weaknesses	Examples of Jurisdictions Using This Model	Examples From Other Products
6. Licensed regulatory system, commercial: Competitive private market, subject to laws and regulations; normally overseen by a cannabis control agency placed in an existing government department.	No particular strengths from a public health perspective; preferred by private businesses and venture capital because of maximum freedom to develop profit-making enterprises	**Pricing:** apart from taxation and minimum pricing, prices set by market competition, which may lead to very low prices for cannabis products, competition for new users, and heavier use among existing customers **Physical availability:** controls may be put in place regarding licensees, density of outlets, etc.; however, as seen with alcohol, such controls are more readily eased over time than tightened **Product restrictions:** pressure to grow market share and profitability may incentivize marketing of stronger products or decreased product quality **Industry influence:** unchecked growth of large companies operating across multiple tiers may harm ability of smaller producers or retailers to survive and may expand lobbying influence of large businesses; without strict regulations, industry members can serve as commission members or on advisory panels	Alaska, California, Colorado, Illinois, Maine, Michigan, Massachusetts, Nevada, Oregon, Vermont, Washington State Manitoba Saskatchewan Uruguay (cannabis social clubs as well)	Alcohol in 33 US states plus the District of Columbia Tobacco retailer licensing in more than 40 US states

Table 4-3. Potential Effectiveness of Systems in Meeting Public Health Goals

	Control the prevalence, frequency, and intensity of cannabis use	Prevent youth cannabis use	Reduce cannabis-related harms	Ensure accurate information about the risks of cannabis use	Reduce industry influence and profit motive
1. Home cultivation only	**	*	**	*	***
2. Cannabis collectives or co-ops	***	**	**	*	***
3. Government wholesale and/or retail monopolies	***	**	**	***	***
4. Public authority	***	**	**	**	**
5. Licensed regulatory system, public health–focused	**	**	**	**	**
5. Licensed regulatory system, commercial	*	*	*	*	*

Note: *low potential for meeting the goal; **moderate potential; ***high potential.

This chapter began by articulating five public health goals of a cannabis regulatory system. States should carefully consider how they plan to meet these goals when creating a regulatory system. Table 4-3 assesses how effectively each of these systems addresses them. Three stars indicate that the system shows high potential for effectiveness in meeting the goals, two stars suggests moderate potential, and one star denotes low potential.

Public health reform succeeds when it can articulate a clear moral vision and illustrate that a new view is possible.[81] In this light, states considering a nonmedical cannabis regulatory system should do the following:

- Move slowly. Take a cautious approach to developing a regulatory system, knowing that regulations can be relaxed over time if public health concerns are mitigated.
- Put protections in place to reduce profit motives by the cannabis industry and to keep businesses small, or provide cannabis without creating a private cannabis industry.
- Assume that the illegal market will not disappear immediately after implementation of a regulated system and ensure that steps taken to eliminate the illegal market do not undercut public health goals such as preventing youth access and reducing excessive consumption or exacerbate social injustices (see Chapter 5).
- Consider co-ops or CSCs that remove the profit motive but allow cannabis users to access the product.
- Adopt some version of the large-scale regulatory systems most conducive to addressing public health concerns: a wholesale and retail monopoly, a wholesale-only monopoly model, or a public authority with similar powers.

- If adopting a licensing system, make it public health-focused and adopt measures that
  - Guard against industry regulatory capture;
  - Prohibit vertical integration;
  - Prevent industry influence over policy decisions;
  - Keep businesses small and diverse; and
  - Permit local jurisdictions to place additional requirements on cannabis businesses.

Meeting these public health goals is just one part of the challenge faced by would-be regulators. The next chapter looks at how cannabis law reform can and has attempted to accomplish another important goal: addressing past and current social disparities and injustices that have been perpetrated and perpetuated by the nation's cannabis laws.

REFERENCES

1. Fosdick R, Scott A. *Toward Liquor Control.* New York: Harper and Brothers; 1933.

2. Caulkins JP, Kilmer B, Kleinman MAR. *Marijuana Legalization: What Everyone Needs to Know.* 2nd ed: Oxford University Press; 2016.

3. Barry RA, Glantz S. A public health framework for legalized retail marijuana based on the US experience: avoiding a new tobacco industry. *PLoS Med.* 2016;13(9):e1002131.

4. Rehm J, Fischer B. Cannabis legalization with strict regulation, the overall superior policy option for public health. *Clin Pharmacol Ther.* 2015;97(6):541–544.

5. Barry RA, Glantz SA. Marijuana regulatory frameworks in four US states: an analysis against a public health standard. *Am J Public Health.* 2018;108(7):914–923.

6. Room R. Legalizing a market for cannabis for pleasure: Colorado, Washington, Uruguay and beyond. *Addiction.* 2014;109(3):345–351.

7. White AM, Slater ME, Ng G, Hingson R, Breslow R. Trends in alcohol-related emergency department visits in the United States: results from the Nationwide Emergency Department Sample, 2006 to 2014. *Alcohol Clin Exp Res.* 2018;42(2):352–359.

8. White AM, Castle IP, Hingson RW, Powell PA. Using death certificates to explore changes in alcohol-related mortality in the United States, 1999 to 2017. *Alcohol Clin Exp Res.* 2020;44(1):178–187.

9. Blanchette JG, Lira MC, Heeren TC, Naimi TS. Alcohol policies in US states, 1999–2018. *J Stud Alcohol Drugs.* 2020;81(1):58–67.

10. Mokdad AH, Marks JS, Stroup DF, Gerberding JL. Actual causes of death in the United States, 2000. *JAMA.* 2004;291(10):1238–1245.

11. Caulkins JP, Kilmer B, Kleiman MAR, et al. *Considering Marijuana Legalization: Insights for Vermont and Other Jurisdictions.* Santa Monica, CA: RAND Corporation; 2015.

12. Caulkins JP, Kilmer B. Considering marijuana legalization carefully: insights for other jurisdictions from analysis for Vermont. *Addiction*. 2016;111(12):2082–2089.

13. Rolles S, Murkin G. *How to Regulate Cannabis: A Practical Guide*. 2nd ed. Bristol, UK: Transform Drug Policy Foundation; 2016.

14. Emmons KM, Kawachi I, Barclay G. Tobacco control: a brief review of its history and prospects for the future. *Hematol Oncol Clin North Am*. 1997;11(2):177–195.

15. Institute of Medicine. *Ending the Tobacco Problem: A Blueprint for the Nation*. Washington, DC: Institute of Medicine; 2007.

16. Centers for Disease Control and Prevention. STATE System smokefree indoor air fact sheet. 2020. Available at: https://www.cdc.gov/statesystem/Factsheets.html. Accessed April 5, 2021.

17. US Department of Health and Human Services. *Preventing Tobacco Use Among Youth and Young Adults: A Report of the Surgeon General*. Atlanta, GA: US Dept of Health and Human Services, Centers for Disease Control and Prevention, National Center for Chronic Disease Prevention and Health Promotion, Office on Smoking and Health; 2012.

18. Centers for Disease Control and Prevention. STATE System licensure fact sheet. November 2018. Available at: https://www.cdc.gov/statesystem/factsheets/licensure/Licensure.html. Accessed April 2, 2021.

19. US Department of Health and Human Services. *The Health Consequences of Smoking—50 Years of Progress: A Report of the Surgeon General*. Atlanta, GA: US Dept of Health and Human Services, Centers for Disease Control and Prevention, National Center for Chronic Disease Prevention and Health Promotion, Office on Smoking and Health; 2014.

20. Jernigan D, Ross CS. The alcohol marketing landscape: alcohol industry size, structure, strategies, and public health responses. *J Stud Alcohol Drugs Suppl*. 2020;Sup 19(suppl 19):13–25.

21. Centers for Disease Control and Prevention. *Alcohol-Related Disease Impact (ARDI), Average for United States 2006–2010 Alcohol-Attributable Deaths Due to Excessive Alcohol Use*. Atlanta, GA: Centers for Disease Control and Prevention; 2017.

22. Cole J. *Guidance Regarding Marijuana Enforcement*. Washington, DC: US Dept of Justice; 2013.

23. Sessions J. *Marijuana Enforcement*. Washington, DC: US Dept of Justice; 2018.

24. Selsky A. Oregon preparing for possible interstate pot commerce. *Associated Press*. June 11, 2019.

25. Pacula RL, Kilmer B, Wagenaar AC, Chaloupka FJ, Caulkins JP. Developing public health regulations for marijuana: lessons from alcohol and tobacco. *Am J Public Health*. 2014;104(6):1021–1028.

26. Mäkelä K, Viikari M. Notes on alcohol and the state. *Acta Sociologica*. 1977;20:155–178.

27. Carnevale JT, Kagan R, Murphy PJ, Esrick J. A practical framework for regulating for-profit recreational marijuana in US States: lessons from Colorado and Washington. *Int J Drug Policy.* 2017;42:71–85.

28. Arcview Market Research. *The State of Legal Cannabis Markets.* 8th ed. Oakland, CA: Arcview Group; 2020.

29. Caulkins JP, Pardo B, Kilmer B. Intensity of cannabis use: findings from three online surveys. *Int J Drug Policy.* 2020;79:102740.

30. Cook PJ. *Paying the Tab: The Costs and Benefits of Alcohol Control.* Princeton, NJ: Princeton University Press; 2007.

31. Mosher J. *Protecting Our Youth: Options for Marijuana Regulation in California.* Ventura, CA: Ventura County Behavioral Health, Alcohol and Drug Programs; 2015.

32. World Health Organization. *WHO Framework Convention on Tobacco Control.* Geneva, Switzerland: World Health Organization; 2003.

33. Carpenter D, Moss D. *Preventing Regulatory Capture.* New York: Cambridge University Press; 2014.

34. Erickson P. *When Suppliers Morph Into Retailers.* May 2018. Available at: http://healthyalcoholmarket.com/pdf/NewsletterMay2018.pdf. Accessed May 20, 2021.

35. Erickson P. *Regulate Marijuana Like Alcohol in 1934 or Skip to 2018?* June 2018. Available at: http://healthyalcoholmarket.com/pdf/NewsletterJune2018.pdf. Accessed May 20, 2021.

36. Washington State Liquor and Cannabis Board. Year one canopy report. 2019. Available at: https://lcb.wa.gov/sites/default/files/publications/Marijuana/YearOneCanopy.pdf. Accessed April 2, 2021.

37. Quinton S. Too much weed? Oregon's got a marijuana surplus and officials aren't too happy. *USA Today.* July 12, 2019.

38. Washington State Liquor and Cannabis Board. FAQs on marijuana. 2019. Available at: https://lcb.wa.gov/mj2015/faqs_i-502. Accessed March 25, 2021.

39. Peña J. Jack of all trades or master of one. *Marijuana Business Magazine.* March 2019; *Marijuana Business Daily.* 2019:77–82.

40. Bowling C, Glantz SA. Civic engagement in California cannabis policy development. *J Psychoactive Drugs.* 2019;51(5):391–399.

41. Gorovitz E, Mosher J, Pertschuk M. Preemption or prevention? lessons from efforts to control firearms, alcohol, and tobacco. *J Public Health Policy.* 1998;19(1):36–50.

42. Crosbie E, Schmidt LA. Preemption in tobacco control: a framework for other areas of public health. *Am J Public Health.* 2020;110(3):345–350.

43. Dilley JA, Hitchcock L, McGroder N, Greto LA, Richardson SM. Community-level policy responses to state marijuana legalization in Washington State. *Int J Drug Policy.* 2017;42:102–108.

44. National Institute on Alcohol Abuse and Alcoholism, Alcohol Policy Information System (APIS). Recreational use of cannabis: volume 1. National Institutes of Health. 2019. Available at: https://alcoholpolicy.niaaa.nih.gov/cannabis-policy-topics/recreational-use-of-cannabis-volume-1/104. Accessed March 25, 2021.

45. Mosher J, Sparks M, Treffers R. *Safeguarding Our Communities: Municipal Regulation of Medical Marijuana Cultivation.* Ventura, CA: Ventura County Behavioral Health; 2016.

46. Public Health Institute, Getting it Right from the Start. Our model ordinances. 2019. Available at: https://www.gettingitrightfromthestart.org/our-model-ordinances. Accessed March 25, 2021.

47. The Cannabis Corner. About us. 2019. Available at: www.thecannabiscorner.org/about. Accessed July 11, 2019.

48. Elder R, Lawrence B, Janes G, et al. Enhanced enforcement of laws prohibiting sale of alcohol to minors: systematic review of effectiveness for reducing sales and underage drinking. *Transportation Res.* 2007;(E-C123):181–188.

49. Shults RA, Elder RW, Sleet DA, et al. Reviews of evidence regarding interventions to reduce alcohol-impaired driving. *Am J Prev Med.* 2001;21(Suppl 4):66–88.

50. Kilmer B, Davenport S, Smart R, Caulkins J, Midgette G. *After the Grand Opening: Assessing Cannabis Supply and Demand in Washington State.* Santa Monica, CA: RAND Corporation; 2019.

51. Oregon Liquor Control Commission. Recreational marijuana supply and demand. January 31, 2019. https://www.oregon.gov/olcc/marijuana/Documents/Bulletins/2019%20Supply%20and%20Demand%20Legislative%20Report%20FINAL%20for%20Publication(PDFA).pdf. Accessed July 9, 2021.

52. McCoy J. As Colorado's medical market finds a plateau, adult-use climbs 2x higher. *Cannabyte* blog. 2019. Available at: https://newfrontierdata.com/cannabis-insights/blog-as-colorados-medical-market-finds-a-plateau-adult-use-climbs-2x-higher. Accessed March 25, 2021.

53. MacCoun RJ. What can we learn from the Dutch cannabis coffeeshop system? *Addiction.* 2011;106(11):1899–1910.

54. Rolles S. *Cannabis Policy in the Netherlands: Moving Forwards Not Backwards.* Bristol, UK: Transform Drug Policy Foundation; 2014.

55. Korf DJ. *Cannabis Regulation in Europe: County Report Netherlands.* Amsterdam, The Netherlands: Transnational Institute; 2019.

56. Government of the Netherlands. Controlled cannabis supply chain experiment. 2020. Available at: https://www.government.nl/topics/drugs/controlled-cannabis-supply-chain-experiment. Accessed March 25, 2021.

57. Pascual A. Netherlands clarifies application process to grow adult-use cannabis. *Marijuana Business Daily.* July 16, 2020.

58. Belackova V, Roubalova Stefunkova M, van de Ven K. Overview of "home" cultivation policies and the case for community-based cannabis supply. *Int J Drug Policy*. 2019;71:36–46.

59. MacCoun R. *Estimating the Non-Price Effects of Legalization on Cannabis Consumption*. Santa Monica, CA: RAND Drug Policy Research Center; July 2010. WR-767-RC.

60. Decorte T, Pardal M, Queirolo R, Boidi MF, Sanchez Aviles C, Pares Franquero O. Regulating cannabis social clubs: a comparative analysis of legal and self-regulatory practices in Spain, Belgium and Uruguay. *Int J Drug Policy*. 2017;(43):44–56.

61. Malsbury A. California announces end date for collectives and cooperatives. Harris Bricken *Canna Law Blog* blog. 2018. Vol 2019.

62. Washington State Senate. History of Washington State Marijuana Laws. National Conference of State Legislatures; 2015.

63. Caplan G. Medical marijuana: a study of unintended consequences. *43 McGeorge Law Rev.* 2012;127:126–143.

64. Queirolo R, Boidi MF, Cruz JM. Cannabis clubs in Uruguay: the challenges of regulation. *Int J Drug Policy*. 2016;34:41–48.

65. Instituto de Regulación y Control del Cannabis. Clubes de Membresía con habilitación vigente. 2020. Available at: https://www.ircca.gub.uy/clubesaprobados. Accessed March 25, 2021.

66. Decorte T. Cannabis social clubs in Belgium: organizational strengths and weaknesses, and threats to the model. *Int J Drug Policy*. 2015;26(2):122–130.

67. Pardal M, Decorte T, Bone M, Parés Ò, Johansson J. Mapping cannabis social clubs in Europe. *Eur J Criminology*. 2020:1–24.

68. Pardal M. An analysis of Belgian cannabis social clubs' supply practices: a shapeshifting model? *Int J Drug Policy*. 2018;57:32–41.

69. Borland R. A strategy for controlling the marketing of tobacco products: a regulated market model. *Tob Control*. 2003;12(4):374–382.

70. Grossman ER, Binakonsky J, Jernigan D. The use of regulatory power by US state and local alcohol control agencies to ban problematic products. *Subst Use Misuse*. 2018;53(8): 1229–1238.

71. Hahn RA, Middleton JC, Elder R, et al. Effects of alcohol retail privatization on excessive alcohol consumption and related harms: a community guide systematic review. *Am J Prev Med*. 2012;42(4):418–427.

72. Canadian Centre on Substance Abuse and Addiction. Interactive map of provincial and territorial cannabis regulations. 2020. Available at: https://www.ccsa.ca/policy-and-regulations-cannabis. Accessed March 25, 2021.

73. Government of Canada. Cannabis in Canada: What you need to know about cannabis. 2019. Available at: https://www.canada.ca/en/services/health/campaigns/cannabis/canadians. html#a9. Accessed March 25, 2021.

74. Kilmer B, MacCoun RJ. How medical marijuana smoothed the transition to the marijuana legalization in the United States. *Annu Rev Law Social Sci.* 2017;13:181–202.

75. Virginia Alcoholic Beverage Control Authority. Authority FAQs. 2019. available at: https://www.abc.virginia.gov/about/agency-overview/authority-faqs. Accessed March 25, 2021.

76. Orenstein DG, Glantz S. Cannabis legalization in state legislatures: public health opportunity and risk. *Marquette Law Rev.* 2020;103(4).

77. Prescription Drug Abuse Policy System. Medical marijuana dispensaries: 2. Are dispensaries required to operate as not-for-profit entitites? 2019. Available at: http://pdaps.org/datasets/dispensaries-medical-marijuana-1501611712. Accessed March 25, 2021.

78. Orenstein DG, Glantz SA. Regulating cannabis manufacturing: applying public health best practices from tobacco control. *J Psychoactive Drugs.* 2018;50(1):19–32.

79. California Bureau of Cannabis Control. Cannabis Advisory Committee members. 2019. Available at: https://bcc.ca.gov/about_us/committee_members.html. Accessed March 25, 2021.

80. Maybin S. Uruguay: The world's marijuana pioneer. *BBC News.* April 4, 2019.

81. Freudenberg N. The manufacture of lifestyle: the role of corporations in unhealthy living. *J Public Health Policy.* 2012;33(2):244–256.

5

Cannabis Regulation and Social Justice: Effects and Implications for Communities

There is no doubt that the nation's cannabis policies have exacerbated inequities and discrimination against certain populations. It is critical that updates and changes to current cannabis policies take into account reforms to prevent further harm and advance social justice.

–Maryland State Senator Clarence Lam, MD, MPH, email communication, December 26, 2020

SUMMARY AND INTRODUCTION

- Cannabis law enforcement, both before and after legalization, disproportionately affects poor—and particularly Black and Latinx—communities, with long-term effects on both individuals and communities.
- Legalization of nonmedical cannabis use has been driven at least in part by concerns about these disproportionate effects.
- Decriminalizing arrests for cannabis use and possession can address this injustice, without full legalization of nonmedical cannabis for commercial sale.
- Research suggests that legalizing cannabis for nonmedical use greatly decreases the overall number of cannabis-related arrests but does not eliminate racial inequalities among those arrested.
- Some states with legalized nonmedical cannabis have implemented well-intentioned programs promoting entry into the cannabis market by members of groups harmed by cannabis prohibition. These programs may have the unintended effect of increasing cannabis consumption and harms in these communities by concentrating cannabis investment and retail outlets there.
- A better approach to rectifying past cannabis-related injustices would be to reinvest cannabis revenues in affected communities in non-cannabis businesses and services.

Rectifying past social injustices has been a major driver of efforts to reform the nation's cannabis laws. The United States has a long history of drug wars that discriminate against specific populations, particularly immigrant and racial minorities.[1-3] There is little doubt that cannabis laws have historically harmed these populations. This chapter reviews the research evidence that sheds light on these issues and provides evidence-based recommendations that show promise in addressing this history of social injustice.

CANNABIS PROHIBITION IN THE UNITED STATES

While a full history of cannabis in the United States is beyond the scope of this book, it should be noted that cannabis products were generally available in the latter half of the 19th century, primarily for medicinal use. They were mostly swallowed, not smoked, and the frequency with which this could lead to unpleasant overdoses may be one reason why medicinal use declined.[4] With waves of Mexican immigrants entering the United States in the early 20th century, cannabis smoking became more common, as this was the primary way that Mexican people ingested the drug. However, the "Mexican hypothesis" that both cannabis use and anti-cannabis sentiment in the first decades of the 20th century originated with Mexican immigrants turns out to be another example of racism infecting US drug policy, since cannabis use in Mexico itself at that time was limited, being common only among soldiers and prisoners.[5]

The Pure Food and Drug Act of 1906 required the listing of cannabis, along with other narcotics, on labels of medicinal preparations shipped in interstate commerce. The Harrison Act of 1914 further restricted pharmaceutical trade in cannabis products, requiring physicians and pharmacists handling cannabis to register, pay special taxes, and keep careful records. State-level prohibitions of cannabis use occurred in the Northeast, the Midwest, and the West (California) between 1912 and 1915, long before Mexican immigrants reached many of those states, but concomitant with efforts to reduce access to alcohol and other intoxicants.[4]

By the 1930s, cannabis use had become identified with "suspect marginal groups," including artists, intellectuals, jazz musicians, petty criminals, and Black and Mexican people.[6] Leadership of the Federal Bureau of Narcotics used rising anti-immigrant sentiment to encourage states to pass the Uniform State Narcotic Act, and 48 states had done so by 1936, making cannabis available solely by prescription. In 1937 Congress found a way to effectively ban cannabis use at the federal level through the Marihuana Tax Act, which set prohibitive taxes on the transfer of cannabis products. While marijuana had appeared in every edition of the *United States Pharmacopeia* since 1850, the 1941 edition removed it.[7]

Prohibitive attitudes toward cannabis began to ebb in the 1960s and reached their nadir in 1970, when Congress passed the Comprehensive Drug Abuse Prevention and Control Act. This act reduced simple possession of any illegal drug to a misdemeanor and moved away from mandatory sentencing guidelines but left cannabis in the newly created Schedule I category of drugs—those with no known medicinal value and with a high potential for addiction. When the country shifted to the right with the election of Ronald Reagan as president in 1980, the pendulum swung back to criminal justice and punitive approaches to illegal drug use. Definition of cannabis as a Schedule I drug left its users vulnerable to the newly strengthened mandatory minimum sentences and three-strikes laws—punishments far out of proportion to the damage done by cannabis to its users or society as a whole and contributing to what would become the racially biased mass incarceration phenomenon of today.

RACIAL INEQUALITIES IN CANNABIS LAW ENFORCEMENT

The shift to punitive approaches intensified in the 1990s, with serious consequences in particular for the Black community. Between 1990 and 2002 alone, arrests for drug offenses grew by 41%, an increase of 450,000 arrests; 82% of the growth stemmed from cannabis arrests and 79% from arrests for cannabis possession only.[8] While only a very small percentage of these resulted in felony convictions, the arrests occurred disproportionately among Black people, who comprised 14% of cannabis users but 30% of those arrested for cannabis law violations.[8]

The 2018 National Incident-Based Reporting System (NIBRS) numbers show that 497,093 individuals were arrested for cannabis possession that year. Figure 5-1 shows arrests for cannabis possession as reported to the NIBRS system from 2008 through 2018.[9] Not all law enforcement agencies routinely report their data to this system,[10] and comparisons across years are discouraged. What remains clear is that there are still hundreds of thousands of cannabis arrests each year. The large increase in the number of daily/near-daily users means that the number of days on which Americans use cannabis is on the rise. However, while there are still large numbers of arrests, these have not kept up with the rise in days of use. This has been interpreted as a decrease in intensity of cannabis enforcement. A 2015 analysis estimated that there was one arrest for every 2,900 days of use in 2007; by 2013, this had fallen to one arrest for every 5,800 days of use.[11]

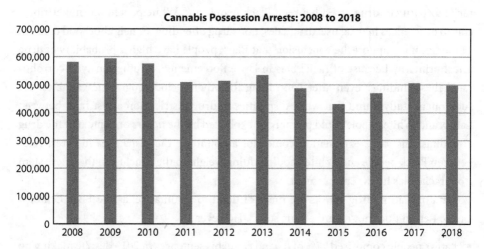

Source: Based on Federal Bureau of Investigation.[9]

Figure 5-1. Cannabis Possession Arrests in the United States: 2008–2018

A 2012 study analyzed arrest probabilities for cannabis possession and differences by age, race, and gender between 1982 and 2008. It found that

- In most years, a cannabis user's probability of being arrested for cannabis possession was less than 1% per year;
- In 2008, arrest rates were more than three times what they were in 1991;
- As of 2008, Black people were more than three times as likely to be arrested compared with White people, despite almost identical rates of cannabis use; and
- Among young males, 15- to 19-year-olds were arrested at almost twice the rate of 20- to 29-year-olds.[12]

A 2013 report found that between 2001 and 2010, cannabis arrests increased by 18% and accounted for 52% of all drug arrests in this country. Black people were 3.73 times more likely to be arrested for cannabis possession than White people; data on Latinx people were not available.[13] A 2020 report updated these findings: cannabis arrests decreased by 18% from 2010 to 2018, but Black people were still 3.64 times more likely than White people to be arrested for cannabis possession, a slight decrease from the 2010 ratio.[14]

There are at least three possible explanations for racial disparities in drug arrests: the *extent* of drug offending by race; the *nature* of drug offending in lower-income neighborhoods; and conscious or subconscious *racial bias* by police.[15] For cannabis, use is fairly similar across racial groups (see Chapter 1), debunking the first explanation. Compared with White people, Black people were twice as likely in 2002 to buy cannabis outdoors, three times more likely to buy from a stranger, and nearly 50% more likely to buy cannabis away from their home; these purchase patterns may explain a relatively modest portion of the difference in arrest rates.[16] However, according to one study, 85% of the racial disparity of drug arrest between Black people and White people was not attributable to differences in drug use, drug sales, non-drug offending, or neighborhood context. These findings support the conclusion that Black people have higher probability of drug arrest primarily because of racial bias in law enforcement.[15] Another analysis corroborated these findings, even after controlling for other sociodemographic variables.[17] A subsequent study found that while disparities in drug distribution arrest rates between Latinx and White people could possibly be explained by the *nature* or context of the drug offending, this same explanation could not account for the disparities in arrest rates between Black people and White people, adding weight to the conclusion that these stem from racial bias in law enforcement.[18]

Data on Latinx drug arrests are more difficult to summarize, as the FBI's Uniform Crime Report does not record ethnic status. However

- Latinx people comprised 77% of federal cannabis sentences in 2015 despite making up less than 20% of the US population.[19]

- In 2009, Latinx people in Arizona had a drug possession (all drugs) arrest rate of 516.5 per 100,000, compared with 450.8 for White people.[20]
- In New York City from 2015 to 2017, Latinx people were arrested on low-level cannabis charges at five times the rate of White people; in the first three months of 2018, of 4,000 people arrested for cannabis possession, 89% were Black or Latinx.[21]

A 2014 National Academy of Sciences report noted that from 1973 to 2009, state and federal prison populations increased from 200,000 to 1.5 million, giving the United States the largest penal population in the world and a rate of incarceration 5 to 50 times higher than that of Western European and other democracies. The report pointed to "extraordinary rates of incarceration in Black and Latinx communities" and concluded that "Intensified enforcement of drug laws subject Black people, more than White people, to new mandatory minimum sentences—despite lower levels of drug use and no higher demonstrated levels of trafficking."[22]

Involvement with the criminal justice system has exacerbated other disparities. Arrest and felony convictions can have further harsh consequences, including denial of federal financial aid for postsecondary education, of access to food stamps and public housing, and of the right to vote. A history of incarceration reduces employment prospects and lowers wages; these losses in aggregate lifetime earnings are greater for Black and Latino men.[23] Both current and formerly incarcerated persons are at elevated risk of chronic health conditions (e.g., cardiovascular disease, infectious diseases, cancer) compared with the general population.[24] These consequences may extend through generations; a longitudinal study found that young adults with an incarcerated parent during childhood were at higher risk of a host of negative outcomes, including anxiety disorder, illicit drug use disorder, having a felony charge, incarceration, not completing high school, early parenthood, and being socially isolated, even after controlling for childhood psychiatric diagnoses and adversity exposure.[25]

Impact of Decriminalization on Cannabis Arrests

Researchers have used the term *decriminalization* to describe a wide range of policy changes, to the point that some consider it too broad to accurately identify how states treat low-level cannabis-related offenses in their criminal justice systems.[26] This terminology problem has complicated efforts to assess effects of cannabis law reform on a variety of outcomes, including racial disparities (see Box 5-1). As of 2020, there were 27 states and the District of Columbia that had decriminalized small amounts of cannabis intended for personal use, meaning that possession was still illegal but was treated as a civil or local infraction with no possibility of jail time.[28] Conviction could lead to small fines, treatment mandates, community service, or other civil penalties, but not the harsher consequences associated with criminal penalties described previously.

Box 5-1. Depenalization, Decriminalization, and Other Terms

The term *depenalization* refers to any policy that reduces the penalties associated with the possession or use of cannabis. These penalties can be criminal or civil in nature. *Decriminalization* refers specifically to policies that change the offense type from criminal to noncriminal. *Defelonization*, another term sometimes used, generally describes changing a drug possession offense from a felony to a misdemeanor; California did this in 2014 for offenses related to the possession of narcotics, controlled substances, and concentrated cannabis in California through Proposition 47.[27] Decriminalization and defelonization policies may be considered more specific forms, or even subsets, of depenalization; however, some researchers have termed states *decriminalized* even when they have not statutorily removed the criminal status for cannabis possession offenses.[28]

Analysis of 2014 Uniform Crime Reporting data for all 50 US states found no significant differences in arrest rates for property crime, violent crime, murder, robbery, rape, burglary, motor vehicle theft, or drug abuse between states that had decriminalized and those that had not.[29] This suggests that decriminalization has not worsened other forms of crime; however, it has had a significant impact on cannabis-related arrest rates. Analysis of data from five states that decriminalized cannabis showed a 75% reduction in the rate of cannabis possession arrests for youth and similar effects on adult arrests between 2008 and 2014; there was no apparent impact on rates of cannabis use in the past 30 days.[30]

Impact of Legalization on Cannabis Arrests

Recent reports from states that have legalized cannabis for nonmedical use indicate that while cannabis arrests have decreased, racial disparities in cannabis arrest rates persist.[14] In Colorado, cannabis arrests decreased by 52% between 2012 and 2017 (from 12,709 to 6,153), but in 2017 the cannabis arrest rate for Black people (233 per 100,000) remained nearly double that of White people.[31] Washington State legalized via ballot initiative in November 2012; analysis of arrest data from 2012 to 2015 found that

- Cannabis arrest rates for Black adults age 21 and older dropped following legalization, but disparities relative to White adults grew from 2.5 to 5 times higher.
- Arrest rates for 18- to 20-year-old Black adults also decreased but remained nearly twice as high as those of White young people.
- Arrests for distributing or selling fell by 67% among White people and by just 5% for Black people.[32]

It is important to note that states that have legalized cannabis for nonmedical use have not necessarily decriminalized or reduced the penalties given to young people for cannabis possession. Analysis of Uniform Crime Reporting data on arrests in 38 states between 2000 and 2016 found that while legalization of cannabis for non-medical use benefited adults through fewer arrests, it did not appear to reduce arrests for cannabis possession among youth.[33] To the contrary, in Oregon, youth cannabis-related allegations (offenses referred by law enforcement to juvenile departments before appearing in court) increased by 32% after legalization of cannabis for non-medical use, even after adjusting for cannabis use trends among youth. The largest disparities were found among Native Americans/Alaska Natives compared with White youth. A possible explanation for the increase in youth arrests could be changes in statutory language made in 2015 that defined possession as consumption within the past 24 hours.[34]

In summary, research suggests that legalizing cannabis for nonmedical use greatly decreases the overall number of cannabis-related arrests but does not eliminate racial or age disparities among those arrested.

Efforts to Mitigate Community Effects of Cannabis Regulation

Expungement

As of 2020, at least 23 states and the District of Columbia had enacted laws facilitating cannabis conviction expungement and other forms of record relief, such as sealing and set-aside, to mitigate some of the adverse effects criminal records can have on individuals.[35] Illinois, for example, now directs local law enforcement and the Illinois State Police to expunge arrests automatically for residents who were convicted for possessing up to 30 grams of cannabis, provided that certain conditions (e.g., nonviolent crime, not involving a minor) apply.[36]

Social Equity Programs

The City of Oakland, California, pioneered cannabis equity programs in 2017 when it instituted a system to award half of all available cannabis licenses to applicants who were prosecuted for cannabis-related crimes or harmed by broad impacts of the War on Drugs.[37] By April 2020, at least six states and some local communities (particularly in California[38]) had taken steps to facilitate equitable participation in the legal cannabis industry by individuals and communities disproportionately harmed by prior cannabis laws. These programs establish criteria for eligibility, often provide additional training and technical assistance on license applications to qualified individuals, and in some cases reduce licensing and application fees. Table 5-1 outlines cannabis industry social equity programs in the six states that have adopted them thus far.

Table 5-1. Cannabis Industry Social Equity Programs

State	Key Program Components	Eligibility
California	Grant funds are for the purpose of assisting local equity applicants and local equity licensees in that local jurisdiction to gain entry to, and successfully operate in, the state's regulated cannabis marketplace. Assistance that grant funds may be used for includes, but is not limited to, any of the following: • Providing a loan or grant to a local equity applicant or local equity licensee to assist with start-up and ongoing costs, including but not limited to rent, leases, local and state application and licensing fees, regulatory adherence, testing of cannabis, equipment, capital improvements, and training and retention of a qualified and diverse workforce • Supporting local equity program efforts to provide sources of capital to qualified applicants and licensees • Providing direct technical assistance to local equity applicants and licensees • Assisting in the administration of local equity programs	To qualify for equity grant funding, a local jurisdiction must meet the following criteria: • Allows commercial cannabis businesses to operate within its jurisdictional boundaries; • Has adopted or operates a local equity program; • Has identified a local equity applicant or a local equity licensee that the local jurisdiction could assist through use of grant funding; and • Has demonstrated the ability to provide, or created a plan to provide, services as identified in Provision 4 of the Budget Act of 2019, Item 1111-490 —Reappropriation.

Illinois	Social equity applicants can receive the following supports and services:
	• Technical assistance and support provided through the Illinois Department of Commerce and Economic Opportunity to social equity applicants on everything from creating a business plan to applying for a license at locations throughout the state
	• 50 points (out of a possible total of 250) on their dispensary license application score or 200 points (out of a possible 1,000) on their craft grower, infuser, or transporter license application score
	• Reduced license and application fees
	• Access to low-interest loans from the state for starting and operating a cannabis-related business
		Social equity applicants must meet the following criteria:
		• Have at least 51% ownership and control by one or more individuals who
		  ○ Lived in a disproportionately impacted area for 5 of the past 10 years; and
		  ○ Was personally or has a parent, child, or spouse who was convicted of or adjudicated delinquent for cannabis-related offenses eligible for expungement, including possession of up to 500 grams or intent to deliver up to 30 grams.
		• Have more than 10 full-time employees, more than half of whom
		  ○ Currently reside in a disproportionately impacted area; and
		  ○ Have personally or has a parent, child, or spouse who has been arrested for, convicted of, or adjudicated delinquent for cannabis-related offenses eligible for expungement, including possession of up to 500 grams or intent to deliver up to 30 grams.

(Continued)

Table 5-1. (Continued)

State	Key Program Components	Eligibility
Massachusetts	The Social Equity Program (SEP) is a free, statewide technical assistance and training program that provides education, skill-based training, and tools for success in the cannabis industry. The SEP focuses on those most impacted by the War on Drugs, marijuana prohibition, and/or disproportionate arrests and incarceration. It provides education and entry across four areas: entrepreneurship, entry-level and managerial-level workforce development, and ancillary business support.	Massachusetts gives priority to economic empowerment applicants who demonstrate at least three of the following criteria: • Majority of ownership belongs to people who have lived in areas of disproportionate impact for 5 of the last 10 years. • Majority of ownership has held one or more previous positions where the primary population served were disproportionately impacted or where primary responsibilities included economic education, resource provision, or empowerment to disproportionately impacted individuals or communities. • At least 51% of current employees/subcontractors reside in areas of disproportionate impact and will increase to 75% by first day of business. • At least 51% of employees or subcontractors have drug-related court arraignment records but are otherwise legally employable in a cannabis-related enterprise. • A majority of the ownership comprises Black and Hispanic/Latinx individuals. • Owners can demonstrate significant past experience in or business practices that promote economic empowerment in areas of disproportionate impact.
Michigan	Qualified applicants can receive discounts on their application, initial license, and renewal fees, including • 25% reduction for meeting residency requirement (required) • Additional 25% reduction if they have a cannabis-related conviction (except for distribution to a minor) • Additional 10% reduction if they were a licensed caregiver for at least two years between 2008 and 2017 A social equity program team assists qualified applicants with applications and potential partners for assistance.	Disproportionately impacted communities are identified through two criteria: • Marijuana-related convictions—average number per county • Poverty—30% or more of the population living below the federal poverty level Applicants must have lived in one of the 41 identified communities for five consecutive years and commit to operating a business in one of those communities.
Oregon	No statewide initiative; local jurisdictions may have programs.	

(Continued)

Table 5-1. (Continued)

State	Key Program Components	Eligibility
Washington (legislation passed in March 2020)	34 retail licenses costing $1,480, with an application fee of $250, will be available from December 1, 2020, until July 1, 2028.	Retail licenses to be awarded to members of the community disproportionately impacted by "the enforcement of cannabis-related laws" (guidelines still to be determined).

Source: Based on Malsbury,[39] California Bureau of Cannabis Control,[40] Siam,[41] Massachusetts Cannabis Control Commission,[42] California Bureau of Cannabis Control,[43] and Michigan Department of Licensing and Regulatory Affairs.[44]

Such programs in Illinois, Michigan, and Washington State have only recently begun; the Massachusetts program has faced significant implementation hurdles, including funding challenges and logistical barriers. At least initially, few equity applicants in that state have managed to get their business off the ground, as large corporate interests dominate the market.[45] As of November 2020, almost 75% of the registered agents with the Massachusetts Cannabis Control Commission were White and only 10% of the businesses were minority owned.[46] While there are little national data on industry representation,[47] a 2017 anonymous online survey of self-identified cannabis industry senior executives and owners/founders found that 19% of those who launched a cannabis business and/or have an ownership stake in a business were racial minorities (5.7% Latinx, 4.3% Black, 2.4% Asian, and 6.7% Other)[48] and about a quarter of cannabis businesses were owned or founded by women.[49]

Some states have allocated dedicated revenue to support these programs. The ballot initiative that brought about legalization of nonmedical cannabis in California promised that cannabis revenues would fund drug abuse prevention and treatment, public safety, protecting the environment from the harms of cannabis cultivation, and economic development. The state set as its initial revenue priority funding cannabis regulation, with financial support for social equity programs and university research in a second tier. The remaining discretionary income was intended for the community programs, but initial revenues have fallen short of projections, leaving many of the programs without state funding, although some localities have used their share of cannabis tax revenues to support them.[50] Because California permits local governments to tax cannabis, some jurisdictions have used this revenue to fund a variety of youth, mental health, and other social services focused on disadvantaged communities. However, the bulk of these local revenues has gone to law enforcement.[51]

In 2019 California dedicated $10 million to local jurisdictions for social equity programs, and by October of that year, 10 jurisdictions had received grants ranging from $100,000 to $1.6 million.[39] By April 2020, the funding amount had grown to $30 million, and 16 jurisdictions had received funding.[52] The California funding was explicitly for helping individuals from communities negatively affected by cannabis criminalization to engage in the cannabis marketplace (see Table 5-1). In 2020, Washington State set aside $1.1 million annually to help aspiring cannabis licensees with such issues as the application process, business plan development, and assistance for microloans.

If these programs are to succeed, they need clear definitions of the groups or communities they target. It is not always clear whether the beneficiaries are individuals or neighborhoods or zip codes. Without such clarity, the amount of money to be made from cannabis sales may incentivize "gaming" the system, which could lead to benefits accruing to the wrong parties.

These social equity efforts may also have unintended consequences. Prioritizing and subsidizing licenses of multiple small operators in a community will increase competition among them, driving prices down and imperiling their ability to survive. As Dr. Timothy Naimi, formerly of Boston Medical Center and now director of the Canadian Institute for Substance Use Research, observed

> It's not unlike 30 or 40 years ago when they put a lot of alcohol outlets in inner city neighborhoods. I'm in general, very skeptical of selling substances as a means of economic growth, or that we can't think of anything better to do. It's a zero-sum game; it creates some revenue, there are going to be a lot of people penalized by it, either by economics or just in terms of health outcomes. Putting a bunch of outlets in poor neighborhoods is likely to exacerbate health disparities and will probably actually suck money out of that community when you look at the aggregate economy. (Tim Naimi, MD, Canadian Institute for Substance Use Research, and Jason Blanchette, JD, MPH, Boston University School of Public Health, in person interview, June 18, 2019.)

Dr. Beau Kilmer, director of the Drug Policy Research Center at RAND, has encouraged consideration of an alternative:

> We're already seeing some of the mom-and-pop businesses in Washington going out of business because they gave out way too many producer licenses in Washington and Oregon. The prices are going down, so if you think by giving preferences to certain groups that it is going to help build wealth in these communities, you need to think about price decline. . . . Another option is to just do a state-store model where you can keep the prices inflated, and say, for example, that 30% of this revenue is going to be put into evidence-based programs that we know can build wealth. (Beau Kilmer, PhD, RAND, in person interview, September 11, 2019.)

As discussed in Chapter 7, cannabis retail outlets can have negative consequences for the communities in which they are located, particularly when they are concentrated in relatively small geographic areas. Low-income communities are already the most likely locales for high concentrations of cannabis retail outlets, for the simple reason that wealthier communities are more likely to organize to keep them out. An overconcentration of cannabis outlets in poor neighborhoods may hamper their efforts to develop diverse and successful local economies. Dr. Naimi has argued that when state governments prioritize cannabis businesses in low-income neighborhoods, it

> helps them make it appear that they are addressing this wrong with something that may actually further worsen substance abuse problems in that community. They are also getting around the issue of the NIMBY ("not in my backyard") problem, because all the rich White people would prefer that these be located in nearby communities that aren't their own. (Tim Naimi, MD, Canadian Institute for Substance Use Research, and Jason Blanchette, JD, MPH, Boston University School of Public Health, in person interview, June 18, 2019.)

The Massachusetts program does not require placement of outlets in disproportionately affected neighborhoods, but it does ask applicants what they will do to benefit those areas, according to Shawn Collins, Executive Director of the Massachusetts Cannabis Control Commission. This could include prioritizing hiring from those areas, even if the outlet is placed elsewhere. (Shawn Collins, JD, Cannabis Control Commission, in person interview, June 19, 2019.)

While legislators and regulators clearly show good intentions in creating social equity programs that provide assistance to communities harmed by the War on Drugs, the long-term outcomes of these approaches are not known. If the programs result in additional cannabis outlets in socially disadvantaged communities, the harms may not be worth the anticipated economic benefits.

In contrast, programs that involve reinvestment of cannabis revenues in disproportionately affected neighborhoods have the potential to encourage wealth creation in those neighborhoods without the risk of increased harm related to drug use. Community-level wealth building employs two central tactics: *leveraging* existing spending of local public and nonprofit institutions such as hospitals, universities, city government, museums, and local foundations; and *anchoring* that spending in the local community by designing and supporting local businesses, with ownership structures embedded in the community that meet the institutions' needs.[53] While this approach has gained adherents and spawned experiments in cities as diverse as Cleveland, Ohio, Austin, Texas, and Richmond, Virginia, no state as of this writing has moved to designate cannabis revenues to non-cannabis-related wealth-creation activities.

POLICY RECOMMENDATIONS

- To continue to reduce what have become very high arrest rates for cannabis use, states should decriminalize cannabis possession for both adults and youth.
- States should establish expungement programs for previous cannabis-related criminal convictions, placing the burden of the expungement process on the criminal justice system and not on previously convicted individuals.
- Disparities in arrests of Black and Latinx persons should be addressed in and of themselves and separately from changes in cannabis policy.

- Social equity programs promoting cannabis industry involvement by members of communities disproportionately affected by prior punitive approaches to cannabis regulation should be carefully examined for possible unintended adverse consequences.
- Jurisdictions should explore options for reinvesting cannabis revenue into socially disadvantaged communities without linking these initiatives to cannabis businesses.

REFERENCES

1. Lusane C, Desmond D. *Pipe Dream Blues: Racism and the War on Drugs.* Boston, MA: South End Press; 1991.

2. Gusfield J. *Symbolic Crusade: Status Politics and the American Temperance Movement.* Urbana: University of Illinois Press; 1963.

3. Provine DM. Race and inequality in the War on Drugs. *Annu Rev Law Social Sci.* 2011;7(1):41–60.

4. Campos I. Mexicans and the origins of marijuana prohibition in the United States: a reassessment. *Social Hist Alcohol Drugs (SHAD).* 2018;32:6–37.

5. Campos I. *Home Grown: Marijuana and the Origins of Mexico's War on Drugs.* Chapel Hill: University of North Carolina Press; 2012.

6. Morgan HW. *Drugs in America: A Social History, 1800–1980.* Syracuse, NY: Syracuse University Press; 1981.

7. Ferraiolo K. From killer weed to popular medicine: the evolution of American drug control policy, 1937–2000. *J Policy History.* 2007;19(2):147–179.

8. King RS, Mauer M. The war on marijuana: the transformation of the war on drugs in the 1990s. *Harm Reduct J.* 2006;3:6.

9. Federal Bureau of Investigation. Crime data explorer. 2019. Available at: https://crime-data-explorer.fr.cloud.gov/explorer/national/united-states/arrest. Accessed March 30, 2021.

10. Doonan SM, Hamilton JR, Johnson JK. Using the National Incident-Based Reporting System (NIBRS) to examine racial and ethnic disparities in cannabis incidents. *Am J Drug Alcohol Abuse.* 2020;46(5):513–519.

11. Humphreys K. Even as marijuana use rises, arrests are falling. *Washington Post.* 2015.

12. Nguyen H, Reuter P. How risky is marijuana possession? considering the role of age, race, and gender. *Crime & Delinquency.* 2012;58(6):879–910.

13. American Civil Liberties Union (ACLU). *The War on Marijuana in Black and White.* New York: ACLU; 2013.

14. American Civil Liberties Union (ACLU). *A Tale of Two Countries: Racially Targeted Arrests in the Era of Marijuana Reform.* New York: ACLU; 2020.

15. Mitchell O, Caudy MS. Examining racial disparities in drug arrests. *Justice Q.* 2015;32(2): 288–313.

16. Ramchand R, Pacula RL, Iguchi MY. Racial differences in marijuana-users' risk of arrest in the United States. *Drug Alcohol Depend.* 2006;84(3):264–272.

17. Koch DW, Lee J, Lee K. Coloring the War on Drugs: arrest disparities in black, brown, and white. *Race Soc Problems.* 2016;8:313–325.

18. Mitchell O, Caudy MS. Race differences in drug offending and drug distribution arrests. *Crime & Delinquency.* 2017;63(2):91–112.

19. Nelson S. Latinos got 77 percent of federal pot sentences last year. *US News & World Report.* March 15, 2017.

20. Males M, Macallair D. *Scapegoating Immigrants: Arizona's Real Crisis Is Rooted in State Residents' Soaring Drug Abuse.* San Francisco, CA: Center on Juvenile and Criminal Justice; 2010.

21. Mueller B, Gebeloff R, Chinoy S. Surest way to face marijuana charges in New York: be black or hispanic. *New York Times.* May 13, 2018.

22. National Research Council. *The Growth of Incarceration in the United States: Exploring Causes and Consequences.* Washington, DC: National Research Council; 2014.

23. Wakefield S, Uggen C. Incarceration and stratification. *Annu Rev Sociol.* 2010;36:387–406.

24. Massoglia M, Remster B. Linkages between incarceration and health. *Public Health Rep.* 2019;134(suppl 1):8S–14S.

25. Gifford EJ, Eldred Kozecke L, Golonka M, et al. Association of parental incarceration with psychiatric and functional outcomes of young adults. *JAMA Netw Open.* 2019;2(8):e1910005.

26. Pacula RL, MacCoun R, Reuter P, et al. What does it mean to decriminalize marijuana? a cross-national empirical examination. *Adv Health Econ Health Serv Res.* 2005;16:347–369.

27. Mooney AC, Giannella E, Glymour MM, et al. Racial/ethnic disparities in arrests for drug possession after California Proposition 47, 2011–2016. *Am J Public Health.* 2018;108(8):987–993.

28. National Conference of State Legislatures (NCSL). Marijuana overview. 2020. Available at: https://www.ncsl.org/research/civil-and-criminal-justice/marijuana-overview.aspx#3. Accessed March 25, 2021.

29. Maier SL, Mannes, S., Koppenhofer, EL. The implication of marijuana decriminalization and legalization on crime in the United States. *Contemp Drug Problems.* 2017;44(2).

30. Grucza RA, Vuolo M, Krauss MJ, et al. Cannabis decriminalization: a study of recent policy change in five US states. *Int J Drug Policy.* 2018;59:67–75.

31. Reed JK. Impacts of marijuana legalization in Colorado: a report pursuant to Senate Bill 13-283. Colorado Department of Public Safety DoCJ; 2018. available at: https://cdpsdocs.state.co.us/ors/docs/reports/2018-SB13-283_Rpt.pdf. Accessed April 2, 2021.

32. Firth CL, Maher JE, Dilley JA, Darnell A, Lovrich NP. Did marijuana legalization in Washington State reduce racial disparities in adult marijuana arrests? *Subst Use Misuse.* 2019;54(9): 1582–1587.

33. Plunk AD, Peglow SL, Harrell PT, Grucza RA. Youth and adult arrests for cannabis possession after decriminalization and legalization of cannabis. *JAMA Pediatr.* 2019.

34. Firth CL, Hajat A, Dilley JA, Braun M, Maher JE. Implications of cannabis legalization on juvenile justice outcomes and racial disparities. *Am J Prev Med.* 2020;58(4):562–569.

35. Schlussel D. Marijuana expungement accelerates across the country. Collateral Consequences Resource Center; 2020. Available at: https://ccresourcecenter.org/2020/11/20/marijuana-expungement-accelerates-across-the-country. Accessed March 30, 2021.

36. McCoppin R. Getting marijuana convictions expunged in Illinois: what you need to know about the process. *Chicago Tribune.* August 30, 2019.

37. Ravani S. Oakland's groundbreaking cannabis equity program showing modest results so far. *San Francisco Chronicle.* May 25, 2019.

38. Silver LD, Naprawa AZ, Padon AA. Assessment of incorporation of lessons from tobacco control in city and county laws regulating legal marijuana in California. *JAMA Netw Open.* 2020;3(6):e208393.

39. Malsbury A. California cannabis equity programs are getting a boost from state and private sources. Harris Bricken, *Canna Law Blog* blog. October 16, 2019. Available at: https:// harrisbricken.com/cannalawblog/california-cannabis-equity-programs-are-getting-a-boost-from-state-and-private-sources. Accessed March 30, 2021.

40. California Bureau of Cannabis Control. Overview of California cannabis equity programs. 2018.

41. Siam K. Social equity programs in cannabis—worth their weight? Seyfarth. *The Blunt Truth* blog. 2020. A blog chronicling the evolution and implementation of marijuana laws in the United States.

42. Massachusetts Cannabis Control Commission (CCC). Guidance for equity provisions. 2019. Updated June 2020. Available at https://mass-cannabis-control.com/wp-content/uploads/2018/04/FINAL-Social-Provisions-Guidance-1PGR-1.pdf. Accessed March 27, 2021.

43. California Bureau of Cannabis Control. *Local Equity Grant Program Guidelines.* 2019:8.

44. Marijuana Regulatory Agency. Michigan Department of Licensing and Regulatory Affairs. Social equity (adult use). 2020. Available at: https://www.michigan.gov/lara/0,4601,7-154-89334_79571_93535---,00.html. Accessed March 30, 2021.

45. Healy B. You can't own more than three pot shops, but these companies are testing the limit and bragging about it. *Boston Globe.* March 21, 2019.

46. Massachusetts Cannabis Control Commission. Adult-use agent registration and ownership. 2020. Available at: https://opendata.mass-cannabis-control.com/stories/s/Agent-and-Owner-Registration/49ku-9nf3. Accessed March 30, 2021.

47. Adinoff B, Reiman A. Implementing social justice in the transition from illicit to legal cannabis. *Am J Drug Alcohol Abuse.* 2019;45(6):673–688.

48. McVey E. Chart: Percentage of cannabis business owners and founders by race. *Marijuana Business Daily.* September 11, 2017.

49. McVey E. Chart: Quarter of cannabis businesses are owned or were founded by women. *Marijuana Business Daily.* August 28, 2017.

50. Krieger LM. Where does California's cannabis tax money go? you might be surprised. *Mercury News.* May 25, 2019.

51. Youth Forward, Getting it Right from the Start. California cannabis tax revenues: a windfall for law enforcement or an opportunity for healing communities? Public Health Institute. 2020. Available at: https://www.phi.org/thought-leadership/california-cannabis-tax-revenues-a-windfall-for-law-enforcement-or-an-opportunity-for-healing-communities. Accessed April 5, 2021.

52. California Cannabis Equity Grants Program provides $30 million in grant funding for local jurisdictions. Press release. California Governor's Office of Business and Economic Development. April 21, 2020. Available at: https://business.ca.gov/california-cannabis-equity-grants-program-provides-30-million-in-grant-funding-for-local-jurisdictions. Accessed March 30, 2021 .

53. Dubb S. Community wealth building forms: what they are and how to use them at the local level. *Acad Manage Perspect.* 2016;30(2):141–152.

6

Cannabis Marketing

Cannabis products are changing and expanding rapidly, and states need to establish and continuously reevaluate a learning regulatory environment for adjusting regulations as new products and health effects emerge.

–Leslie McAhren, ABD, MPH, MFA, New Mexico Licensed Medical Cannabis Producer-Founder & Public Health Researcher, phone interview, September 5, 2019

SUMMARY AND INTRODUCTION

- A comprehensive public health approach to cannabis marketing should begin by defining permissible cannabis products and packaging, as well as the basic consumer information that any product should provide.
- Alcohol and tobacco marketing influence youth consumption; cannabis marketers have been particularly active in digital and social media, and early research indicates that this marketing is associated with youth use.
- US Supreme Court decisions as well as state constitutional provisions protecting commercial speech make regulation of cannabis advertising challenging and underscore the importance of "nonspeech" measures that can mitigate possible harmful effects of cannabis marketing.
- Some regulatory systems incentivize advertising more than others. If substantial marketing activity is likely, states should draw on lessons from alcohol and tobacco regulation to reduce and restrict marketing to the extent possible.
- Marketing restrictions should be accompanied by well-resourced systems of monitoring and enforcement.

This chapter begins to pull apart the components of a public health approach to cannabis regulation through the lens of the "four P's" of marketing. It opens with a broad overview of marketing and then explores in more depth regulation of cannabis products and cannabis promotions. Subsequent chapters outline research about and options for regulation of the physical availability and pricing of cannabis.

WHAT IS MARKETING?

The term *marketing* encompasses a range of activities, only some of which this chapter will cover. The National Cancer Institute and the World Health Organization (WHO) have used the diagram in Figure 6-1 to illustrate the range of tobacco and alcohol marketing, respectively.[1] As discussed in the introduction to Part II, the traditional marketing taxonomy encompasses the four P's: *product* design and labeling, the *place* or *physical availability* of the product, the product's *pricing*, and *promotion* of the product. In this century, corporations have augmented this with sophisticated stakeholder activities—including corporate social responsibility activities, lobbying, and social marketing and health education activities funded, promoted, and implemented by the industry that produced the product—that public health researchers and authorities have increasingly viewed as important parts of the marketing mix.[2]

US cannabis interests have been active in all four levels of marketing shown in Figure 6-1, including stakeholder marketing and specifically, lobbying. For ballot initiatives alone, including measures promoting decriminalization as well as medical and nonmedical legalization, pro-cannabis groups raised $139.1 million between 2004 and 2016;

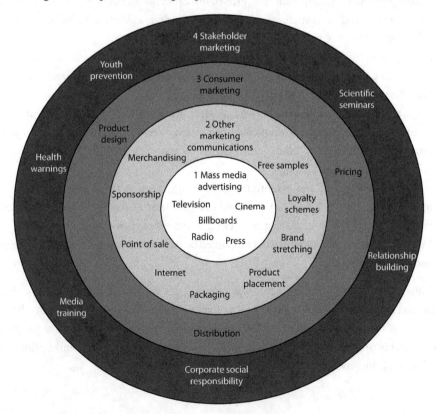

Source: Reprinted from National Cancer Institute.[1]

Figure 6-1. National Cancer Institute Diagram of Marketing Activities

opponents of these measures spent $37.3 million over the same period. In 29 of 32 ballot contests, pro-cannabis groups outraised and outspent opponents of cannabis law reform. While much of the pro-liberalization spending in earlier years came from nonindustry organizations such as the Marijuana Policy Project and the Drug Policy Alliance, the total coming directly from the cannabis industry grew 2.3% per year on average over the 13-year period.[3] From 2016 to 2019, cannabis growers and sellers spent an additional $11 million to lobby state legislatures.[4]

Regulation of marketing, however, is generally a federal rather than a state responsibility. For most products, federal agencies such as the Federal Trade Commission and the Federal Communications Commission have the mandate and the competency to regulate marketing. For products in interstate commerce, states lack both mandate and experience in marketing regulation. This chapter and those following it focus on the three inner circles of Figure 6-1, arenas where states can take regulatory action. The current chapter focuses on product regulation and then on the inner two circles of the diagram, "mass media advertising" and "other marketing communications."

REGULATING THE PRODUCT: POLICY OPTIONS

> *I understand from some perspective that edibles could be helpful in terms of minimizing*
> *people smoking a combustible material, but it seems to me to be the most problematic*
> *publicly, in terms of dose, timing, even the kinds of products that are allowed. I mean, really,*
> *do we have to have edible gummy bears?*
>
> –Michael Botticelli, MEd, Grayken Center for Addiction,
> in person interview, June 17, 2019

As Chapter 3 describes, because of rapid innovation both in the forms of cannabis available for purchase and the methods of consuming them, cannabis products are a complex and moving target for would-be regulators. Policymakers have several options for regulating products to reduce the potential health and safety risks associated with their use, many of which are being used in states that have legalized cannabis for non-medical use. Experiences with alcohol and tobacco products can provide guidance regarding their effectiveness and implementation.

Ban, Restrict, or Delay Introduction of High-Risk Products

While Canada legalized cannabis for nonmedical use in October 2018, its expert Task Force on Cannabis Legalization and Regulation recommended that legal sale of edible cannabis, cannabis extracts, and cannabis topicals be delayed until a year later. Beginning in October 2019, Canada allowed these products under certain conditions, including the following:

- For edibles, no added vitamins, minerals, nicotine, or alcohol is allowed, and there are limits on caffeine.

- Extracts (both ingested and inhaled) have the same restrictions as edibles and may have no added sugars, sweeteners, or colors.
- Topicals cannot contain nicotine or alcohol and may be used only on skin, hair, and nails.
- Edibles, extracts, and topicals also must list the equivalency to dried cannabis.

In addition, the newly available products should not be appealing to youth; make health, dietary, or cosmetic claims; or have any elements associated with alcoholic beverages, tobacco products, or vaping products.[5]

Colorado and Washington State, by contrast, allowed the purchase of edibles prior to formulating regulations regarding which products would be prohibited, as well as the labeling, packaging, and THC content by serving size of the products to be allowed (see Figure 6-2 and Figure 6-3).[6-8] A number of states now prohibit the manufacture of products that may appeal to children.[8] Washington State also prohibits "potentially hazardous foods" (as defined in WAC 246-215-01115) from being infused with cannabis. This restriction includes any foods that require refrigeration, freezing, or a hot holding unit to keep them safe for human consumption.[9]

From their experience with alcohol, states have ready precedents available to them for controlling problematic products. Some state alcohol control agencies have banned or restricted high-potency grain alcohol and alcoholic energy drinks that posed public health risks.[10] Some states distinguish alcohol products by strength and permit sales of the

Source: Reprinted from US Drug Enforcement Administration.[6]

Figure 6-2. Shop Window With Cannabis Products

Source: Reprinted from Ticer.[7]
Figure 6-3. Early Example of Prepackaged Marijuana Edibles

strongest form—distilled spirits—only in government-controlled retail outlets or in fewer types of outlets. This allows states both to limit the number of stores selling the stronger products and, in the case of state-run stores, to permit the sale of these products only in government-controlled retail stores. Doing this reduces availability through the limited number of state stores and provides the opportunity for added retail protections while still permitting the sale of weaker beverages (beer and wine) in private retail outlets.

In January 2020, legislators in Washington State introduced HB 2546 to prohibit retailers from selling marijuana concentrates with a THC concentration greater than 10%, except for medical cannabis retailers, who may continue to sell these products to qualifying patients in the Medical Marijuana Authorization Database. It would also prohibit cannabis processors from processing and selling concentrates with greater than 10% THC, except when the concentrates are intended for sale to a medical cannabis retailer. As of December 2020, the bill had not moved out of the House Committee on Commerce and Gaming.[11]

Packaging

Warning Labels Regarding Health and Safety Risks

Canada currently requires plain packaging for cannabis—that is, no brands or images; uniform, transparent color; and clear contrast between the yellow health warning message and the red color of the standardized cannabis symbol (see Figure 6-4).[12] Each package must display excise stamps, a standardized cannabis symbol, and a mandatory health

Source: Reprinted with permission from Government of Canada.[12]

Figure 6-4. Canada's Standardized Cannabis Packaging Symbol

warning message from a rotating list, which ensures that each warning is displayed an equal number of times.[13,14] A preliminary study of plain packaging in Canada found that viewing cannabis packages with such packaging and health warnings significantly increased knowledge of the health effects of cannabis and reduced the appeal of the products.[15] These requirements mirror the American Public Health Association's recommendations for cannabis product warning labels.[16]

Research on health warnings on cigarette packaging has found that they increase health knowledge and perceptions of risk and are associated with greater motivation to quit smoking.[17,18] The Framework Convention on Tobacco Control—the WHO's global tobacco treaty—requires tobacco health warnings that cover at least 30% and ideally 50% or more of a package's principal display area.[19] By contrast, the congressionally mandated warning labels on alcohol containers in the United States are a cautionary tale in failed warnings. Compared with research on effective tobacco warning labels, the alcohol labels are too small, too vague, not rotated, and with insufficient contrast to the rest of the package information. It is therefore not surprising that there is no evidence that alcohol warning labels change drinking patterns, although they may affect knowledge and attitudes.[20,21]

One research team recruited an expert panel of cannabis researchers to develop a list of recommended warning label messages. The panel reached consensus on six key topics:[22]

1. Safety (e.g., Don't drive or operate machinery while under the influence.)
2. Physical health (e.g., Cannabis use can cause negative long-term physical effects, including heart and lung disease.)
3. Fetal harm (e.g., Cannabis use can cause fetal harm.)
4. Mental health (e.g., Cannabis use creates a risk of harm to mental health and psychological functioning)
5. Drug dependence (e.g., Cannabis use may lead to dependence, addiction, or abuse.)
6. Negative effects on development (e.g., Cannabis use can have negative effects on adolescent development.)

The team also recruited a panel of cannabis users to conduct the same exercise. The user panel's recommendations largely overlapped with the experts' list, with some key differences: users recommended messages saying that cannabis can cause short-term physical side effects (e.g., dizziness, nausea, and drowsiness) and that cannabis should be used responsibly.[23] Users did not recommend fetal harm or heart disease warnings, suggesting that there may be a need for further education, including on warning labels, regarding these risks.

Labeling

Labels should include, in addition to warning messages, information about the source of the product (including the lot number); the packaging date; an ingredient list and nutritional facts; the amount of THC in the product; whether pesticides were applied at any point during cultivation or processing, with additional information as appropriate; testing procedures; and where appropriate, an expiration date. Canada requires the majority of this information on most of its cannabis products, although differences apply between types of product.[5,14]

Packaging and Serving Sizes

States that have legalized cannabis for nonmedical use and allowed edibles have developed their regulations in this area over time as they became aware of the problems described in Chapter 3. Most require child-resistant packaging and information about standard serving size (generally varying between 5 and 10 mg of THC per serving). The majority have set limits on the maximum allowable total THC in edible products.[8] Most states also prohibit the manufacture and packaging of products that may appeal to children. The American Public Health Association recommends plain and opaque packaging, with limited brand elements.[16] Some states require manufacturers to disclose on the label any use of pesticides.

By comparison, everything on alcohol labels requires preapproval from the Alcohol and Tobacco Tax and Trade Bureau of the US Department of the Treasury.

POLICY RECOMMENDATIONS

Products

- Prohibit concentrates.
- Prohibit any products that contain alcohol or tobacco.
- Establish a THC ceiling of 15%.
- If high-potency products are allowed, regulate and make them available separately, for instance through government-controlled stores with additional purchasing requirements and safety standards.

- Plan for and permit regulatory flexibility as the industry's evolution necessitates fresh regulatory responses to new products and methods of consumption.
- Establish a minimum CBD-to-THC ratio with flexibility to alter this as research emerges.
- Ban use of all but an approved list of pesticides.
- Ban edibles and drinkables, or if permitted, follow Canada's example and phase in the sale of edibles after legalization of cannabis for nonmedical use if they are not already available.
- If edibles are allowed, prohibit their sale in outlets within 1,500 feet of schools, a more stringent prohibition than for outlets that do not sell edibles.
- Prohibit any product deemed to be "appealing to children."*
- Prohibit free giveaways of products or branded items.

Packaging

- Require childproof or child-resistant packaging.
- Require on all product packaging rotating and specific health and safety warnings that cover at least 30% and ideally 50% or more of a package's principal display area.
- Require plain packaging (i.e., no branding) and permit inclusion of strain name, amounts of THC and CBD, and warnings.
- Develop a standardized dosage for adults and put recommended dosage information (i.e., serving size) on the label.
- Require clearly visible labels that list the percent concentration and THC-to-CBD ratio.
- Require labeling that indicates whether pesticides were used in cultivation of the product and that indicates organic (pesticide-free) cultivation, if applicable.

REGULATING MARKETING AND PROMOTION: AN INTRODUCTION

The Framework Convention on Tobacco Control has defined tobacco advertising and promotion as "any form of commercial communication, recommendation or action with the aim, effect or likely effect of promoting a tobacco product or tobacco use either

---

*Oregon regulations (OAR 845-025-7000(1)) define "attractive to minors" as packaging, labeling, and marketing that feature
  - Cartoons (see OAR 845-025-7000 for definition);
  - A design, brand, or name that resembles a non-cannabis-consumer product of the type typically marketed to minors;
  - Symbols or celebrities commonly used to market products to minors;
  - Images of minors; or
  - Words that refer to products commonly associated with minors or marketed by minors.

directly or indirectly."[19] The Pan American Health Organization built on this definition to define alcohol marketing as including

> the design of products, brand stretching (using an established brand for a new product in another product category), co-branding (collaboration between different brands with the same advertising goals), depiction of products and brands in entertainment media, [and] corporate social responsibility activities undertaken by the industry. . . . Trademarks and trade dress (label design, product configuration, and product packaging), which can serve multiple functions, are included when their goals align with those already mentioned previously.[24]

This mass of synergistic activities makes marketing a difficult area for regulators—notoriously a "balloon" that when pushed or restricted in one area likely expands elsewhere if marketing is still permitted. In the United States, the US Supreme Court's decisions regarding commercial speech, most notably *Central Hudson Gas and Electric Corp. v. Public Service Commission*, have made regulation of marketing even more complex. If commercial expression is lawful and not misleading, then regulation of this kind of speech must pass three tests: government must have substantial interest in regulating the speech, such regulation must directly advance that substantial interest, and the regulation must not be more extensive than necessary to serve that interest. State constitutions may also contain provisions interpreted as protecting commercial speech (see Box 6-1).[25]

States that have already legalized nonmedical cannabis have established a variety of marketing restrictions (see below for details). Whether these restrictions lie outside of the federal protections for commercial speech remains unclear. Under federal law,

---

Box 6-1. Advertising Regulation and the First Amendment

Jacobs[25] provides a useful set of guidelines for constructing advertising regulation to comply with Supreme Court decisions regarding commercial speech:

1. Identify clear and precise objectives for regulating advertising, with reference to specific harms being avoided, and state each objective specifically and separately.
2. Collect evidence showing that
   a. The adverse effect to be avoided exists;
   b. The persuasive messaging being restricted causes that adverse effect;
   c. The entire scheme of regulation is pointed at eliminating the adverse effect;
   d. Restrictions are tailored to only restrict the speech causing the adverse effect and not any "extra" speech not having that effect; and
   e. Alternative approaches less restrictive of speech are too expensive, politically infeasible, or significantly less effective.

Source: Adapted with permission from Jacobs.[25]

commercial expression promoting cannabis use may not be lawful because it promotes use of a substance that is illegal at the federal level. Just one court case has challenged cannabis marketing regulations. This Colorado case, *Colorado Press Association, Inc., and We Are Pueblo v. Brohl*, was dismissed by the US District Court after it determined that the plaintiffs lacked sufficient standing to bring their complaint. The judge thus elected not to rule on the question of applicability of the First Amendment.

Research Findings on Alcohol and Tobacco Marketing

The alcohol and tobacco research literature clearly demonstrates that marketing can affect youth use of psychoactive and addictive substances. Three systematic reviews of studies on alcohol marketing found that youth with greater exposure to alcohol marketing are more likely to initiate alcohol use and engage in binge or hazardous drinking.[26-28] A "review of reviews" of the alcohol literature published in 2020 used the Bradford Hill criteria for causation to establish that the relationship between youth exposure to alcohol marketing and youth alcohol use is actually causal—that is, exposure causes youth to be more likely to drink.[29] The tobacco literature demonstrates that exposure to tobacco promotions enhances the appeal of smoking to many adolescents and increases their risk for initiation, with greater exposure resulting in higher risk.[30-32] These results hold true for online tobacco marketing as well as more traditional forms of advertising.[33]

The introduction of e-cigarettes as a new tobacco product also has demonstrated the reach of marketing in influencing youth use. A systematic review of 124 publications on e-cigarette marketing and communication found that e-cigarette marketing content is attractive and accessible to youth and that exposure to these ads is associated with greater likelihood of adolescents and young adults trying e-cigarettes.[34] A study of college students in Texas found that exposure to e-cigarette advertising was associated with use of cannabis in these devices one year later,[35] indicating that the marketing of products using one delivery device may affect use of other substances in a similar delivery device.

There is less available research on the effectiveness of restrictions on marketing. In developed nations, researchers found that comprehensive tobacco advertising bans can reduce per capita cigarette consumption by about 7% but that a more limited set of advertising bans will have little or no effect.[36] In the United States specifically, restrictions on billboard and magazine advertising, branded promotional items, and sponsored events as part of the Master Settlement Agreement were associated with declines in adolescent smoking following 10 years of increasing rates.[37] However, note that these restrictions were a result of a voluntary contract between tobacco companies and state attorneys general and were thus not subject to First Amendment protections. Whether taking a similar approach with regard to cannabis advertising is constitutionally feasible remains untested in the courts.

CANNABIS MARKETING

Advertising and promotions include direct advertising (e.g., broadcast and print media, billboards, storefront signs, point-of-sale items, and online social media) as well as indirect advertising such as branded merchandise and sponsorship of events, product placements, influencer marketing, direct mail, in-cinema advertising, and social responsibility programs and messages. Although the cannabis industry is relatively new in the legal marketplace, early research suggests that it is an active marketer. One research group looking at this has highlighted a key difference between the alcohol and tobacco industries and the cannabis industry, in that "while the alcohol and tobacco industries crafted their original marketing campaigns decades ago using traditional media (e.g., print, billboards, radio), cannabis businesses have their origins in the digital age and consequently, they rely largely on social media to sell their products."[38] Digital media may be the primary focus of cannabis industry marketing efforts, but the research reveals that the industry is using in some fashion all the modes of marketing available to it.

Marketing Content

Several studies have analyzed and summarized the content prevalent in cannabis marketing. Researchers examined the advertising practices of retailers listed on Weedmaps (an online platform where consumers can find and rate cannabis sellers) in 2015 that were selling for nonmedical use in Colorado and Washington State and had independent operational websites. They found that 61% of dispensaries in Colorado and 44% in Washington State advertised health claims that have not yet been scientifically substantiated, with the most common being use of the product to reduce anxiety, as well as claims of effectiveness in treatment of depression, insomnia, and pain. They also found that none of the stores listed any harmful or adverse effects of cannabis use. In addition, 35% to 41% of these dispensary websites lacked any restrictions to verify a person's age before permitting access to the website, despite regulations in each of these states that limit online marketing to adult viewing only.[39]

Analysis of point-of-sale cannabis marketing around California schools in 2018 revealed that 74% of dispensaries located within three miles of a middle or high school had at least one instance of interior marketing of products, packages, paraphernalia, or advertisements that could appeal to youth. More than a quarter (28%) of dispensaries violated the state's ban on free samples, and 84% lacked age-limit signs.[40]

A 2016 study of just under 100 medical and nonmedical cannabis store websites in 10 states found that 63 made health claims related to specific products. While some of the claims had what experts from the National Academies of Sciences, Engineering, and Medicine (NASEM) would have termed conclusive evidence, others had only moderate, limited, or insufficient evidence as indicated by the NASEM report (see Chapter 2).[41] Slightly less than half warned consumers of potential negative effects of cannabis use, such as paranoia, anxiety, and dizziness. Less than a fifth of the websites contained warnings about contraindications, such as not driving after consumption or not using in combination with other drugs/medications or alcohol. Price promotions were not infrequent, with 44% offering reduced prices or coupons, 19% promoting buy-one, get-one-free offers or free gifts, and 31% advertising memberships providing benefits to regular customers.[42]

Social media blur the line between marketing and other content. A systematic review of cannabis marketing studies found that a majority of cannabis-related social media accounts are run by advocacy groups and industry interests, rather than by individuals sharing opinions or experiences.[43] One study analyzed a random sample of 6,620 cannabis-related tweets with the most followers and activity associated with them, out of more than 7.5 million cannabis-related tweets during one month in 2014. The results suggested that approximately 1 of 2,000 tweets being sent on Twitter is about cannabis. Of the cannabis-related tweets analyzed, 77% were in favor of cannabis use and 5% opposed it; the potential reach of the pro-cannabis tweets was 12 times higher than those in opposition. More than half of the pro-cannabis tweeters were under 20 years of age; the majority of these were Black.[44]

Another analysis of more than 2,000 cannabis-related Instagram posts in 2014 found that 9% included advertisements for cannabis-related products; 13% of these advertisements were for cannabis shops/dispensaries.[45] Discounted prices via sales or coupons as well as contests and free giveaways for cannabis products were also seen on the Instagram posts, indicating that the cannabis industry is using social media platforms to endorse their businesses and promote products. The authors noted, "Individuals can create an Instagram account starting at age 13, and because Instagram does not censor explicit content and/or restrict underage viewing, these marijuana-related posts can be seen when searched for by an underage viewer."[45] A study of Instagram posts in 2017–2018 that mentioned any of the three cannabis vaporizers with the most Instagram followers found that while the makers of the vaporizers do not sell cannabis, they directly or indirectly communicated the intended use of their products, including by tagging "cannabis influencers"—Instagram users with established relationships with cannabis companies or brands.[46]

Indeed, a number of Instagram influencers appear to be doing paid work for cannabis companies despite a ban on cannabis businesses advertising directly on Instagram, Twitter, and Facebook. A quote from one news article reports,

They appear to be getting products for free from various shops, and doing reviews and giveaways,' says James Lange, a researcher at San Diego State University who has been following drug use in online videos for several years. 'But when you look at the style of videos and the types of people who are doing well, they fit into what you'd expect from just about any other similar content: young, attractive and upbeat.'[47]

In Washington State, researchers found that between 2% and 13% of posts by Washington cannabis businesses on Facebook and Twitter violated regulations prohibiting advertising that encourages overconsumption, promotes therapeutic benefits, or appeals to youth, with a small number of businesses repeatedly violating these provisions. For example, 41% of the posts encouraging overconsumption came from one business. In comparison, the required warnings were present on only approximately 11% of the posts.[48]

Marketing Exposure

A cross-sectional survey conducted among adult Oregonians shortly after retail cannabis sales began found that 55% reported seeing cannabis advertising in the past month, including more than half of young people and young adults between the ages of 18 and 24. Respondents most frequently saw storefront advertising (75%), followed by streetside advertising (67%) and billboards (56%). Exposure to advertising was also significantly higher for those living in counties with retail sales (57%) compared with those who did not (32.5%). The researchers concluded, "Our results confirm that exposure to marijuana advertising will be prevalent following legalization of retail marijuana, absent strong regulations to restrict it."[49]

Users report similar levels of exposure to cannabis marketing. A 2015 national cross-sectional survey of past-month cannabis users ages 18 to 34 found that over half of participants were exposed to cannabis advertising in the past month. In states where cannabis for nonmedical use is allowed, 66% of participants reported seeing or hearing advertisements, compared with 47% in medical cannabis-only states and 46% in states where cannabis use is not legal. The most common sources of advertisements were social media (67%), print media (30%), and online sources other than social media (26%).[50]

Youth Exposure and Its Effects

What we're also seeing with marijuana in the parallels between alcohol and tobacco and marijuana is that billboards are back. Billboards advertising marijuana events, marijuana delivery services, marijuana retail stores. [What] we know from past research on tobacco and alcohol is with more social cues, and particularly billboards, you have a higher recognition and then youth and young adults are more likely to want to experiment and to purchase.

–Cynthia Hallett, MPH, Americans for Nonsmokers' Rights, phone interview, November 25, 2019

While there clearly is an abundance of cannabis marketing, the key public health question is what effect it has on those exposed to it. A number of cross-sectional studies have revealed that, similar to alcohol and tobacco marketing, exposure to cannabis marketing is associated with youth use. As with all cross-sectional studies, the direction of the association cannot be determined: it is possible either that exposure to marketing is leading to use or that users are more likely to pay more attention to the marketing. Nevertheless, policymakers need to recognize the association found in both national and state-specific studies between exposure to cannabis marketing and cannabis use as they develop cannabis marketing policies.

A 2018 survey of 15- to 19-year-olds in states that had legalized cannabis for nonmedical use found that 90% reported exposure to at least one type of cannabis ad or promotion; one-third of youth in these states reported interacting with cannabis marketing. Youth who engaged with cannabis business pages on social media had five times higher likelihood of past-year cannabis use compared with youth who did not engage with these pages; those who reported a favorite cannabis brand had eight times the likelihood of past-month cannabis use.[38]

Another cross-sectional study, of young people and young adults (18- to 25-year-olds) and their exposure to pro-cannabis content on Twitter, found the likelihood of being a current (past-month) cannabis user substantially greater for participants with both active and passive exposure to pro-cannabis content.[51] Yet another found that individuals who reported having seen a social media message about the benefits of cannabis had 6% greater likelihood of having used cannabis themselves.[52]

Only one study has used a longitudinal design to assess the impact of youth exposure on cannabis use over time. The researchers interviewed students of middle school-age from Southern California in 2010–2011, when only medical cannabis was legally allowed. Nearly a quarter of respondents at baseline (22%) and nearly a third of respondents at one-year follow-up (30%) reported seeing a medical cannabis advertisement in the prior three months. Longitudinally, those who saw the ads were twice as likely as those who saw no ads both to use and to report intent to use cannabis during the next year.[53] The researchers interviewed the students again in 2017 and found that those with higher-than-average exposure to medical cannabis ads in 2010–2011 reported greater cannabis use and more negative consequences from use in the follow-up survey.[54]

Young people are also exposed to cannabis marketing through advertising signage on cannabis dispensaries. A study of 18- to 22-year-olds in Los Angeles County found an association between living near a higher number of medical cannabis dispensaries and increased past-month use, an important consideration in evaluating the impact of outlet density (see Chapter 7). The association had a four- to six-times greater effect on the number of times used per day and positive expectancies if respondents lived near more dispensaries with storefront signage.[55]

These findings build on research demonstrating that e-cigarette retailer density around schools was positively associated with ever and past-month use of e-cigarettes by high school students and that there was a dose-response relationship: every additional e-cigarette advertisement within a half mile of a young person's school was associated with a 1% greater probability of past-month e-cigarette use.[56] Similarly, cross-sectional alcohol research conducted with middle school students found that exposure to alcohol marketing in liquor, convenience, or small grocery stores was widespread and associated with higher odds of ever drinking.[57]

STRATEGIES TO REDUCE NEGATIVE EFFECTS OF MARKETING
Provisions From Self-Regulatory Codes

Current state policies regarding cannabis marketing fall into two principal categories: restricting content and regulating placement, usually in order to reduce youth exposure. Regarding placement, Colorado has taken specific provisions of the alcohol industry self-regulatory codes and written them into law, including prohibitions on placing cannabis outdoor advertisements in places where adults 21 and older are less than 71.6% of the audience or within 500 feet of a school, church, or playground. Regarding content, Washington State's regulations also borrow from alcohol industry voluntary codes, including prohibitions on text that is false or misleading, encourages overconsumption, may be attractive to children, or makes curative or therapeutic claims.[58]

Relying on the alcohol industry's voluntary provisions in state marketing codes for cannabis has at least two problems. First, research suggests that voluntary compliance with these state-level cannabis marketing codes is low and that enforcement is difficult and requires enforcement resources beyond current state allocations.[40,48,49,59,60] Second, and more importantly, the code provisions themselves are ineffective. Research from the alcohol field has found that the industry codes are routinely violated and have little or no effect on youth exposure to alcohol marketing.[61,62] The voluntary codes often rely on vague language, loopholes, and lax guidelines for enforcement.[63] The main purpose of the self-regulatory policies and programs, from the industry's point of view, may be to delay statutory regulations.

Other Statutory Regulation

Perhaps the most effective way to prevent or reduce negative effects of cannabis marketing is to adopt a regulatory system that removes or reduces the profit motive, and by extension the incentive to advertise. As described in Chapter 4, some regulatory systems, such as state monopolies and public authorities or cannabis social collectives, remove cannabis from many of the free-market pressures that incentivize and reward advertising and marketing.

If the regulatory system is likely to create pressure for advertising and promotion, the best practice in tobacco and alcohol marketing regulation begins with as complete a ban as constitutionally feasible. This is what WHO recommends for alcohol marketing,[2,24] while its Framework Convention on Tobacco Control, which was signed by 168 nations, reads,

"Each Party shall, in accordance with its constitution or constitutional principles, undertake a comprehensive ban of all tobacco advertising, promotion and sponsorship."[19]

Short of the ability to implement a comprehensive ban, best practice in alcohol control follows the model of the French Loi Evin of 1991, which banned all marketing and then explicitly named marketing activities that were permitted. This approach makes it easier for regulators to keep abreast of marketing innovations, for any innovations require changes in the law itself if they are to be permissible. With this approach, the French were able to limit both placement—such as a ban on alcohol advertising at sporting events—and content, permitting only certain basic product characteristics to be advertised, as opposed to advertising that places the product in lifestyles and contexts that may be attractive to youth.

In practice, content restrictions tend to be difficult to monitor and enforce. Nonetheless, Washington State's ban on cannabis content that makes curative or therapeutic claims, is false or misleading, or encourages overconsumption is a good start. The tobacco field has pioneered in the use of plain packaging, as well as detailed and graphic warnings about health risks inherent in use of the product—these also could be explored for cannabis.

Experience in the alcohol field has shown that placement restrictions have great potential for protecting youth from problematic content.[64] The 71.6% adult audience standard used in Colorado comes from the alcohol industry's voluntary ad placement code and is based on the percentage of the US population under age 21. However, as public health researchers as well as 24 state and territorial attorneys general have argued, a more appropriate standard would focus on protecting adolescents (age 12 and above); such a standard would ban advertising anywhere that young people ages 12 to 20 constitute more than 15% of the viewing, reading, or listening audience.[65,66]

Other regulatory options affecting exposure include Washington State's ban on outdoor advertising within 1,000 feet of sensitive land uses such as schools or playgrounds; restrictions or bans on signage at retail locations; bans on event sponsorship; and limits on the use of social media—for instance, banning influencers or use of platforms such as Snapchat that are likely to be popular among young people.

In digital and social media, states should require use of state-of-the-art age verification systems to limit youth access to cannabis sites and marketing. While online age verification does not guarantee that minors will not access age-inappropriate content online or be able to purchase age-restricted products,[67-72] age verification tools to prohibit those under 21 from entering cannabis-related websites are an important first step in restricting youth access to both marketing and products.

Current marketing regulations in states that have legalized cannabis for nonmedical use contain some but not all of these provisions. Appendix 2 provides examples from California, Colorado, and Washington State regulatory codes and the penalties for violations.

To be effective, all these measures will need accompanying and well-resourced monitoring and enforcement. Similar to the review boards that some cannabis control agencies have instituted to assess product packaging and labeling, review bodies comprising public health officials and substance abuse prevention professionals could be established to review and approve all cannabis advertising content and placement/exposure.

Policymakers also should consider potential loopholes that cannabis industry members could exploit. Researchers analyzing marketing restrictions in Washington State found that some retailers had separate storefronts adjacent to the cannabis dispensaries where they sold branded apparel and could use larger exterior signage.[59] Lessons from the tobacco field illustrate tactics that industry used to thwart marketing regulations, including adopting weak voluntary advertising codes to avoid stronger measures, hiring consultants to discredit the evidence base for restrictions, and lobbying against restrictions.[73] It stands to reason that the cannabis industry will learn from the strategies utilized by the tobacco industry and likely improve upon them.

Other Regulatory Options in Light of First Amendment Protections

While commercial free-speech protections afforded by the First Amendment make advertising restrictions challenging in the United States, restrictions aimed at adolescents and children will likely be allowed.[74] Other strong regulatory approaches to limit cannabis advertising may face constitutional challenges under either state or federal law.

Another way of limiting cannabis advertising is through the tax code. Currently, sellers must pay federal taxes even on illegal transactions, and they may take business expense deductions against this liability. However, Section 280E of the federal tax code expressly fences off expenses, other than from costs of production or of purchasing inventory, for "trafficking in controlled substances" from this deduction, including the costs of advertising.[25] This provision functions as a disincentive to cannabis advertising; in contrast, advertising costs for most other goods are tax-deductible. There may be equivalent provisions in state tax codes. This offers a means of discouraging cannabis advertising without raising First Amendment issues.

Similarly, directly regulating pricing techniques (see Chapter 8) such as discounting, sampling, or bulk purchase incentives can obviate the need to ban advertising for such promotions. The same logic applies to restrictions on potentially harmful products—bans on production or sale of these would make restrictions on advertising them unnecessary.[25]

Warnings in Advertising

It is also possible to counter the impact of advertising by embedding health warning messages in the advertising itself. In the United States, alcohol companies often voluntarily include warning messages in their advertising; however, analysis of these messages concluded that they were overwhelmingly being used to promote the product rather than to achieve any public health goal.[75] Worldwide, 56 countries report mandating health warnings on alcohol advertisements.[76] Warnings on tobacco advertising also have been widely used. Research into the effectiveness of such warnings in influencing viewer behavior suggests that the devil is in the details. Qualitative research into the impact of warnings on alcohol advertising in France found that the messages suffered from lack of visibility and credibility, as well as being overly vague.[77] Eye-tracking studies of warnings in tobacco ads have shown on the one hand that the messages are consistently ignored and on the other that novel or graphic warnings can increase attention, particularly in the context of otherwise plain packaging, and that greater visual attention to the warning is associated with greater recall of the messages.[78]

Countering Marketing: Public Awareness Campaigns

Beyond regulation, other forms of communication have attempted to counter the effects of marketing. In the tobacco context historically, and regarding alcohol currently, educational campaigns have been largely unsuccessful, in part because young people are so heavily exposed to the marketing. Indeed, abundant research in both the alcohol and tobacco fields has shown that educating youth about the risks of using these substances is ineffective in the absence of other strategies that reduce youth access.[79-82] A systematic review of mass media campaigns to reduce alcohol consumption and related harms found that while these campaigns have achieved changes in knowledge, attitudes, and beliefs about alcohol, there is little evidence of any reduction in alcohol consumption.[80]

Efforts to use public awareness campaigns to influence illegal drug use also have been largely unsuccessful. A systematic review and meta-analysis of the literature on anti-illegal-drug public service announcements through 2010 showed mixed results, with the meta-analysis finding no significant effects and the review of observational studies showing evidence of both harmful and beneficial effects.[83] A study of the impact on adolescents of pro-cannabis messages in social media found that exposure to messages about cannabis harms was unrelated to youth cannabis use.[52] And a survey evaluation of a national campaign to encourage adolescents to view antidrug informational websites found that only a small percentage of respondents visited antidrug websites; those who did were more likely to use cannabis within the next 12 months.[84]

Between 1998 and 2004, the US Congress appropriated nearly $1 billion for the National Youth Anti-Drug Campaign and incorporated a "Marijuana Initiative" four years into the campaign. An evaluation of the Marijuana Initiative conducted with high-sensation-seeking adolescents, a subset of the target population, found significant changes in attitudes, beliefs, and cannabis use in this population in two communities.[85] A larger evaluation of the entire campaign, however, concluded that despite 94% of adolescents reporting general exposure to the campaign, there were very few favorable effects on youth and there may have been delayed negative effects, such as pro-cannabis cognitions and increases in initiation of use.[86] Additional analyses indicated that positive ad evaluations were followed one year later by reductions in both intentions to use and actual use of cannabis, but only for youth already using cannabis and not for vulnerable youth—that is, those who are contemplating cannabis use.[87] Some researchers have noted a potential "boomerang" effect, in that antidrug messages may increase adolescents' curiosity about the substance in question or their beliefs that drug use is commonplace.[86,88]

There is strong evidence, however, from other areas of public health that well-designed and well-funded public awareness campaigns using the mass media can result in changes in health behavior at the population level if such campaigns occur in the context of complementary, community-wide interventions.[89,90] Effective campaigns likely need to (1) achieve high levels of exposure among the intended target audience over a long period of time, (2) happen at the same time as other effective interventions such as tax increases or increased enforcement of availability and purchasing restrictions, and (3) be guided in their design by behavior change theory and formative research.[91]

Despite the poor track record for alcohol and tobacco, and thus far for cannabis, there is a continued need for efforts at public awareness campaigns and other dedicated resources to educate young people on the short- and long-term risks of cannabis use. Misinformation about cannabis is widespread, and youth perceptions of risks associated with cannabis use have been steadily falling.[92] One group of researchers, having conducted a qualitative assessment of youth protection in the Colorado cannabis market, suggested that prevention messaging campaigns may need to evolve from abstinence-only and toward harm reduction, as public health officials have concluded that abstinence-only approaches are not effective.[93] Careful use of behavior change theory and formative research may assist campaigns in making decisions about the messaging most likely to be effective.

Countering Marketing: Counteradvertising Campaigns

As opposed to public awareness campaigns, counteradvertising campaigns focus on the marketing itself. They pose a direct challenge to the legitimacy and credibility of the industry that is marketing a particular product.[94] Evidence of their effectiveness in tobacco control is strong: the Community Preventive Services Task Force evaluated almost 100 studies and concluded that counteradvertising (primarily done through television) can help decrease the prevalence of tobacco use, increase cessation and use of services such as quit lines, and decrease initiation among young people.[95] An evaluation of the more recent *The Real Cost* media campaign on tobacco, which began in 2014, found that the likelihood of reporting smoking initiation was lower among youth in media markets with higher levels of campaign advertisements and that the campaign was associated with preventing 380,000 to 587,000 US youth ages 11 to 19 from initiating smoking between 2014 and 2016.[96]

In addition, the US Supreme Court has held that taxing commodity producers to pay for advertising relevant to that commodity is permissible. Specifically, if the speech paid for by the tax comes from the government, with the government controlling the content of the message, then "[c]itizens have no First Amendment right not to fund [it]."[97] Because it does not in any way ban or restrict commercial communications but rather promotes more communication in the public sphere, this "more speech" approach is another way to avoid constitutional challenges to efforts to counteract the public health impact of cannabis advertising.

MARKETING AND INDUSTRY CONCENTRATION

As mature industries, both alcohol and tobacco are highly concentrated in their ownership. For instance, two companies sell close to 80% of the beer consumed in the United States.[98] Despite multiple restrictions on tobacco marketing, the Federal Trade Commission (FTC) reported that in 2018, the major manufacturers in that industry spent $8.6 billion on advertising and promotion of its products.[99] The most recent FTC report on alcohol advertising looked at 2011 expenditures by 14 major alcohol companies and found that they spent $3.45 billion on marketing activities in that year.[100]

These high marketing expenditures function as an economic barrier to entry into these two industries. Because they sell so much more than any smaller competitor seeking to enter the market, the major companies' cost of marketing per unit sold will be much lower[101]; they also have the ability to overwhelm or purchase outright competitors that threaten their market dominance. This dominance in turn helps them to extract oligopoly profits from the marketplace; these profits then support the large marketing budgets that help to keep their oligopoly status intact.[98]

Without restrictions on cannabis marketing, and without a regulatory system structured to keep cannabis companies small (see Chapter 4), this market concentration and dominance, supported and reproduced by high marketing spending, will likely occur in the cannabis marketplace as well. Already, the world's largest cannabis producer, Curaleaf, has a market capitalization of $7.7 billion, and its shares rose by 85% between January and December of 2020. Green Thumb, a close competitor, is valued at $4.6 billion, with shares up 120% during 2020.[102] In the absence of meaningful regulation, market forces will favor the largest companies, which will in turn have incentives similar to those of alcohol and tobacco to market heavily in the effort to maintain their dominance.

POLICY RECOMMENDATIONS

- If the regulatory system chosen by a state incentivizes advertising, the most effective regulatory response to cannabis marketing will be as comprehensive a ban as possible.

- Short of an outright ban, restrictions on marketing content and placement should focus on what is allowed instead of what is prohibited, so that industry efforts at innovation outside of what is permitted would require changes in the advertising law.
- Bans on problematic products or pricing practices will obviate the need to restrict advertising related to them.
- Putting the current federal ban on tax deductibility of cannabis advertising into state law will disincentivize cannabis advertising without raising First Amendment issues.[25]
- Approaches that put "more speech" into the public sphere, such as counteradvertising or mandated and highly visible warning messages in all advertising, offer opportunities for reducing the impact of advertising without running afoul of the First Amendment.
- Regarding exposure, advertising should be restricted to media and events where audiences contain 15% or fewer youth under 21, roughly the percentage of 12- to 20-year-olds in the general population, and the standard recommended for alcohol advertising by 24 state and territorial attorneys general.
- State-of-the-art age verification software should be used to reduce the likelihood that youth under 21 can access cannabis business and marketing websites.
- Health-related marketing claims that are not conclusively supported by scientific research should be banned, and a state cannabis scientific advisory board established to review the scientific literature in order to approve/reject health claims.
- A compliance unit should be adequately funded within a cannabis control agency to oversee marketing and advertising compliance. A review board comprising public health officials and substance abuse prevention professionals should review and approve all cannabis advertising for content and exposure.
- A portion of cannabis tax revenues should be used to support the robust monitoring and enforcement capacity that is needed and to pay for robust and research-based public awareness and counteradvertising campaigns.
- There should be strong administrative penalties for violations of marketing restrictions.

Products that are designed for and promoted to a target audience must also be available for that audience to purchase and consume. The next chapter moves on from consideration of product and promotion to the third "P" of traditional marketing: place, or physical availability. The chapter discusses both why physical availability matters and what a regulatory approach to it informed by public health research and experience would look like.

REFERENCES

1. National Cancer Institute. *The Role of the Media in Promoting and Reducing Tobacco Use*. Bethesda, MD: US Dept of Health and Human Service, National Institutes of Health, National Cancer Institute; 2008.

2. World Health Organization. *Regulate Alcohol Marketing: Alcohol Policy Brief No. 6*. Geneva, Switzerland: World Health Organization;forthcoming.

3. Orenstein DG, Glantz SA. The grassroots of grass: cannabis legalization ballot initiative campaign contributions and outcomes, 2004–2016. *J Health Polit Policy Law*. 2020;45(1):73–109.

4. National Institute on Money in Politics. State-level lobbyist spending by marijuana growers and product sales spenders. 2020. Available at: https://www.followthemoney.org/show-me?dt-=3&lby-f-fc=2&lby-f-cci=151#[{1|gro=lby-y. Accessed April 1, 2021.

5. Government of Canada. Final regulations: edible cannabis, cannabis extracts, cannabis topicals. Canada Go. 2019.

6. US Drug Enforcement Administration. Drug Alert: Marijuana Edibles. Get the Facts about Drugs | Just Think Twice. January 1, 2018. Available at: www.justthinktwice.gov/article/drug-alert-marijuana-edibles. Accessed May 20, 2021.

7. Ticer RL. Legalized Recreational Marijuana: a View from the Colorado Association of Chiefs of Police. Colorado Association of Chiefs of Police. 2016. Available at: https://dot.nebraska.gov/media/7872/7-legalization-of-marijuana-chief-robert-l-ticer.pdf. Accessed May 20, 2021.

8. Gourdet C, Giombi KC, Kosa K, Wiley J, Cates S. How four US states are regulating recreational marijuana edibles. *Int J Drug Policy*. 2017;43:83–90.

9. Washington Administrative Code. Marijuana processor license—privileges, requirements, and fees. WAC 314-55-0772020.

10. Grossman ER, Binakonsky J, Jernigan D. The use of regulatory power by US state and local alcohol control agencies to ban problematic products. *Subst Use Misuse*. 2018;53(8): 1229–1238.

11. Washington State Legislature. Concerning the potency of marijuana products. 2020.

12. Government of Canada. Standardized Cannabis Symbol. July 11, 2018. Available at: https://www.canada.ca/en/health-canada/services/drugs-medication/cannabis/laws-regulations/regulations-support-cannabis-act/standardized-symbol.html. Accessed May 20, 2021.

13. Government of Canada. Cannabis in Canada: what you need to know about cannabis. 2019. Available at: https://www.canada.ca/en/services/health/campaigns/cannabis/canadians.html#a9. Accessed April 1, 2021.

14. Government of Canada. Cannabis regulations, part 7, packaging and labelling. 2019. Available at: https://laws-lois.justice.gc.ca/eng/regulations/SOR-2018-144/page-13.html#h-848579. Accessed April 1, 2021.

15. Mutti-Packer S, Collyer B, Hodgins DC. Perceptions of plain packaging and health warning labels for cannabis among young adults: findings from an experimental study. *BMC Public Health*. 2018;18(1):1361.

16. American Public Health Association. A public health approach to regulating commercially legalized cannabis. October 24, 2020. Policy 20206. Available at: https://www.apha.org/ Policies-and-Advocacy/Public-Health-Policy-Statements/Policy-Database/2021/01/13/ A-Public-Health-Approach-to-Regulating-Commercially-Legalized-Cannabis. Accessed April 5, 2021.

17. Hammond D. Health warning messages on tobacco products: a review. *Tob Control.* 2011;20(5):327–337.

18. Noar SM, Hall MG, Francis DB, Ribisl KM, Pepper JK, Brewer NT. Pictorial cigarette pack warnings: a meta-analysis of experimental studies. *Tob Control.* 2016;25(3):341–354.

19. World Health Organization. *WHO Framework Convention on Tobacco Control.* Geneva, Switzerland: World Health Organization; 2003.

20. Wilkinson C, Room R. Warnings on alcohol containers and advertisements: international experience and evidence on effects. *Drug Alcohol Rev.* 2009;28(4):426–435.

21. Hassan LM, Shiu E. A systematic review of the efficacy of alcohol warning labels: Insights from qualitative and quantitative research in the new millenium. *J Social Marketing.* 2018;8(3):333–352.

22. Malouff JM, Rooke SE. Expert-recommended warnings for medical marijuana. *Subst Abus.* 2013;34(2):92–93.

23. Malouff JM, Johnson CE, Rooke SE. Cannabis users' recommended warnings for packages of legally sold cannabis: an Australia-centered study. *Cannabis Cannabinoid Res.* 2016;1(1):239–243.

24. Pan American Health Organization. Technical note: background on alcohol marketing regulation and monitoring for the protection of public health. 2017.

25. Jacobs LG. Regulating marijuana advertising and marketing to promote public health: navigating the constitutional minefield. *Lewis & Clark Law Rev.* 2018;21(4):1082–1133.

26. Anderson P, de Bruijn A, Angus K, Gordon R, Hastings G. Impact of alcohol advertising and media exposure on adolescent alcohol use: a systematic review of longitudinal studies. *Alcohol Alcohol.* 2009;44(3):229–243.

27. Jernigan D, Noel J, Landon J, Thornton N, Lobstein T. Alcohol marketing and youth alcohol consumption: a systematic review of longitudinal studies published since 2008. *Addiction.* 2017;112(suppl 1):7–20.

28. Smith LA, Foxcroft DR. The effect of alcohol advertising, marketing and portrayal on drinking behaviour in young people: systematic review of prospective cohort studies. *BMC Public Health.* 2009;9:51.

29. Sargent JD, Cukier S, Babor TF. Alcohol marketing and youth drinking: is there a causal relationship, and why does it matter? *J Stud Alcohol Drugs Suppl.* 2020;(suppl 19):5–12.

30. DiFranza JR, Wellman RJ, Sargent JD, et al. Tobacco promotion and the initiation of tobacco use: assessing the evidence for causality. *Pediatrics.* 2006;117(6):e1237–e1248.

31. Arnett JJ, Terhanian G. Adolescents' responses to cigarette advertisements: links between exposure, liking, and the appeal of smoking. *Tob Control.* 1998;7(2):129–133.

32. Paynter J, Edwards R. The impact of tobacco promotion at the point of sale: a systematic review. *Nicotine Tob Res.* 2009;11(1):25–35.

33. Soneji S, Pierce JP, Choi K, et al. Engagement with online tobacco marketing and associations with tobacco product use among US youth. *J Adolesc Health.* 2017;61(1):61–69.

34. Collins L, Glasser AM, Abudayyeh H, Pearson JL, Villanti AC. e-cigarette marketing and communication: how e-cigarette companies market e-cigarettes and the public engages with e-cigarette Information. *Nicotine Tob Res.* 2019;21(1):14–24.

35. Kreitzberg DS, Hinds JT, Pasch KE, Loukas A, Perry CL. Exposure to ENDS advertising and use of marijuana in ENDS among college students. *Addict Behavi.* 2019;93:9–13.

36. Saffer H, Chaloupka F. The effect of tobacco advertising bans on tobacco consumption. *J Health Econ.* 2000;19(6):1117–1137.

37. Pierce JP. Tobacco industry marketing, population-based tobacco control, and smoking behavior. *Am J Prev Med.* 2007;33(suppl 6):S327–334.

38. Trangenstein PJ, Whitehill JM, Jenkins MC, Jernigan DH, Moreno MA. Active cannabis marketing and adolescent past-year cannabis use. *Drug Alcohol Depend.* 2019;204:107548.

39. Bierut T, Krauss MJ, Sowles SJ, Cavazos-Rehg PA. Exploring marijuana advertising on Weedmaps, a popular online directory. *Prev Sci.* 2017;18(2):183–192.

40. Cao Y, Carrillo AS, Zhu SH, Shi Y. Point-of-sale marketing in recreational marijuana dispensaries around California schools. *J Adolesc Health.* 2020;66(1):72–78.

41. National Academies of Sciences, Engineering, and Medicine. *The Health Effects of Cannabis and Cannabinoids: The Current State of Evidence and Recommendations for Research.* Washington, DC: National Academies Press; 2017.

42. Cavazos-Rehg PA, Krauss MJ, Cahn E, et al. Marijuana promotion online: an investigation of dispensary practices. *Prev Sci.* 2019;20(2):280–290.

43. Park SY, Holody KJ. Content, exposure, and effects of public discourses about marijuana: a systematic review. *J Health Commun.* 2018;23(12):1036–1043.

44. Cavazos-Rehg PA, Krauss M, Fisher SL, Salyer P, Grucza RA, Bierut LJ. Twitter chatter about marijuana. *J Adolesc Health.* 2015;56(2):139–145.

45. Cavazos-Rehg PA, Krauss MJ, Sowles SJ, Bierut LJ. Marijuana-related posts on Instagram. *Prev Sci.* 2016;17(6):710–720.

46. Spillane TE, Wong BA, Giovenco DP. Content analysis of Instagram posts by leading cannabis vaporizer brands. *Drug Alcohol Depend.* 2020;218:108353.

47. Varghese S. Weed firms are using Instagram influencers to dodge regulations. *Wired UK.* January 19, 2019.

48. Moreno MA, Gower AD, Jenkins MC, et al. Social media posts by recreational marijuana companies and administrative code regulations in Washington State. *JAMA Netw Open.* 2018;1(7):e182242.

49. Fiala SC, Dilley JA, Firth CL, Maher JE. Exposure to marijuana marketing after legalization of retail sales: Oregonians' experiences, 2015–2016. *Am J Public Health.* 2018;108(1):120–127.

50. Krauss MJ, Sowles SJ, Sehi A, et al. Marijuana advertising exposure among current marijuana users in the US. *Drug Alcohol Depend.* 2017;174:192–200.

51. Cabrera-Nguyen EP, Cavazos-Rehg P, Krauss M, Bierut LJ, Moreno MA. Young adults' exposure to alcohol- and marijuana-related content on Twitter. *J Stud Alcohol Drugs.* 2016;77(2):349–353.

52. Roditis ML, Delucchi K, Chang A, Halpern-Felsher B. Perceptions of social norms and exposure to pro-marijuana messages are associated with adolescent marijuana use. *Prev Med.* 2016;93:171–176.

53. D'Amico EJ, Miles JN, Tucker JS. Gateway to curiosity: medical marijuana ads and intention and use during middle school. *Psychol Addict Behav.* 2015;29(3):613–619.

54. D'Amico EJ, Rodriguez A, Tucker JS, Pedersen ER, Shih RA. Planting the seed for marijuana use: changes in exposure to medical marijuana advertising and subsequent adolescent marijuana use, cognitions, and consequences over seven years. *Drug Alcohol Depend.* 2018;188:385–391.

55. Shih RA, Rodriguez A, Parast L, et al. Associations between young adult marijuana outcomes and availability of medical marijuana dispensaries and storefront signage. *Addiction.* 2019;114(12):2162–2170.

56. Giovenco DP, Casseus M, Duncan DT, Coups EJ, Lewis MJ, Delnevo CD. Association between electronic cigarette marketing near schools and e-cigarette use among youth. *J Adolesc Health.* 2016;59(6):627–634.

57. Hurtz SQ, Henriksen L, Wang Y, Feighery EC, Fortmann SP. The relationship between exposure to alcohol advertising in stores, owning alcohol promotional items, and adolescent alcohol use. *Alcohol Alcohol.* 2007;42(2):143–149.

58. Noel JK, Babor TF. Predicting regulatory compliance in beer advertising on Facebook. *Alcohol Alcohol.* 2017;52(6):730–736.

59. Berg CJ, Henriksen L, Cavazos-Rehg P, Schauer GL, Freisthler B. Point-of-sale marketing and context of marijuana retailers: assessing reliability and generalizability of the marijuana retail surveillance tool. *Prev Med Rep.* 2018;11:37–41.

60. Berg CJ, Henriksen L, Cavazos-Rehg P, Schauer GL, Freisthler B. The development and pilot testing of the marijuana retail surveillance tool (MRST): assessing marketing and point-of-sale practices among recreational marijuana retailers. *Health Educ Res.* 2017;32(6):465–472.

61. Noel JK, Babor TF, Robaina K. Industry self-regulation of alcohol marketing: a systematic review of content and exposure research. *Addiction.* 2017;112 (suppl 1):28–50.

62. Noel JK, Babor TF. Does industry self-regulation protect young people from exposure to alcohol marketing? a review of compliance and complaint studies. *Addiction.* 2017;112(suppl 1): 51–56.

63. Noel J, Lazzarini Z, Robaina K, Vendrame A. Alcohol industry self-regulation: who is it really protecting? *Addiction.* 2017;112(suppl 1):57–63.

64. Jernigan DH, Ostroff J, Ross C. Alcohol advertising and youth: a measured approach. *J Public Health Policy.* 2005;26(3):312–325.

65. Jernigan DH. Framing a public health debate over alcohol advertising: the Center on Alcohol Marketing and Youth, 2002–2008. *J Public Health Policy.* 2011;32(2):165–179.

66. Shurtleff ML, Gansler DF, Horne T, et al. Re: alcohol reports, paperwork comment; Project No. P114503. A communication from the chief legal officers of the following states: Arizona, Connecticut, Delaware, Guam, Hawaii, Idaho, Illinois, Iowa, Maryland, Massachusetts, Mississippi, Nevada, New Hampshire, New Mexico, New York, Oklahoma, Oregon, Rhode Island, South Carolina, Tennessee, Utah, Vermont, Washington, Wyoming. 2011. Available at: https://www.ftc.gov/sites/default/files/documents/public_comments/alcohol-reports-project-no.p114503-00071%C2%A0/00071-58515.pdf. Accessed March 30, 2021.

67. Jones SC, Thom JA, Davoren S, Barrie L. Internet filters and entry pages do not protect children from online alcohol marketing. *J Public Health Policy.* 2014;35(1):75–90.

68. Williams RS, Ribisl KM. Internet alcohol sales to minors. *Arch Pediatr Adolesc Med.* 2012;166(9):808–813.

69. Williams RS, Derrick J, Ribisl KM. Electronic cigarette sales to minors via the internet. *JAMA Pediatr.* 2015;169(3):e1563.

70. Williams RS, Derrick J, Phillips KJ. Cigarette sales to minors via the internet: how the story has changed in the wake of federal regulation. *Tob Control.* 2017;26(4):415–420.

71. Ribisl KM, Williams RS, Kim AE. Internet sales of cigarettes to minors. *JAMA.* 2003;290(10):1356–1359.

72. Ribisl KM, Kim AE, Williams RS. Are the sales practices of internet cigarette vendors good enough to prevent sales to minors? *Am J Public Health.* 2002;92(6):940–941.

73. Henriksen L. Comprehensive tobacco marketing restrictions: promotion, packaging, price and place. *Tob Control.* 2012;21(2):147–153.

74. American Public Health Association. Regulating commercially legalized marijuana as a public health priority. November 18, 2014. Policy 201410. Available at: https://www.apha.org/policies-and-advocacy/public-health-policy-statements/policy-database. Accessed April 5, 2021.

75. Smith KC, Cukier S, Jernigan DH. Defining strategies for promoting product through "drink responsibly" messages in magazine ads for beer, spirits and alcopops. *Drug Alcohol Depend.* 2014;142:168–173.

76. World Health Organization. *Global Status Report on Alcohol and Health, 2018*. Geneva, Switzerland: World Health Organization; 2018.

77. Dossou G, Gallopel-Morvan K, Diouf JF. The effectiveness of current French health warnings displayed on alcohol advertisements and alcoholic beverages. *Eur J Public Health*. 2017;27(4):699–704.

78. Meernik C, Jarman K, Wright ST, Klein EG, Goldstein AO, Ranney L. Eye tracking outcomes in tobacco control regulation and communication: a systematic review. *Tob Regul Sci*. 2016;2(4):377–403.

79. Carson KV, Ameer F, Sayehmiri K, et al. Mass media interventions for preventing smoking in young people. *Cochrane Database Syst Rev*. 2017;6:CD001006.

80. Young B, Lewis S, Katikireddi SV, et al. Effectiveness of mass media campaigns to reduce alcohol consumption and harm: a systematic review. *Alcohol Alcohol*. 2018;53(3):302–316.

81. Babor T, Caetano R, Casswell S, et al. *Alcohol: No Ordinary Commodity—Research and Public Policy*. 2nd ed. New York: Oxford University Press; 2010.

82. US Department of Health and Human Services. *Preventing Tobacco Use Among Youth and Young Adults: A Report of the Surgeon General*. Atlanta, GA: US Dept of Health and Human Services, Centers for Disease Control and Prevention, National Center for Chronic Disease Prevention and Health Promotion, Office on Smoking and Health; 2012.

83. Werb D, Mills EJ, Debeck K, Kerr T, Montaner JS, Wood E. The effectiveness of anti-illicit-drug public-service announcements: a systematic review and meta-analysis. *J Epidemiol Community Health*. 2011;65(10):834–840.

84. Belenko S, Dugosh KL, Lynch K, Mericle AA, Pich M, Forman RF. Online illegal drug use information: an exploratory analysis of drug-related website viewing by adolescents. *J Health Commun*. 2009;14(7):612–630.

85. Palmgreen P, Lorch EP, Stephenson MT, Hoyle RH, Donohew L. Effects of the Office of National Drug Control Policy's Marijuana Initiative Campaign on high-sensation-seeking adolescents. *Am J Public Health*. 2007;97(9):1644–1649.

86. Hornik R, Jacobsohn L, Orwin R, Piesse A, Kalton G. Effects of the National Youth Anti-Drug Media Campaign on youths. *Am J Public Health*. 2008;98(12):2229–2236.

87. Alvaro EM, Crano WD, Siegel JT, Hohman Z, Johnson I, Nakawaki B. Adolescents' attitudes toward antimarijuana ads, usage intentions, and actual marijuana usage. *Psychol Addict Behav*. 2013;27(4):1027–1035.

88. Czyzewska M, Ginsburg HJ. Explicit and implicit effects of anti-marijuana and anti-tobacco TV advertisements. *Addict Behav*. 2007;32(1):114–127.

89. Wakefield MA, Loken B, Hornik RC. Use of mass media campaigns to change health behaviour. *Lancet*. 2010;376(9748):1261–1271.

90. Hornik R. Evaluation design for public health communication programs. In: Hornik R, ed. *Public Health Commun.* Mahwah, NJ: Lawrence Erlbaum Associates; 2002:385–408.

91. National Academies of Sciences, Engineering, and Medicine (NASEM). *Getting to Zero Alcohol-Impaired Driving Fatalities: A Comprehensive Approach to a Persistent Problem.* Washington, DC: NASEM, 2018.

92. Azofeifa A MM, Schauer G, McAfee T, Grant A, Lyerla R. National estimates of marijuana use and related indicators—National Survey on Drug Use and Health, United States, 2002–2014. *MMWR Surveill Summ 2016;65(SS-11):1–25.*

93. Subritzky T, Lenton S, Pettigrew S. Cannabis and youth protection in Colorado's commercial adult-use market: a qualitative investigation. *Int J Drug Policy.* 2019;74:116–126.

94. Dorfman L, Wallack L. Advertising health: the case for counter-ads. *Public Health Rep.* 1993;108(6):716–726.

95. Community Preventive Services Task Force. Reducing tobacco use and secondhand smoke exposure: mass-reach health communication interventions. April 2013. Updated June 3, 2013. Available at: https://www.thecommunityguide.org/sites/default/files/assets/Tobacco-Mass-Reach-Health-Communication.pdf. Accessed March 30, 2021.

96. Duke JC, MacMonegle AJ, Nonnemaker JM, et al. Impact of The Real Cost media campaign on youth smoking initiation. *Am J Prev Med.* 2019;57(5):645–651.

97. *Johanns v. Livestock Marketing Association,* 544 US 550 (2005).

98. Jernigan D, Ross CS. The alcohol marketing landscape: alcohol industry size, structure, strategies, and public health responses. *J Stud Alcohol Drugs Suppl.* 2020;(suppl 19):13–25.

99. Federal Trade Commission. *Cigarette Report for 2018.* Washington, DC: Federal Trade Commission; 2019.

100. Federal Trade Commission. *Self-Regulation in the Alcohol Industry.* Washington, DC: Federal Trade Commission; 2014.

101. Jain SC. *Global Competitveness in the Beer Industry: A Case Study.* University of Connecticut, Dept of Agriculture and Resource Economics, Food Marketing Policy Center; 1994.

102. TipRanks. 3 US cannabis stocks gearing up for growth; Cantor says 'buy.' *Yahoo!finance.* December 8, 2020.

7

Physical Availability: Public Health and Community Effects of Legal Cannabis Outlets

A well-crafted cannabis legal framework preserves the authority of local jurisdictions to regulate business operations within their borders in keeping with community needs and values.

–Orenstein and Glantz[1]

SUMMARY AND INTRODUCTION

- Cannabis availability—how easy it is to get—is a significant determinant of cannabis use and associated problems.
- Availability has many facets, including type, number, and location of outlets; outlet retail practices, including days and hours of sale and use of security personnel; and accessibility to youth.
- Historically, alcohol and tobacco outlets have clustered in poor and minority communities, and indications are that cannabis outlets may be doing the same.
- Research has found cannabis outlets to be associated with increased cannabis consumption and related harms, along with increases in crime, either in the immediate vicinity of the stores or in nearby or adjacent areas.
- Cannabis policies regarding physical availability should build on the existing evidence regarding alcohol and tobacco availability, consumption, and harm.

Research in the alcohol field has found that people's perceptions about how available a substance is influences their drug use.[2] Substance availability has multiple facets.[3] Price and discounting determine the economic availability of various substances and are discussed with regard to cannabis in Chapter 8. Social availability arises out of the norms surrounding drug use—the degree of support for it among peer groups, family, and neighborhood social groupings. Subjective, or psychological, availability refers to how people see use of the drug—alcohol, tobacco, cannabis, and so on—fitting into their view of themselves: their lifestyle, culture, and personal identity. This form of availability is often what alcohol marketing, the subject of the previous chapter, seeks to influence.[4]

The final aspect of availability is physical: How easy is it practically and physically to access the substance? Hundreds of studies over the past 60 years have demonstrated that increased availability of alcohol leads to increased drinking, which in turn leads to increased alcohol problems.[5] A range of tobacco studies also has found associations between tobacco availability (including noncombustibles) and smoking behavior, particularly among youth.[6,7]

Studies have consistently found that alcohol and tobacco outlets are more likely to cluster in lower-income and minority neighborhoods.[8-13] This social justice aspect of physical availability merits careful consideration if and when states expand the availability of cannabis.

This chapter focuses on the physical aspect of availability, in particular the facets of it that require regulatory attention, including the type, number, and location of outlets, as well as the sales and service practices within those outlets, including days and hours of sale and presence of security personnel. It begins by reviewing findings about the disproportionate location of outlets selling legal drugs, including cannabis, in particular neighborhoods. Building on research and experience from the alcohol and tobacco fields, the chapter next explores both the evidence of harms from and the regulatory options for controlling the effects of various aspects of commercial as well as private (i.e., in private homes or spaces) availability of cannabis. The chapter closes with a discussion of policy and enforcement best practices for limiting youth access to cannabis.

AVAILABILITY: KEY CONSIDERATIONS

Accessibility to youth is a critical aspect of physical availability. As discussed in Chapter 2, cannabis poses significant risks to young people, including effects on healthy development of young brains (youth through adolescence and into their mid-20s). Recognizing these risks, all states that have legalized cannabis for nonmedical use have adopted a minimum age of 21 to purchase cannabis and a prohibition on youth cannabis possession.[14] In contrast, persons 18 years of age or older may become registered cannabis users in Uruguay,[15] and the minimum legal purchase age in Canada ranges from 18 (Alberta) to 21 (Quebec), with the majority of provinces designating 19 as the minimum legal purchase age.[16]

Many researchers have attempted to evaluate the impact of cannabis policies (from decriminalization to legalizing medical cannabis or cannabis for nonmedical use) on youth cannabis use. A recent systematic review and meta-analysis of these policy options found that cannabis decriminalization led to no statistically significant change in youth patterns of use, either preventing or increasing it, and that the studies evaluating legalization of cannabis for medical use were inconclusive. In six studies with a low or very low risk of bias, the authors found that legalization of cannabis for non-medical use was associated with a small increase in use among youth.[17] The bottom line from this literature is that legalization is not preventing youth use (which already was substantial prior to legalization; see Chapter 1), underscoring the need for a strong policy and enforcement response.

One of the most important determinants of physical availability is the overall regulatory system governing cannabis. As discussed in Chapter 4, a regulatory system prioritizing public health can generally influence cannabis availability by placing sales in the hands of government- or public authority–run outlets or by looking to cannabis social cooperatives to keep the product out of the general marketplace altogether. This chapter assumes that a regulatory system is already in place and then looks to other availability controls that may be important in safeguarding public health.

OUTLET LOCATION

Research conducted in diverse states and communities shows that cannabis outlets are more likely to be found in low-income communities than elsewhere:

- In California, cannabis dispensaries are most likely to be located in block groups with greater cannabis demand, higher rates of poverty, and more alcohol outlets and in areas just outside city boundaries.[18]
- In Washington State, census tracts with more poverty have more cannabis producers, processors, and retailers.[19]
- Also in Washington, between 2014 and 2017 the density of all types of cannabis businesses (producers, processors, and retailers) increased over time. Across all three years, the most economically deprived census tracts had the highest absolute number and average population-adjusted density of the three types of cannabis businesses.[20]
- Cannabis outlets in Colorado were more likely to be located in neighborhoods with a higher proportion of racial and ethnic minority populations, lower household incomes, larger unemployment rates, and higher crime rates.[21]

Findings regarding medical dispensaries in Colorado were slightly different: in Denver, prior to legalization medical cannabis dispensaries were not more likely to be located in communities of color and poor neighborhoods but were still more likely to be in neighborhoods with higher crime rates and more retail employment (i.e., retail jobs as a higher percentage of total jobs in the neighborhood).[22]

With the exception of Denver pre-legalization, location of cannabis outlets mirrors what has happened with alcohol and tobacco outlets. Low-income racial and ethnic minority neighborhoods and communities consistently have greater concentrations of alcohol outlets for off-premises consumption.[8-10] Similarly, tobacco outlets nationwide tend to cluster in urban census tracts with larger proportions of Black and Hispanic residents.[11] At the state and county levels as well, tobacco outlets are more likely to be located in neighborhoods with lower median incomes.[12,13]

Harms Related to Outlet Location

Outlet location and density are important because research has repeatedly shown that they are associated with a range of harms, even after accounting for other factors. The evidence is most clear for alcohol. The US Community Preventive Services Task Force "found sufficient evidence of a positive association between outlet density and excessive alcohol consumption and harms to recommend limiting alcohol outlet density through the use of regulatory authority."[23] Harms from alcohol outlets include public nuisance activities such as disorderly conduct, noise, neighborhood disruption, and property damage as well as more serious problems, including alcohol-impaired driving, pedestrian injuries, interpersonal and domestic violence, and child abuse and neglect.[24] Studies have found associations between outlet density and these harms even after accounting for other possible explanations such as neighborhood disadvantage or social disorganization.[25,26]

The type of outlet and how outlets cluster also matter. For alcohol, off-premises outlets—that is, outlets selling the product for consumption away from the premises— are significantly more likely to be associated with violence than on-premises outlets (see Figure 7-1).[26,27] While it is logical that bars may lead to more violence and other harms than restaurants, studies have generally not explored distinctions between outlets other than on-premises and off-premises.

When outlets cluster, there is more competition, which may lead to more price discounting as well as gatherings of heavier drinkers, creating greater risk of interpersonal violence.[28-30] Clusters, as well as the alcohol outlets themselves, have been found to be more likely to exist in neighborhoods with a history of redlining and other forms of disinvestment.[31,32]

In the case of tobacco, lower neighborhood socioeconomic status and higher concentrations of convenience stores are associated with higher levels of individual smoking generally,[33] while the density of tobacco outlets is associated with greater likelihood of youth smoking.[6,7] For alternative tobacco products as well, living in neighborhoods with greater densities of tobacco retailers is associated with higher odds of youth tobacco initiation, after controlling for individual and school factors.[34]

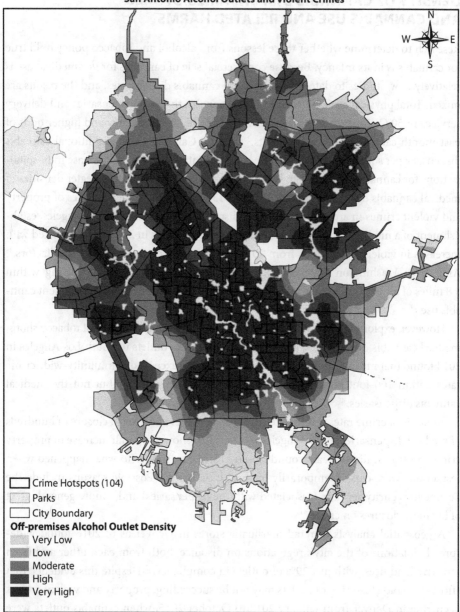

San Antonio Alcohol Outlets and Violent Crimes

▢ Crime Hotspots (104)
▨ Parks
▢ City Boundary
Off-premises Alcohol Outlet Density
▨ Very Low
▨ Low
▨ Moderate
▨ High
▨ Very High

Source: Reprinted with permission from Lu et al.[27]
Note: Darker areas have greater density of alcohol outlets; dark-bordered shapes are census tracts with more violent crime than their surrounding neighbors.

Figure 7-1. Alcohol Outlets and Violent Crime in San Antonio, Texas

DENSITY OF CANNABIS DISPENSARIES/STORES
AND CANNABIS USE AND RELATED HARMS

Research to determine whether these lessons from alcohol and tobacco policy hold true for cannabis is in its infancy. Because commercial sale of cannabis for nonmedical use is relatively new, studies to date include medical cannabis dispensaries, and the results are mixed. Total physical availability of medical cannabis through dispensaries and delivery services in 50 California cities was associated with higher frequency and higher odds of past-month cannabis use among adults.[35] Also in California, each additional cannabis dispensary per square mile in a zip code was associated with a 6.8% increase in hospitalizations for cannabis use or dependence.[36] In Long Beach, California, greater densities of medical cannabis dispensaries in 2012 and 2013 were related to higher rates of property and violent crimes in areas adjacent to the dispensary locations.[37] In Los Angeles, establishment of a medical cannabis dispensary in a census block in 2013 was associated with increases in violent crime rates from 2013 to 2014, after controlling for other factors.[38] And when Washington State opened its retail cannabis stores, adults living within 0.8 miles of a cannabis retailer increased both current (past 30 days) and frequent cannabis use.[39]

However, exploration of geographic associations between the density of tobacco shops, medical cannabis dispensaries, and off-premises alcohol outlets in South Los Angeles in 2014 found that mean property and violent crime rates exceeded community-wide crime rates within 100-foot buffers of the tobacco and alcohol outlets but not the medical cannabis dispensaries.[40]

Analysis of crime rates immediately prior to and after short-term closure of hundreds of medical dispensaries in Los Angeles in June 2010 showed a small increase in property crime in very localized areas around closed businesses, similar to what happened when restaurants were closed temporarily for health violations. Possible reasons include the decline in security services (associated with the dispensaries) and a more general effect of business closures on crime.[41]

A geospatial analysis of retail marijuana stores in Denver as of 2016 found widespread violations of the city's regulations on distance, both from each other and from sensitive land uses, with just 29% of outlets in compliance.[42] Despite this evidence that efforts to avoid clustering of outlets may not be succeeding, property and violent crimes occurring in Denver from January 2013 to October 2015, when cannabis outlets were opening for nonmedical as well as medical use, were unrelated to densities of cannabis outlets within census block groups (CBGs); however, CBGs with higher local as well as adjacent-area cannabis outlet densities had at least 9.8% higher property crime rates and higher rates of cannabis-specific crimes, compared with those without cannabis outlets.[43] Yet, using different methods and excluding murder and auto theft, a separate examination of crime in Denver from 2012 to 2015 found both medical and nonmedical cannabis outlets associated with statistically significant increases in rates of neighbor-hood crime and disorder.[44]

This diversity of findings suggests the need for greater methodological rigor and consistency across studies. The unit of analysis is important: authors of a study that found density of medical cannabis dispensaries in census tracts in Sacramento, California, in 2009 unrelated to rates of property or violent crimes surmised that census tracts may be too large a unit to show these relationships.[45]

Despite the preliminary and mixed nature of research on the relationship between cannabis outlet density and harm, the experience of cities like Baltimore, Maryland, where alcohol outlet density is high and numerous studies have shown clear links to harms,[46] demonstrates that it is much easier to limit outlet density before large numbers of retailers have established themselves than to reduce density and the number of outlets later.

OUTLET PRACTICES

Researchers in the Sacramento study did not initially measure on-site security or guardianship at the dispensaries, which may affect crime immediately surrounding these locations. This illustrates the importance of addressing specific outlet practices. In a subsequent study, the same research team surveyed all the dispensaries in Sacramento and found that some measures, such as security cameras and having security staff outside, might be effective in reducing crime within the outlets' immediate vicinity.[47]

Research on alcohol sales has concluded that extending hours and days of sale is likely to increase alcohol-related problems.[48,49] While there has not been any research on this regarding cannabis outlets, the logic holds: the more days and times cannabis is available for purchase, the higher consumption is likely to be.

Another outlet practice is allowing cannabis consumption on the premises. Commercial spaces permitting cannabis consumption on site are proliferating. These include cannabis lounges, cannabis tour or party buses, and retailers with on-site sampling, as well as special events, concerts, or festivals with a cannabis focus. Some states already regulate on-premises consumption under existing smoke-free laws. Analysis of cannabis use allowances in smoke-free laws in seven states as of August 2019 (see Table 7-1) found five that met criteria for being smoke-free in workplaces, restaurants, bars, and gambling sites and six that included electronic vaping devices in their smoke-free laws.[50]

Alaska, California, and Colorado now delegate to local jurisdictions the authority to permit cannabis smoking or vaping on the premises of a cannabis retail establishment provided the store meets certain criteria, including adequate ventilation, availability of smoke-free areas for employees, lack of public visibility from outside the premises, and no alcohol consumption.[50] California and Colorado also allow cannabis consumption in

Table 7-1. Smoke-Free Laws and Cannabis Use Allowances Among US States that Regulate Adult-Use Retail Sales

State	100% Smoke-Free Workplaces, Restaurants, Bars, Gambling (WRBG) Sites	Allowable Exemptions to Smoke-Free Law[a]	Electronic Vaping Devices Included in State Smoke-Free Law	Prohibits Public Cannabis Smoking or Vaping	Cannabis Retail Establishments	Social Consumption Lounges	Indoor Tourist Venues (Buses, Public Event)
Alaska	Not 100% WRBG because of local opt-out provision	1, 4	√	√	√+	X	X
California	100% WRBG	1, 6	√	√	√+	√+	√+
Colorado	100% WRBG	1, 6	√	√	√+	√+	√+
Massachusetts	100% WRBG	1, 2, 3, 6	√	√	X	X	X
Nevada	100% WR	1, 5	X	√	X	X	X
Oregon	100% WRBG	1, 2, 3, 6	√	√	X	X	X
Washington	100% WRBG	3, 6	√	√	X	X	X

Source: Reprinted with permission from Steinberg et al.[50]

Note: As of August 20, 2019. √ = yes; √+ = yes, per approval by local jurisdiction; X = no.

[a]Allowable exemptions to state smoke-free law: 1 = tobacco or electronic cigarette (or "vape") shops; 2 = cigar bars; 3 = private clubs; 4= licensed cannabis establishments; 5 = cigarette or e-cigarette use in bars, casinos, tobacco shops, strip clubs, brothels, hotel rooms; 6 = smoking allowed in a designated percentage of hotel rooms.

indoor tourist venues, such as tour or party buses, and public events, pending local jurisdiction approval.[50] No state allows cannabis consumption in commercial spaces that do not have a cannabis-related business license, such as bars or restaurants.

Direct-to-Consumer Sales and Delivery

The other big issue is whether you let Amazon get involved. We've seen what it's done to main street America already, so if you let cannabis be delivered, that could have significant implications.

–Beau Kilmer, PhD, RAND, in person interview, September 11, 2019

Direct-to-consumer sales and delivery includes home delivery, internet sales, third-person delivery, and even delivery by mail. These sales and delivery avenues raise public health concerns because of their potential to circumvent local decisions about cannabis availability and to increase availability to youth. Research from the alcohol and tobacco fields suggests caution in permitting this form of sale. Two small studies have found that minors successfully used home delivery to purchase 45% of the time for alcohol orders and 32.4% of the time for online tobacco purchases.[51,52]

Recently, in the wake of the COVID-19 pandemic, many states loosened regulations regarding home delivery of alcohol. In May 2020, the California Department of Alcoholic Beverage Control reported the results of a test of approximately 200 alcoholic beverage orders for delivery to decoys under age 21. Bars and restaurants failed the test (i.e., delivered alcohol to a minor) 25% of the time; delivery apps failed 80% of the time.[53]

These experiences point to the challenges of policing direct-to-consumer delivery of cannabis, which some states allow. In September 2019, Massachusetts, for example, approved new rules for home delivery under a separate delivery license. Delivery companies must sign contracts with licensed retailers, and delivery employees must wear body cameras. They must also adhere to restrictions applicable to outlet licensees, including limited delivery hours (8 a.m. to 9 p.m.), age verification requirements, and a ceiling on the amount of product permitted in one sale. Deliveries are prohibited in local jurisdictions that have banned nonmedical cannabis sales.[54] California also allows home delivery; unlike Massachusetts, however, it permits deliveries anywhere in the state regardless of local bans—a recent law currently being challenged by several local jurisdictions.[55] After it legalized cannabis for nonmedical use nationwide, Canada permitted online sales, but most jurisdictions control those sales through provincial or territorial government distribution systems, which in theory should facilitate a higher level of compliance with relevant laws and regulations.[56]

UNDERAGE ACCESS TO CANNABIS

States that permit the sale of cannabis for nonmedical use must reckon with social as well as commercial access to cannabis. To deter youth alcohol use, law enforcement has used strategies such as underage compliance checks (which test whether store clerks are complying with requirements to check patron IDs to ensure that buyers are of legal purchase age), shoulder taps (wherein youth, trained and monitored by law enforcement, approach adults 21 and older outside alcohol outlets and ask them to buy alcoholic beverages for them), and false ID laws. While compliance checks have been the most frequently evaluated and are effective in preventing youth access to alcohol,[57] the other strategies also have shown some effectiveness.[58-63]

Cannabis outlets may be doing a better job at preventing youth access. A small 2015 study in Colorado used pseudo-underage buyers (young adults age 21 or over who appear younger and do not carry their IDs) to attempt to purchase cannabis in 20 cannabis retail outlets. All the outlets asked the buyer to show an ID, and only one was willing to sell cannabis after the buyer did not provide proof of age.[64] A follow-up study in Colorado and Washington State found that stores refused pseudo-underage purchasers in 92.6% of purchase attempts. Both states forbid customers to enter a store or to be on the sales floor without a valid ID showing they are 21 or older; buyers were asked to present their ID at some point in all the purchase attempts.[65] However, youth and young adults themselves report being able to purchase cannabis in retail outlets. In a recent survey of 758 past-month cannabis users ages 18 to 25 (average age 21.6 years) in Los Angeles County, 59% reported obtaining cannabis from nonmedical cannabis retailers and 39% reporting buying it from medical dispensaries.[66]

SOCIAL USE LOCATIONS

As summarized in Chapter 2, a small and evolving body of evidence shows that secondhand cannabis smoke can put nonusers at risk for health-related harms. As such, there is considerable debate about whether to expand places where cannabis consumption may occur. All states that have legalized cannabis for nonmedical use have confined consumption to private property and prohibited use in public, although there are numerous exceptions. Some states allow consumption in private clubs or social club settings, while others permit it in retail environments and tourist venues or omit vaping devices from their bans.[50,67] Public spaces may include buildings (auditoriums, government buildings, and so on), parks, public streets or highways, and public higher-education facilities. Interior spaces may be covered by existing smoke-free laws or ordinances (see Table 7-1). Proponents of cannabis use argue that the limitations make it difficult or impossible for tourists and some local citizens who live in dense housing arrangements to find a place to use the product. Opponents respond that the discussion should include the health risks to nonusers.

While states generally are permitting cannabis use in personal residences, challenging issues arise in multiunit housing, rental properties, government subsidized housing, and vehicles. While some have argued that prohibiting cannabis consumption in multiunit housing or government-subsidized housing places an unfair burden on lower-income residents who use cannabis, making them vulnerable to eviction, others are concerned about the effects of secondhand smoke, particularly on children.

This area of research and policymaking is still evolving, and lessons from the alcohol experience are unclear. Communities around the world have advocated for bans on alcohol use in high-risk public settings such as public beaches.[68] However, a systematic review of public drinking bans found that while they improve popular perceptions of safety and the environment, they may have negative effects on marginalized groups and simply displace the behavior to other venues. Whether they actually reduce public drinking or alcohol-related crime or harm remains unclear.[69]

REGULATORY OPTIONS

Given the numerous physical availability challenges laid out above, what are the regulatory options? As discussed in Chapter 4, states can allow local jurisdictions to regulate various aspects of the cannabis market. Local authority is particularly important in addressing availability in retail and social or private settings. Local governments typically play a primary role in addressing land use, and these are the powers typically used to establish distance and density requirements for private businesses. At least 10 states authorize localities to opt out of allowing cannabis outlets in their jurisdictions, and/or these states permit local governments to establish time, place, and manner restrictions through local zoning or other regulations.[14,70]

Outlet Location and Density

Land use regulations for businesses such as cannabis retail stores may be divided into three subcategories: zoning restrictions, proximity buffers, and density controls.[71] In Washington State, 83 cities have enacted zoning regulations regarding cannabis; 10 have established caps on the number of cannabis businesses allowed in their jurisdiction; and 15 have mandated distance requirements more stringent than those set by the state for proximity to "sensitive uses," including elementary or secondary schools or playgrounds, churches and religious facilities, government complexes, correctional facilities, and substance abuse treatment facilities. A law change in 2015 permitted local jurisdictions to reduce the default 1,000-foot buffer distance from youth-serving uses other than schools and playgrounds (e.g., recreational facilities, child care centers, public parks); seven cities have reduced their buffer distances to anywhere from 500 feet to 100 feet from these locations.[70] In California, 42 jurisdictions increased the distance required between cannabis outlets and schools beyond the state-specified 600 feet, while 6 jurisdictions decreased the buffer. More than 100 jurisdictions added new sites to the list of sensitive uses requiring such a buffer, including colleges, public beaches, libraries, and recreation centers.[72]

Experience from the alcohol field suggests that greater local control provides public health with more leverage to put in place protective measures.[73] States and localities can work together to establish caps on how many outlets are permitted as well as requirements on how far outlets must be from sensitive uses. Nevada, for example, has established tiered caps on numbers of outlets, basing the caps on population size of the county in which an outlet would be located.[74]

Outlet Practices

Local jurisdictions can also determine outlet practices such as hours and days of sale, often in the context of the state setting a maximum that is reflective of public health concerns. Using their land use powers, localities can also require security and exterior lighting, ban signage or advertising visible outside the store, mandate a minimum age for sellers, set the maximum amount permissible in a single purchase, require cannabis retailer education, ban or restrict consumption or entertainment on site, establish minimum requirements for checking age and identification, and prohibit sampling and giveaways.

The Public Health Institute of California's Getting It Right from the Start initiative produced a model local ordinance, applicable to California cities but also influencing policy elsewhere, that lays out the rationale for and details of an effective conditional use (zoning) permitting process specific to cannabis retailing. The ordinance covers many of the store practices described in the preceding paragraph, along with three more: requiring that no use permit be issued if the outlets in a geographic area already exceed 1 per 15,000 people; banning home delivery; and requiring outlets to be a minimum distance away from youth-serving facilities.[75]

States that have legalized cannabis for nonmedical use have limited sales to licensed cannabis-only retail outlets. This facilitates monitoring and enforcement, and maintenance of an orderly and safe cannabis trade (see Chapter 4 for more detail on best practices for cannabis distribution systems).

Residential Spaces

The National Housing Law Project has produced *A Guide to Equitable Smoke-Free Public Housing*, which makes the following suggestions:

1. Create designated smoking areas on the housing property grounds.
2. Establish graduated enforcement that includes at least three verbal and written warnings prior to a termination notice.
3. Discourage the use of fees and fines for violations.
4. Allow residents to "reset the clock" if they have not had a violation during a set period of time (six months, for example).[76]

While these suggestions were made in relation to tobacco products and public housing (since as a Schedule I drug cannabis is prohibited in any federally subsidized housing), jurisdictions could consider these types of allowances for all multiunit housing and rental properties for cannabis consumption. Alternatively, states could allow landlords to prohibit cannabis smoking via a lease agreement but restrict them from prohibiting consumption of cannabis edibles or other noncombustible forms, as Massachusetts has done.[77]

Limiting Youth Access

Research from the alcohol field demonstrates the potential benefits of minimum purchase age laws[78]; a substantial body of research shows that raising the minimum legal alcohol purchase age to 21 has saved thousands of lives.[79] On December 20, 2019, the federal government followed this experience by raising the minimum age from 18 to 21 for sale of tobacco products to youth. All states that have legalized nonrecreational consumption of cannabis have established a minimum legal purchase and consumption age of 21. Best practice would be to also restrict access to cannabis retail environments to persons age 21 and above.

Regarding social access to cannabis, laws that impose civil and criminal penalties against individuals (social hosts) responsible for underage drinking events on property they own, lease, or otherwise control have been associated with less frequent underage drinking in private settings,[80] as well as with a reduction in alcohol-related traffic fatalities among 18- to 20-year-olds.[81] As these types of parties can increase the risk of problems such as impaired driving, new and existing social host laws could encompass underage parties with cannabis.

The Importance of Enforcement

In addition to strong policies, proactive and routine enforcement is essential to ensure compliance and protect public health and safety.[82] Chapter 9 takes up the topic of enforcement, but it is discussed here as well because restrictions on youth purchases rely on strategic enforcement for their effectiveness.

For tobacco, enhanced enforcement and compliance checks regarding young people's access in retail outlets have clearly reduced cigarette sales to minors.[83] For alcohol, the Task Force on Community Preventive Services, based on its systematic review of the research literature, recommends as an effective intervention enhanced enforcement of laws prohibiting sale of alcohol to minors.[57]

The theory of deterrence posits that effectiveness of deterrent strategies rests on three legs: certainty of apprehension, swiftness of sanctions, and severity of sanctions.[84] Whether thresholds for these elements are being reached for enforcement of laws restricting youth access to cannabis remains unclear. Nationwide in 2018, 80% of 12th graders reported that it would be fairly or very easy to obtain cannabis.[85] Youth perception of lax enforcement of underage cannabis laws predicts increases in youth cannabis use.[86] Parents are often the first line of enforcement, and yet an early survey after the legalization of cannabis for nonmedical use in Washington State showed that one-third of parents incorrectly believed that the legal age for nonmedical cannabis use was 18.[87]

A survey of law enforcement agencies in Colorado and Washington State after cannabis legalization found that while 30% of agencies conducted enforcement related to underage possession and use, only 20% conducted underage compliance checks. Similarly, only 32% of agencies centered their enforcement activities equally on both users and providers, while 40% of agencies made users their primary targets and just 11% focused on providers.[88]

Lessons from the fields of alcohol and tobacco control indicate that it is more effective to focus on the providers/suppliers.[5,57,89,90] Criminal penalties for youth possession may also feed into a narrative favored by alcohol and tobacco producers, shifting blame for underage consumption to young people and away from corporate entities that may benefit from underage sales.[90] As discussed in Chapter 5, a number of states have decriminalized possession of small amounts of cannabis. However, some state laws decriminalized adult but not youth possession. Another policy option is for underage possession laws to levy civil penalties, usually involving fines but not arrests or creation of criminal records. Civil penalties have proved sufficient to deter youth consumption,[90] the major public health goal for these policies.

Leading alcohol policy attorney James Mosher recommends that jurisdictions impose strict license sanctions on retail cannabis businesses that provide cannabis to underage youth, without consideration of retailer intent or actual knowledge of the customer's age.[91] Evidence that the transfer occurred can be sufficient, and all forms of transfer may be included, not just sales. He also recommends that civil or administrative penalties take precedence over criminal penalties for violations because criminal cases require a higher burden of proof and involve a more complex, lengthy legal process.[91]

The Washington State Liquor and Cannabis Board has taken a proactive role in preventing youth access to cannabis by conducting underage compliance checks in each cannabis retail outlet at least three times a year; in fiscal year 2017, the compliance rate was 90%.[92] It also has established a set of administrative penalty guidelines that begin with a 5-day suspension or $1,250 fine for a first violation, increase to a

10-day suspension or $7,500 fine for a second violation, and can eventually result in license revocation if a fourth offense occurs within a two-year window.[93] In contrast, the *Los Angeles Times* reported that as of 2019, California's Bureau of Cannabis Control had not introduced compliance checks in licensed cannabis outlets, instead focusing its enforcement efforts primarily on the almost 3,000 unlicensed dispensaries in the state.[94]

A study of underage purchase attempts in cannabis outlets in Colorado and Washington State found that in 5.4% of the attempts, store personnel actually suggested that the buyer, who was not actually permitted to enter the store, have the person accompanying him or her purchase the cannabis for the buyer.[65] Laws can prohibit this, as well as the use of false identification, in attempts to purchase cannabis, and retailers can be required to check IDs, ideally before patrons enter a cannabis outlet and again at the point of purchase. As in the alcohol and tobacco fields, incentives can be offered to those retailers that choose to use ID scanners or other technology to help validate IDs. (See Box 7-1 for discussion of Responsible Vendor Programs.)

Box 7-1. Responsible Vendor Programs

While evidence is mixed on the effectiveness of responsible beverage service training programs for reducing excessive alcohol consumption and related harms,[95-97] the cannabis retail environment may benefit from analogous training programs. Employees face the dual challenge of providing information and advice that extends beyond their expertise and preventing sales and access to underage persons and service to intoxicated customers. In an online survey of staff in medical and nonmedical cannabis retail outlets across eight states and Washington, DC, (n=55), 55% reported some formal training, although topics covered ranged from customer service to business operations and cannabis information. The majority of respondents reported providing advice to customers, including information on cannabis strains, suggested administration methods, potential side effects, and benefits of cannabis for specific symptoms. Only 20% of respondents, however, reported prior medical and/or scientific training.[98] These findings highlight the need for evidence-based training on cannabis products, health benefits and harms, as well as strategies and techniques for preventing youth access and service to intoxicated customers.

There have been limited efforts to create training programs for cannabis retail staff. In jurisdictions where it was illegal to sell cannabis to alcohol-intoxicated customers, a randomized control trial of a responsible vendor program found that employees' ability to check IDs and identify intoxicated customers improved after the training.[99] Subsequent tests in Washington State, Oregon, and Colorado in which pseudo-customers simulated obvious signs of intoxication revealed that the training did not reduce sales to pseudo-alcohol-intoxicated customers, with only 11% of the pseudo-intoxicated customer purchase attempts refused.[100] Responsible vendor programs without clear policies, consistent enforcement, and appropriately strong penalties may be unlikely to lead to significant changes in retailer behavior.

Unlicensed Cannabis Retailers

Unlicensed cannabis retailers should be considered part of the illegal market. They pose several risks: selling products that have not undergone routine testing and may have pesticides or contaminants; failing to comply with other areas of licensing, such as training of staff and limits on sales of certain products; and possibly facilitating easier access for youth. Unlicensed retailers may also be a manifestation of health and social inequities. An analysis in 2018 of licensed and unlicensed cannabis retailers in California found that neighborhoods with only unlicensed retailers had higher proportions of Latinx and Black Americans compared with neighborhoods with only licensed retailers.[101] Adequate enforcement resources are needed both to shut down unlicensed retail outlets and to conduct regular, proactive compliance checks, licensed premises inspections, and other enforcement operations as needed. Laws may need to be modified to allow law enforcement to use underage operatives in cannabis compliance check operations.

POLICY RECOMMENDATIONS

- Jurisdictions should place population-based caps on the number of cannabis outlets and require at least a 1,000-foot buffer zone from sensitive land uses.
- States should support the ability of local jurisdictions to govern cannabis availability within their borders. This includes permitting local governments to use zoning powers, set proximity buffers, and establish controls over outlet density.
- Any zoning restrictions and proximity buffers should equitably distribute cannabis businesses throughout a community. Implementation of distance requirements from schools and other sensitive areas must be done in ways that ensure that businesses do not end up predominantly located in poor communities and communities of color.
- Minimum purchase age laws should bar anyone under 21 from purchasing cannabis and explicitly state that using a false ID to purchase cannabis is illegal. Sanctions for purchasers should be civil and not criminal, with penalties on par with those for adult violations for possessing cannabis over the maximum allowed amount.
- Unless there is government control over delivery, as is the case in most Canadian jurisdictions, states should ban home delivery of nonmedical cannabis altogether to help keep it out of the hands of young people. If states do not prohibit home delivery, they should give localities the option to do so, especially if they have already banned cannabis retail outlets within their borders.
- Law enforcement should focus on sales to minors by retailers and establish administrative penalties that increase from fines to license suspension and revocation, with a window of no less than three years for consideration of subsequent violations.
- Existing social host laws regarding alcohol should be revised to incorporate cannabis. These and new social host laws should impose civil penalties on individuals who allow parties where underage cannabis consumption occurs on their property.
- No one under age 21 should be permitted to work in cannabis-related businesses, and no one under age 21 should be allowed to enter a cannabis-selling establishment.
- State and local law enforcement agencies should develop protocols and have adequate resources and training to conduct frequent and regular underage compliance checks of cannabis retailers for sales of cannabis to anyone under age 21.

Much of the emphasis in regulation of physical availability is on keeping cannabis out of the hands and minds of young people. The economic availability of cannabis—that is, how affordable it is—is also of critical importance for reducing consumption by youth, who often have less money than adults. The next chapter examines the fourth of the "four P's" of marketing: price.

REFERENCES

1. Orenstein DG, Glantz S. Cannabis legalization in state legislatures: public health opportunity and risk. *Marquette Law Rev.* 2020;103(4):1347.

2. Abbey A, Scott RO, Smith MJ. Physical, subjective, and social availability: their relationship to alcohol consumption in rural and urban areas. *Addiction.* 1993;88(4):489–499.

3. Smart RG. Availability and the prevention of alcohol-related problems. In: Harford TC, Parker DA, Light L, eds. *Normative Approaches to the Prevention of Alcohol Abuse and Alcoholism.* Rockville, MD: National Institute on Alcohol Abuse and Alcoholism; 1980:123–146.

4. Babor TF, Robaina K, Jernigan D. The influence of industry actions to increase availability of alcoholic beverages in the African region. *Addiction.* 2015;110(4):561–571.

5. Babor T, Caetano R, Casswell S, et al. *Alcohol: No Ordinary Commodity—Research and Public Policy.* 2nd ed. New York: Oxford University Press; 2010.

6. Novak SP, Reardon SF, Raudenbush SW, Buka SL. Retail tobacco outlet density and youth cigarette smoking: a propensity-modeling approach. *Am J Public Health.* 2006;96(4):670–676.

7. Cantrell J, Pearson JL, Anesetti-Rothermel A, Xiao H, Kirchner TR, Vallone D. Tobacco retail outlet density and young adult tobacco initiation. *Nicotine Tob Res.* 2016;18(2):130–137.

8. Gorman DM, Speer PW. The concentration of liquor outlets in an economically disadvantaged city in the northeastern United States. *Subst Use Misuse.* 1997;32(14):2033–2046.

9. Morrison C. Exposure to alcohol outlets in rural towns. *Alcohol Clin Exp Res.* 2015;39(1):73–78.

10. Berke EM, Tanski SE, Demidenko E, Alford-Teaster J, Shi X, Sargent JD. Alcohol retail density and demographic predictors of health disparities: a geographic analysis. *Am J Public Health.* 2010;100(10):1967–1971.

11. Rodriguez D, Carlos HA, Adachi-Mejia AM, Berke EM, Sargent JD. Predictors of tobacco outlet density nationwide: a geographic analysis. *Tob Control.* 2013;22(5):349–355.

12. Yu D, Peterson NA, Sheffer MA, Reid RJ, Schnieder JE. Tobacco outlet density and demographics: analysing the relationships with a spatial regression approach. *Public Health.* 2010;124(7):412–416.

13. Schneider JE, Reid RJ, Peterson NA, Lowe JB, Hughey J. Tobacco outlet density and demographics at the tract level of analysis in Iowa: implications for environmentally based prevention initiatives. *Prev Sci.* 2005;6(4):319–325.

14. National Institute on Alcohol Abuse and Alcoholism, Alcohol Policy Information System (APIS). Recreational use of cannabis. Volume 1. 2019; https://alcoholpolicy.niaaa.nih.gov/cannabis-policy-topics/recreational-use-of-cannabis-volume-1/104. Accessed July 14, 2019.

15. Boidi MF, Queirolo R, Cruz JM. Cannabis consumption patterns among frequent consumers in Uruguay. *Int J Drug Policy.* 2016;34:34–40.

16. CBC News. Legal age to buy cannabis in Quebec is now 21, the highest in Canada. *CBC.* January 1, 2020.

17. Melchior M, Nakamura A, Bolze C, et al. Does liberalisation of cannabis policy influence levels of use in adolescents and young adults? A systematic review and meta-analysis. *BMJ Open.* 2019;9.

18. Morrison C, Gruenewald PJ, Freisthler B, Ponicki WR, Remer LG. The economic geography of medical cannabis dispensaries in California. *Int J Drug Policy.* 2014;25(3):508–515.

19. Tabb LP, Fillmore C, Melly S. Location, location, location: assessing the spatial patterning between marijuana licenses, alcohol outlets and neighborhood characteristics within Washington State. *Drug Alcohol Depend.* 2018;185:214–218.

20. Amiri S, Monsivais P, McDonell MG, Amram O. Availability of licensed cannabis businesses in relation to area deprivation in Washington State: a spatiotemporal analysis of cannabis business presence between 2014 and 2017. *Drug Alcohol Rev.* 2019;38(7):790–797.

21. Shi Y, Meseck K, Jankowska MM. Availability of medical and recreational marijuana stores and neighborhood characteristics in Colorado. *J Addict.* 2016;2016:7193740.

22. Boggess LN, Pérez DM, Cope K, Root C, Stretesky PB. Do medical marijuana centers behave like locally undesirable land uses? implications for the geography of health and environmental justice. *Urban Geography.* 2014;35(3):315–336.

23. Task Force on Community Preventive Services. Recommendations for reducing excessive alcohol consumption and alcohol-related harms by limiting alcohol outlet density. *Am J Prev Med.* 2009;37(6):570–571.

24. Campbell CA, Hahn RA, Elder R, et al. The effectiveness of limiting alcohol outlet density as a means of reducing excessive alcohol consumption and alcohol-related harms. *Am J Prev Med.* 2009;37(6):556–569.

25. Toomey TL, Erickson DJ, Carlin BP, et al. The association between density of alcohol establishments and violent crime within urban neighborhoods. *Alcohol Clin Exp Res.* 2012;36(8):1468–1473.

26. Trangenstein PJ, Curriero FC, Webster D, et al. Outlet type, access to alcohol, and violent crime. *Alcohol Clin Exp Res.* 2018;42(11):2234–2245.

27. Lu Y, Trangenstein P, Jernigan DH. Policy-maker relevant metrics to break the link between alcohol outlets and violence. Paper presented at: Annual Meeting of the American Public Health Association; October 24, 2020. Virtual.

28. Scribner RA, MacKinnon DP, Dwyer JH. The risk of assaultive violence and alcohol availability in Los Angeles County. *Am J Public Health.* 1995;85(3):335–340.

29. Grubesic TH, Pridemore WA. Alcohol outlets and clusters of violence. *Int J Health Geogr.* 2011;10:30.

30. Zhang X, Hatcher B, Clarkson L, et al. Changes in density of on-premises alcohol outlets and impact on violent crime, Atlanta, Georgia, 1997–2007. *Prev Chronic Dis.* 2015;12:E84.

31. Trangenstein PJ, Gray C, Rossheim ME, Sadler R, Jernigan DH. Alcohol outlet clusters and population disparities. *J Urban Health.* 2020;97(1):123–136.

32. Lee JP, Ponicki W, Mair C, Gruenewald P, Ghanem L. What explains the concentration of off-premise alcohol outlets in Black neighborhoods? *SSM Popul Health.* 2020;12:100669.

33. Chuang YC, Cubbin C, Ahn D, Winkleby MA. Effects of neighbourhood socioeconomic status and convenience store concentration on individual level smoking. *J Epidemiol Community Health.* 2005;59(7):568–573.

34. Abdel Magid HS, Halpern-Felsher B, Ling PM, Bradshaw PT, Mujahid MS, Henriksen L. Tobacco retail density and initiation of alternative tobacco product use among teens. *J Adolesc Health.* 2020;66(4):423–430.

35. Freisthler B, Gruenewald PJ. Examining the relationship between the physical availability of medical marijuana and marijuana use across fifty California cities. *Drug Alcohol Depend.* 2014;143:244–250.

36. Mair C, Freisthler B, Ponicki WR, Gaidus A. The impacts of marijuana dispensary density and neighborhood ecology on marijuana abuse and dependence. *Drug Alcohol Depend.* 2015;154:111–116.

37. Freisthler B, Ponicki WR, Gaidus A, Gruenewald PJ. A micro-temporal geospatial analysis of medical marijuana dispensaries and crime in Long Beach, California. *Addiction.* 2016;111(6):1027–1035.

38. Contreras C. A block-level analysis of medical marijuana dispensaries and crime in the city of Los Angeles. *Justice Q.* 2017;34(6):1069–1095.

39. Everson EM, Dilley JA, Maher JE, Mack CE. Post-legalization opening of retail cannabis stores and adult cannabis use in Washington State, 2009–2016. *Am J Public Health.* 2019;109(9):1294–1301.

40. Subica AM, Douglas JA, Kepple NJ, Villanueva S, Grills CT. The geography of crime and violence surrounding tobacco shops, medical marijuana dispensaries, and off-sale alcohol outlets in a large, urban low-income community of color. *Prev Med.* 2018;108:8–16.

41. Chang T, Jacobson M. Going to pot? the impact of dispensary closures on crime. *J Urban Econ.* 2017;100:120–136.

42. Akpanekong AO. GIS Suitability analysis to situate recreational/retail marijuana stores in Denver, Colorado. *Walden DIssertations and Doctoral Studies.* 2019. Available at: https://scholarworks.waldenu.edu/dissertations/7525. Accessed April 1, 2021.

43. Freisthler B, Gaidus A, Tam C, Ponicki WR, Gruenewald PJ. From medical to recreational marijuana sales: marijuana outlets and crime in an era of changing marijuana legislation. *J Prim Prev.* 2017;38(3):249–263.

44. Hughes LA, Schaible LM, Jimmerson K. Marijuana dispensaries and neighborhood crime and disorder in Denver, Colorado. *Justice Q.* 2020;37:461–485.

45. Kepple NJ, Freisthler B. Exploring the ecological association between crime and medical marijuana dispensaries. *J Stud Alcohol Drugs.* 2012;73(4):523–530.

46. Trangenstein PJ, Eck RH, Lu Y, et al. The violence prevention potential of reducing alcohol outlet access in Baltimore, Maryland. *J Stud Alcohol Drugs.* 2020;81(1):24–33.

47. Freisthler B, Kepple NJ, Sims R, Martin SE. Evaluating medical marijuana dispensary policies: spatial methods for the study of environmentally-based interventions. *Am J Community Psychol.* 2013;51(1–2):278–288.

48. Hahn RA, Kuzara JL, Elder R, et al. Effectiveness of policies restricting hours of alcohol sales in preventing excessive alcohol consumption and related harms. *Am J Prev Med.* 2010;39(6):590–604.

49. Sherk A, Stockwell T, Chikritzhs T, et al. Alcohol consumption and the physical availability of take-away alcohol: systematic reviews and meta-analyses of the days and hours of sale and outlet density. *J Stud Alcohol Drugs.* 2018;79(1):58–67.

50. Steinberg J, Unger JB, Hallett C, Williams E, Baezconde-Garbanati L, Cousineau MR. A tobacco control framework for regulating public consumption of cannabis: multistate analysis and policy implications. *Am J Public Health.* 2019;e1–e6.

51. Williams RS, Ribisl KM. Internet alcohol sales to minors. *Arch Pediatr Adolesc Med.* 2012;166(9):808–813.

52. Williams RS, Derrick J, Phillips KJ. Cigarette sales to minors via the internet: how the story has changed in the wake of federal regulation. *Tob Control.* 2017;26(4):415–420.

53. Siddiqui F. Food delivery apps fueled alcohol sales to minors, California regulators find. *Washington Post.* May 8, 2020.

54. DeCosta-Klipa N. Massachusetts is going ahead with marijuana delivery. Here's how it will work. *Boston.com.* October 1, 2019.

55. McGreevy P. California officials side with marijuana company in new fight over home deliveries. *Los Angeles Times.* November 26, 2019.

56. Lancione S, Wade K, Windle SB, Filion KB, Thombs BD, Eisenberg MJ. Non-medical cannabis in North America: an overview of regulatory approaches. *Public Health.* 2020;178:7–14.

57. Elder R, Lawrence B, Janes G, et al. Enhanced enforcement of laws prohibiting sale of alcohol to minors: systematic review of effectiveness for reducing sales and underage drinking. *Transportation Research.* 2007;(E-C123):181–188.

58. Toomey TL, Fabian LE, Erickson DJ, Lenk KM. Propensity for obtaining alcohol through shoulder tapping. *Alcohol Clin Exp Res.* 2007;31(7):1218–1223.

59. Fell JC, Tanenbaum E, Chelluri D. Evaluation of a combination of community initiatives to reduce driving while intoxicated and other alcohol-related harms. *Traffic Inj Prev.* 2018;19(suppl 1):S176–S179.

60. Fell JC, Scherer M, Thomas S, Voas RB. Effectiveness of social host and fake identification laws on reducing underage drinking driver fatal crashes. *Traffic Inj Prev.* 2014;15(suppl 1): S64–S73.

61. Grube JW. Preventing sales of alcohol to minors: results from a community trial. *Addiction.* 1997;92(suppl 2):S251–S260.

62. Stogner J, Martinez JA, Miller BL, Sher KJ. How strong is the "fake ID effect"? an examination using propensity score matching in two samples. *Alcohol Clin Exp Res.* 2016;40(12): 2648–2655.

63. Yoruk BK. Can technology help to reduce underage drinking? Evidence from the false ID laws with scanner provision. *J Health Econ.* 2014;36:33–46.

64. Buller DB, Woodall WG, Saltz R, Starling R. Pseudo-underage assessment of compliance with identification regulations at retail marijuana outlets in Colorado. *J Stud Alcohol Drugs.* 2016;77(6):868–872.

65. Buller DB, Woodall WG, Saltz R, Buller MK. Compliance with personal ID regulations by recreational marijuana stores in two US states. *J Stud Alcohol Drugs.* 2019;80(6): 679–686.

66. D'Amico EJ, Rodriguez A, Dunbar MS, et al. Sources of cannabis among young adults and associations with cannabis-related outcomes. *Int J Drug Policy.* 2020;86:102971.

67. National Institute on Alcohol Abuse and Alcoholism, Alcohol Policy Information System (APIS). Recreational use of cannabis. Volume 2. 2020. Available at: https://alcoholpolicy. niaaa.nih.gov/cannabis-policy-topics/recreational-use-of-cannabis-volume-2/105. Accessed April 1, 2021.

68. Conway K. Booze and beach bans: turning the tide through community action in New Zealand. *Health Promot Int.* 2002;17(2):171–177.

69. Pennay A, Room R. Prohibiting public drinking in urban public spaces: a review of the evidence. *Drugs: Educ, Prev Policy.* 2012;19(2):91–101.

70. Dilley JA, Hitchcock L, McGroder N, Greto LA, Richardson SM. Community-level policy responses to state marijuana legalization in Washington State. *Int J Drug Policy.* 2017;42: 102–108.

71. Németh J, Ross E. Planning for marijuana: the cannabis conundrum. *J Am Plann Assoc.* 2014;80(1):6–20.

72. Silver LD, Naprawa AZ, Padon AA. Assessment of incorporation of lessons from tobacco control in city and county laws regulating legal marijuana in California. *JAMA Netw Open.* 2020;3(6):e208393.

73. Jernigan DH, Sparks M, Yang E, Schwartz R. Using public health and community partnerships to reduce density of alcohol outlets. *Prev Chronic Dis.* 2013;10:E53.

74. Nevada Department of Taxation. Nevada Marijuana Program. February 15, 2019. Available at: https://tax.nv.gov/uploadedFiles/taxnvgov/Content/Meetings/Marijuana-Ovcrview-2-14-19.pdf. Accessed April 1, 2021.

75. Public Health Institute, Getting it Right from the Start. Retail & marketing model ordinance. 2020. Available at: https://www.gettingitrightfromthestart.org/our-model-ordinances. Accessed April 1, 2021.

76. National Housing Law Project. *A Guide to Equitable Smoke-Free Public Housing.* January 2020. Available at: https://www.nhlp.org/wp-content/uploads/FINAL_-A-Guide-to-Equitable-Smoke-Free-Public-Housing-2020.01.14.pdf. Accessed August 25, 2021.

77. Public Health Law Center. *Marijuana in Multi-Unit Residential Settings.* St Paul, MN: Public Health Law Center, Mitchell Hamline School of Law; August 2019.

78. Ammerman S, Ryan S, Adelman WP, Committee on Substance Abuse, Committee on Adolescence. The impact of marijuana policies on youth: clinical, research, and legal update. *Pediatrics.* 2015;135(3):e769–e785.

79. DeJong W, Blanchette J. Case closed: research evidence on the positive public health impact of the age 21 minimum legal drinking age in the United States. *J Stud Alcohol Drugs Suppl.* 2014;75(suppl 17):108–115.

80. Paschall MJ, Lipperman-Kreda S, Grube JW, Thomas S. Relationships between social host laws and underage drinking: findings from a study of 50 California cities. *J Stud Alcohol Drugs.* 2014;75(6):901–907.

81. Dills AK. Social host liability for minors and underage drunk-driving accidents. *J Health Econ.* 2010;29(2):241–249.

82. Wagenaar AC, Toomey TL, Erickson DJ. Preventing youth access to alcohol: outcomes from a multi-community time-series trial. *Addiction.* 2005;100(3):335–345.

83. Friend KB, Lipperman-Kreda S, Grube JW. The impact of local US tobacco policies on youth tobacco use: a critical review. *Open J Prev Med.* 2011;1(2):34–43.

84. Stafford MC. Deterrence theory: crime. In: Wright JD, ed. *International Encyclopedia of the Social & Behavioral Sciences.* 2nd ed. Oxford, UK: Elsevier; 2015:255–259.

85. Johnston LD, Miech RA, O'Malley PM, Bachman JG, Schulenberg JE, Patrick ME. *Monitoring the Future National Survey Results on Drug Use, 1975–2018: Overview, Key Findings on Adolescent Drug Use.* Ann Arbor, MI: Institute for Social Research, University of Michigan; 2019.

86. Guttmannova K, Skinner ML, Oesterle S, White HR, Catalano RF, Hawkins JD. The interplay between marijuana-specific risk factors and marijuana use over the course of adolescence. *Prev Sci.* 2019;20(2):235–245.

87. Kosterman R, Bailey JA, Guttmannova K, et al. Marijuana legalization and parents' attitudes, use, and parenting in Washington State. *J Adolesc Health*. 2016;59(4):450–456.

88. Wiens T, Lenk KM, Fabian LEA, Erickson DJ. Law enforcement practices in the first two states in US to legalize recreational marijuana. *Int J Drug Policy*. 2018;61:38–43.

89. Lantz PM, Jacobson PD, Warner KE, et al. Investing in youth tobacco control: a review of smoking prevention and control strategies. *Tob Control*. 2000;9(1):47–63.

90. Mosher JF. The merchants, not the customers: resisting the alcohol and tobacco industries' strategy to blame young people for illegal alcohol and tobacco sales. *J Public Health Policy*. 1995;16(4):412–432.

91. Mosher J. *The 2016 California Marijuana Initiative and Youth: Lessons from Alcohol Policy*. San Francisco, CA: UC San Francisco; 2 016.

92. Washington State Liquor and Cannabis Board. *Washington State Liquor and Cannabis Board Annual Report: Fiscal Year 2018*. Olympia, WA: 2018.

93. Washington Administrative Code. Title 314 WAC. Liquor and Cannabis Board. 2020.

94. McGreevy P. California isn't using minors to bust illegal pot sales as it does with tobacco and alcohol. *Los Angeles Times*. November 18, 2019.

95. Community Preventive Services Task Force. Preventing excessive alcohol consumption: responsible beverage service training. 2012. Available at: https://beta.thecommunityguide.org/sites/default/files/assets/Alcohol-Beverage-Service-Training.pdf. Accessed April 3, 2021.

96. Lenk KM, Erickson DJ, Nelson TF, et al. Changes in alcohol policies and practices in bars and restaurants after completion of manager-focused responsible service training. *Drug Alcohol Rev*. 2018;37(3):356–364.

97. Ker K, Chinnock P. Interventions in the alcohol server setting for preventing injuries. *Cochrane Database Syst Rev*. 2008(3). Available at: https://www.cochranelibrary.com/cdsr/doi/10.1002/14651858.CD005244.pub3. Accessed March 30, 2021.

98. Haug NA, Kieschnick D, Sottile JE, Babson KA, Vandrey R, Bonn-Miller MO. Training and practices of cannabis dispensary staff. *Cannabis Cannabinoid Res*. 2016;1(1):244–251.

99. Buller DB, Woodall WG, Saltz R, Grayson A, Buller MK. Implementation and effectiveness of an online responsible vendor training program for recreational marijuana stores in Colorado, Oregon, and Washington State. *J Public Health Manag Pract*. 2019;25(3):238–244.

100. Buller DB, Woodall WG, Saltz R, Grayson A, Svendsen S, Cutter GR. Sales to apparently alcohol-intoxicated customers and online responsible vendor training in recreational cannabis stores in a randomized trial. *Int J Drug Policy*. 2020;83:102860.

101. Unger JB, Vos RO, Wu JS, et al. Locations of licensed and unlicensed cannabis retailers in California: a threat to health equity? *Prev Med Rep*. 2020;19:101165.

8

Cannabis Taxes and Prices

As we see a number of states engaging around the country in a retail market, this is no longer an experiment. It is also no secret that we are heading into some rough economic waters and we need to explore every possible revenue stream.

−Texas State Rep. Joe Moody (D-El Paso)[1]

SUMMARY AND INTRODUCTION

- State legislators considering legalizing cannabis for adult nonmedical use are often drawn to its potential for raising revenues, but taxation of cannabis is complex and requires robust administration and enforcement.
- Research on alcohol and tobacco has found that users, including those who are dependent, are sensitive to price, and that price increases will decrease consumption and related harms.
- Cannabis consumers, including youth and regular users, also are sensitive to price.
- Commonly considered taxation options for cannabis include taxing by weight, potency, or price; each has the potential to affect cannabis prices and consumption patterns.
- Prohibiting or limiting price discounts, couponing, and other discount schemes, and requiring minimum unit markups, can also discourage consumption.
- States that have legalized cannabis for nonmedical use have allocated revenues from cannabis to a variety of programs and services. However, cannabis prices have generally fallen in the wake of legalization, so future government revenues may decline.

This chapter reviews the public health goals of cannabis taxation and pricing policies in a regulated market. Policies and policy options regarding cannabis taxation will differ based on whether states elect to create a public government-controlled monopoly or public authority or to eliminate profit motives altogether through cannabis social clubs or home cultivation (see Chapter 4). While the latter may obviate the opportunity and need for cannabis taxation, public monopolies or authorities may still levy taxes at the producer level. For states considering public health–focused or commercially-focused licensing, this chapter provides an overview of the taxation and pricing policy options and their potential effects on public health. It concludes with a discussion of options for revenue allocation, which should also be considered in light of potential conflicts of interest with regulatory efforts.

TAXATION AND PRICING GOALS

The public health goals of cannabis taxation and pricing policies are identical to the first three of the five goals articulated in the Introduction:

- Preventing youth cannabis use;
- Controlling the prevalence, frequency, and intensity of cannabis use; and
- Reducing cannabis-related harms to individuals and communities.

Historically, however, at least in the United States, governments have viewed taxes on commodities such as alcohol, tobacco, and cannabis primarily as revenue opportunities and not as public health tools. Revenue generation in and of itself is not a public health goal, unless those revenues are earmarked to address the problems associated with use of the products being taxed. Governments are vulnerable to a conflict of interest: on one hand they are responsible for reducing problems associated with the product; on the other they can increase revenues accruing to them by encouraging consumption.[2-4]

LESSONS FROM OTHER PRODUCTS

Higher taxes increase the prices of alcohol and tobacco products, and these price increases in turn reduce alcohol and tobacco consumption.[5-9] Tobacco price increases are associated with preventing smoking initiation by youth, young adults, and those of lower socioeconomic status and encouraging current tobacco users to stop.[8-12] Increases in cigarette taxes in the United States have had the greatest impact on smoking prevalence among youth, followed by young adults. A tax increase of 25 cents per pack was associated with an estimated 1.5% reduction in smoking prevalence among those ages 18 to 24.[10]

Larger price increases will have more significant effects. The Community Preventive Services Task Force found that an intervention that increases the unit price for tobacco products by 20% can reduce overall tobacco consumption by 10.4%, decrease the prevalence of adult tobacco use by 3.6%, and reduce the initiation of tobacco use by young people by 8.6%. Higher tobacco prices may also reduce tobacco-related disparities by income group and by race/ethnicity.[13]

A meta-analysis of the impact of alcohol prices and taxes on consumption concluded that a 10% increase in prices resulted in a 4.4% reduction in drinking.[5] Doubling the alcohol tax would lead to an average reduction of 35% in alcohol-related mortality.[14]

In addition to taxation, other price policies to consider include minimum unit prices, minimum markup requirements, and prohibitions on discounting and coupons.[15] Minimum floor, or unit, prices set a base price for which products must be sold. Minimum markup laws typically prohibit selling products below cost as they move through the supply chain, requiring wholesalers and retailers to increase prices by a minimum percentage—a minimum markup—from what they pay for goods.

The tobacco industry has often offered price discounts such as dollar-off promotions; coupons; buy-one, get-one-free offers; and multipack discounts. Policies prohibiting such practices may be effective in reducing consumption.[16] Heavy tobacco smokers and young adult smokers have been found to use coupons and bulk promotional discounts more than other adult smokers.[17,18] Smokers who utilized a higher number of cost-saving strategies had lower odds of reducing the number of days smoked.[18] These pricing schemes can weaken the effects of taxes and other pricing laws, and jurisdictions may prohibit them.[15] Such bans should be considered as complements to taxation, which has the greatest potential for reducing consumption.

The alcohol and tobacco literatures differentiate between minimum unit price laws and minimum markup laws, although the phrases are sometimes used interchangeably. In this country in 2015, 27 states had minimum markup laws for cigarettes—which require a minimum percentage markup to the base cost of the product—while only 4 states had minimum price laws. The minimum wholesale markups required in these states ranged from 2% to 6%, and minimum retail markups were between 4% and 25%.[19] Evaluations of minimum markup or price policies for tobacco have found that these are more effective when the tobacco industry is not able to adjust what consumers pay for products by offering volume-based discounts, promotions, and coupons and by providing products in different price tiers, which often target specific market segments.[16,20,21]

Several countries have implemented minimum alcohol price policies. The 2018 introduction of minimum unit pricing in Scotland was associated with a small increase in purchase prices and a 7.6% reduction in weekly alcohol purchases per adult, predominantly affecting the top 20% of alcohol-purchasing households.[22] In Canada, a 10% increase in minimum unit prices in Saskatchewan reduced consumption (of all beverage types) by 8.4%.[23] Research conducted over a 20-year period in the province of British Columbia demonstrated that a 10% increase in the mean minimum price of alcohol reduced total consumption by 3.4%, and a 10% increase in the minimum price of any alcoholic beverage reduced its consumption relative to other beverages by 16.1%.[24]

CANNABIS PRICES AND THEIR PUBLIC HEALTH IMPACT

The big takeaway from this report we did about 10 years ago is you have to pay attention to price. For so many of the outcomes that people care about, whether it be size of illicit market, consumption, tax revenues, profitability of businesses, which is especially

important now as the social equity discussion has moved toward giving preferences for
licenses, all of these are shaped by price.

–Beau Kilmer, PhD, RAND, in person interview, September 11, 2019

From a public health perspective, cannabis prices and taxes matter because, as with alcohol and tobacco, governments may be able to use them as a policy lever to reduce consumption and related harms. There is clear evidence that cannabis users are sensitive to price; the effects of prices also vary by subgroup, with light, casual, regular, and heavy users responding differently to price changes.[25-28] Prior to legalization of cannabis for nonmedical use, researchers estimated that a 10% drop in the price of cannabis would lead to a 3% to 5% increase in the number of new, young cannabis users,[29,30] as well as a 2.4% to 2.5% increase in regular users.[26,27] Conversely, price increases reduce consumption. One study conducted in France found that for every 10% increase in cannabis prices there would be a 17% to 21% drop in the amount users purchased. Perceived potency of the product seemed to matter, but actual potency had little effect on price; more important was the quantity purchased, with the price declining 0.21% for every 1% increase in the amount users bought.[31]

There is less evidence of the direct impact of changes in cannabis prices on harms from cannabis use. Because legalization generally leads to lower prices, post-legalization increases in acute harms such as traffic fatalities and hospitalizations point to the impact of prices on such issues in the short term (see Chapter 2 for a fuller discussion of legalization and these harms). For longer-term negative outcomes, such as effects on mental health or employment, the relatively brief time in which cannabis has been legal and states have been experimenting with taxation regimes makes the effect of price hard to assess.

Although "[a]t less than a dollar per stoned hour, today's marijuana prices are already pretty low,"[32] relatively cheap cannabis does not mean that it is a small portion of users' budgets. Analysis of the US cannabis market from 2002 to 2013 revealed that daily or near-daily users accounted for upward of 75% of all reported spending and that daily or near-daily users were, on average, not particularly affluent. Users in this group who were over 21 years old and without college degrees (an estimated 3.5 million people) spent on average 9% of their household income on cannabis purchases.[33]

However, illegal cannabis, the product being purchased when these studies were done, is likely to be more expensive than its legal counterpart, for the following reasons:

1. Legal risks (including risks of violence) associated with every stage of illicit supply, from cultivation and processing to transportation and sale, are passed on as additional costs.
2. Risks (e.g., involving land or workers) are greater in the illegal market, necessitating a higher rate of return in relation to them.
3. Illegal production is also generally less efficient, which raises production costs.[34]

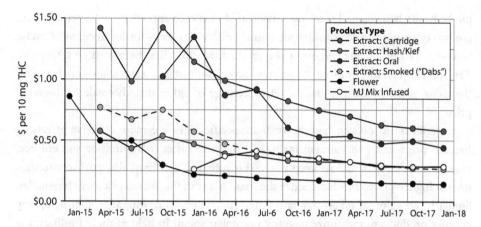

Source: Reprinted with permission from Davenport.[39]

Figure 8-1. Regression-Based Estimates for Price per 10 mg THC by Product/Subtype Over Time in Washington State

One implication of this is that prices are likely to fall after legalization. This is what appears to have happened at least in some states, where prices initially dropped quite dramatically after legalization at the same time that consumers shifted the types of products purchased.[35-38] Figure 8-1 shows what happened to prices by product type in Washington State between July 2014, when nonmedical cannabis outlets opened, and October 2017.[39]

Other researchers have noted the instability and limited effects on price in the early months of legalization of nonmedical cannabis in Colorado and Washington State, and they caution that markets do not stabilize immediately. As such, short-term evaluations of policy effects on cannabis consumption will not necessarily reflect long-term consumption trends.[34]

TAXATION/PRICING OPTIONS

There are some conversations occurring about whether the tax should just be straight-across excise, or whether it should be based on potency. Say you tax higher potency at a higher rate and lower potency at a lower rate. I think that's an interesting concept to be looking at because then we can get to some of those higher risk products and how you tax those appropriately, utilizing taxes as a deterrent for youth access.

–Justin Nordhorn, BA, Washington State Liquor and Cannabis Board, in person interview, August 13, 2019

With taxes as government's principal lever for influencing cannabis prices, public health advocates as well as those in favor of cannabis legalization have proposed various taxation schemes.[40-42] States and countries have implemented a variety of taxation approaches domestically and internationally for sale of alcohol and tobacco products, with specific public health benefits and challenges associated with each approach.[43,44] Generally, there are two types of taxes to consider for cannabis: *Specific taxes*—for instance, most excise taxes—are levied on the *volume* of the product, whether that be measured by weight, THC potency, carton, or piece. *Ad valorem taxes*—for instance, sales taxes—are based on the *value* of the product, usually a set percentage of either the wholesale or the retail price.

Experience in tobacco has shown that specific taxes are more effective at raising tobacco prices than ad valorem taxes, and they are easier to administer and enforce. However, these often fail to keep pace with inflation and may also push consumers toward higher-priced products, since the share of tax in the overall price will be smaller. Similarly, ad valorem taxes may encourage consumers to downgrade—that is, to buy cheaper products to maximize quantity per dollar spent. In light of these findings, the World Health Organization (WHO) recommends that for tobacco, countries rely primarily on specific taxes, regularly adjusted for inflation, combined with a minimum tax floor.[43]

Given the substantial variation in strength and composition of cannabis products, for tax purposes, cannabis may have more in common with alcohol than tobacco. In its technical guide on alcohol taxation, WHO suggests employing a mix of taxation and pricing strategies. Specific taxation may promote consumption of lower-strength products, whereas ad valorem taxes may be more effective in preventing drinking initiation among young people, provided there is some kind of tax floor or minimum price in place.[44]

These examples from tobacco and alcohol illustrate both the range of tax and price tools available to governments and how differently each may influence consumption. Various methods for taxing cannabis are described next. Table 8-1 provides specific examples of jurisdictions using each of the systems. Table 8-2 rates these methods from one to three stars based on their ability to achieve the public health goals articulated at the start of this chapter.

Table 8-1. Examples of Taxation Options Currently in Use

Jurisdiction	By Weight	By Potency	By Price
Alaska	$50 per oz. mature bud, $25 per oz. immature bud, $25 per oz. abnormal bud, $15 per oz. remainder of plant, and clones $1 per plant (producer level)		
California	$9.25 per oz. flowers; $2.75 per oz. leaves; $1.29 per oz. fresh cannabis plant (producer level)		15% of sales (retail level)

(Continued)

Table 8-1. (Continued)

Jurisdiction	By Weight	By Potency	By Price
Canada*	For dried/fresh cannabis, $0.25 per gram of flowering material, and $0.075 per gram of non-flowering material or 2.5% of the dutiable amount of the cannabis product, whichever is higher. For cannabis plants and seeds, $0.25 per plant or seed or 2.5% of the dutiable amount for the cannabis product, whichever is higher. Additional duties may be applied at the provincial level (producer level)	THC-based tax ($0.0025 per milligram of total THC with a possible additional duty of $0.0075 per milligram of total THC) on concentrates, edibles, and topical products (producer level)	
Colorado*	15% of the contract price or the average market rate per pound for cultivation (producer level)		15% of sales (retail level)
Illinois		Smoked (or vaporized) cannabis products (e.g., flowers, buds, dabs, vaping cartridges) taxed at 10% if THC content is below 35% and at 25% if THC content is above 35% (retail level)	7% of sales to retailers (producer level); 20% of sales of noncombustible cannabis products (e.g., beverages, food, oil, ointments, tinctures) (retail level)
Maine	$335 per pound of marijuana flower or mature marijuana plants, $94 per pound of marijuana trim, $1.50 per immature marijuana plant or seedling, and $0.30 per marijuana seed sold to other licensees in the state (producer level)		10% of sales (retail level)
Massachusetts			10.75% of sales (retail level)
Michigan			10% of sales (retail level)
Nevada			15% of sales (producer-level); 10% of sales (retail level)
Oregon			17% of sales (retail level)
Washington State			37% of sales (retail level)

Source: Based on Government of Canada[45] and National Institute on Alcohol Abuse and Alcoholism.[46]

*Colorado and Canada have a portion of their tax structure based on tax by weight, but the jurisdictions also specify options where the product can be taxed by price.

Table 8-2. Taxation Options in Relation to Public Health Goals

	Control the prevalence, frequency, and intensity of cannabis use	Prevent youth cannabis use	Reduce cannabis-related harms
By weight	**	**	**
By potency	***	***	***
By price	**	**	*

Taxing by Weight

While an excise tax based on weight (a specific tax; e.g., $5 per pound) is relatively easy to administer, it diminishes options for using prices to affect the intensity of cannabis use. As RAND researchers noted, "Taxing based on weight creates an incentive to pack the most intoxicating material into each gram, which could be dangerous."[41] Jurisdictions could tie weight-based tax options to product restrictions, ensuring that products with high THC levels are not available in the market and thereby making weight-based taxes easier to administer and harder to avoid. However, the Institute on Taxation and Economic Policy (ITEP), a nonpartisan, nonprofit research organization, recommends taxing by weight and indexing these taxes to grow alongside the rate of inflation each year.[42]

Taxing by Price

Taxation by price (ad valorem taxation) is also relatively easy to implement. Ad valorem taxes can be applied at the producer, wholesaler, and/or retailer level. The primary concern with these taxes is that when the pretax price goes down, so does the tax, leading to an overall price decrease for consumers and a concomitant likely increase in consumption. These taxes may also encourage downtrading, in which consumers purchase products that are cheaper or of lower quality. Another concern highlighted by ITEP is that determining the true price of cannabis can be difficult in states that have allowed vertical integration between producers and retailers.[42] Some researchers have suggested that ad valorem taxes might work best in conjunction with minimum pricing rules.[32] Regulations also need to be in place to prevent the industry from gaming the system by bundling cannabis with other products (e.g., cover charges that include product as a part of the charge, selling other products and pricing cannabis low as a "loss leader").[41]

Taxing by Potency

It appears to me that dabbing solid concentrates generally delivers massive amounts of THC, causing unusually severe intoxication. If a potency tax aims to prevent people from consuming a lot of THC, perhaps it ought to disproportionately affect dabs. Moreover, dab

users tend to be young, lower-income, and report heavy cannabis use, and dabs are generally the cheapest product per unit THC, as they lend towards large-scale extraction and manufacture. Therefore, a tax that raises dab prices would also help to raise the minimum price per THC and discourage heavy use among bargain-seeking users.

–Steven Davenport, PhD, Aperture Research, phone interview, November 5, 2019

Taxing by potency (a specific tax) may be implemented using either an excise or an ad valorem approach. For the purposes of taxation, potency generally means THC content (number of milligrams of THC) or concentration (THC as a percentage of dry weight). Taxing by potency could significantly help achieve the public health goal of preventing cannabis-related harms, as higher prices for more potent products could help encourage consumers to select less potent ones. As a leading substance use economist noted for tobacco products, "In the future, differential taxation for different tobacco products may make sense from a harm-reduction perspective. . . . [A] differential tax structure that taxes the significantly reduced-risk products at lower rates than the riskier products would likely lead many who currently use the most dangerous products to switch to the new, significantly reduced-risk ones."[11] Many states tax alcoholic beverages in tiers roughly based on the percentage of alcohol by volume, thus imposing the equivalent of a potency tax.

Cannabis could be taxed by potency in four ways:

1. **By milligram of THC:** Canada, for example, taxes concentrates, edibles, extracts, and topical products at $0.0025 per milligram of total THC, with an additional cannabis duty of $0.0075 per milligram of total THC applicable in some provinces.[45] A taxation system based on amount of THC will require sophisticated laboratory and testing systems.

2. **By product category:** In states that have tried this approach, taxes are generally collected at the wholesale level. Liquid concentrates tend to be among the most potent cannabis products available; they also are the easiest category to test for THC content.[47] An advantage of this approach is that taxes can be used to make the most potent products more expensive, thereby discouraging their purchase and consumption. However, harms from cannabis use may emanate from factors other than the level of THC in the product (e.g., smoking cannabis, while usually providing a lower THC concentration than vaping or dabbing, introduces other physical harms to the lungs). Another drawback to this approach is that cannabis products are in fairly constant evolution. This tax structure may encourage another form of gaming the system, in this case creating products that resist categorization or deceptively fall into the wrong categories.

3. **By potency range:** This is an appealing option. While there is not sufficient research to determine at what THC concentrations higher tax rates should be applied,

taxing by range instead of by actual THC per milligram could help alleviate, but not eliminate, some testing and laboratory challenges while still discouraging use of higher-potency products. Producers could try to circumvent this approach, however, with products that measure just below the cutoff point for a higher tax. A similar option is to set lower tax rates for products with a lower THC-to-CBD ratio, as CBD is believed to offset some of the intoxicating properties of THC, although results of research in this area are mixed.[48] (Researchers analyzed price data in Oregon and Washington State and found that cannabis products high in THC were less expensive than products high in CBD.[38]) There could be continuous or discontinuous ranges for taxes—that is, taxes that either increase in a linear fashion for each percentage increase in THC or rise from rate to rate based on cutoff points.

4. **Using a hybrid model:** This approach combines aspects of the other three methods. Hybrid potency taxes (used in Canada and Illinois) allow for flexibility in directing tax rates to achieve policy goals. For example, if certain products are attractive to youth or frequent users, they can be taxed at a higher rate while all other products can be taxed at a rate per milligram. Hybrid programs may be more difficult to implement and enforce; adequate resources must be in place to ensure compliance with the tax structures. Hybrid models could also be employed as new products emerge and differential taxation rates potentially are needed. This has proven to be the case in numerous states with the emergence of new tobacco products, such as e-cigarettes.[49] As more information becomes available on the relative harms of different products, higher taxes can be applied to specific products to reduce consumption.

There will be challenges with any potency-based taxation system. Overall, compliance with a potency-based taxation system will rely heavily on a well-designed and well-regulated testing system, as well as the ability to use a seed-to-sale tracking system for audits.[41]

Box 8-1. Potential Federal Tax and Pricing Policies

Should cannabis become legal at the federal level, federal taxation and pricing policies could have large effects in standardizing cannabis prices and leveling the playing field among states through reductions in interstate smuggling and cross-border purchases. However, legalization under federal law would also likely lead to the emergence of large cannabis corporations promoting national or even international brands, which could lead to lower prices as producers reap gains from economies of scale.[32]

(Continued)

Box 8-1. (Continued)

A federal tax on cannabis could be one way to keep prices high. In addition, as researchers have suggested for tobacco, a well-designed mandatory federal minimum price would establish a strict floor price, keeping industry from setting prices that encourage excessive and youth consumption. Complementary measures would include prohibiting coupons, promotions, or discounts that reduce prices below the floor price; adjusting the minimum price consistently; and tying the tax rate to inflation. When researchers modeled the effects of these policies at the federal level for tobacco, they found that setting a federal minimum price requirement (modeled at $5, $7, and $10 a pack) could result in approximately 1.0 million, 4.7 million, and 10.7 million fewer smokers, respectively.[50]

Section 280E of federal tax law currently denies to cannabis producers many routine deductions that other businesses can claim, such as rent, wages, and advertising, as a result of the illegality of cannabis at the federal level.[42] Should cannabis become legal, federal policymakers should consider continuing to ban the deductibility of at least advertising and marketing expenses (see Chapter 6). If these deductions are permitted, cannabis taxes should be sufficiently high to make up for the loss of previous net revenue from Section 280E.

Other Policy Options for Influencing Cannabis Prices

Local Taxes

Some states, including Alaska, California, Colorado, Massachusetts, Nevada, and Washington, allow local jurisdictions to levy cannabis sales taxes.[42] Massachusetts and Oregon, for example, allow local governments to levy cannabis-specific sales (ad valorem) taxes of up to 3%.

Besides these product-specific taxes, some localities have established taxes on the square footage of grow spaces. Rates can vary for indoor and outdoor grows depending on the priorities of the local jurisdiction. As noted in a RAND report produced for Vermont, a square-footage tax correlates poorly with potency, so it should not be a stand-alone tax measure.[41] Similarly, some jurisdictions (e.g., Arcata, California) have established electricity tax rates that increase when a customer exceeds a certain percentage of a baseline designed to reflect normal use.[41] This tax was designed to curb excessive electricity use and may indirectly pressure more indoor growers to move to outdoor locations.

Minimum Unit Pricing

As mentioned in the review of the literature from other fields, setting a minimum unit price helps establish a floor below which prices cannot fall. The minimum price should be tied to inflation to ensure that the effectiveness of the policy does not diminish over time.

Price Discounts

Other pricing discounts, such as coupons, price promotions, and bulk purchases at discount, may be prohibited. If the cannabis industry models itself on tobacco and alcohol, these discounting practices may become widespread if not explicitly limited.

TAX ADMINISTRATION

Jurisdictions need to decide which agency will collect taxes and from whom. Taxes can be collected at the producer/cultivator, processor, wholesaler, and/or retailer level, and the type of tax applied may determine the level at which they are collected. For example, sales taxes are usually applied at the retail level while excise taxes are often applied at the wholesale level.

Different benefits and challenges of tax collection apply at each level of the supply system. Taxes at the cultivation level may prevent less loss of untaxed product than at later points in the system. "Leakage" further down the supply chain—theft from farms or factories, truck hijackings, shoplifting, informal (untaxed) sales to friends, gifts, and theft from retail establishments—will weaken the effect of any taxes collected at retail.[51] Taxes applied at levels of the supply chain where there are fewer companies (e.g., wholesalers versus retailers) may make it easier to collect taxes from this smaller number of businesses, putting less burden on government and facilitating audits.[41] Another benefit of applying taxes earlier in the supply chain is that those costs are often passed on, with additional markups that increase the ultimate price of products. This approach falls in line with the public health goals of preventing youth cannabis use and reducing overall cannabis use.

Tax avoidance and tax evasion are two issues that can be indirectly related to tax administration systems. Tax avoidance is legal and usually involves a change in economic or other activity to reduce tax payments. For example, a tax system may inadvertently provide incentives for manufacturers to alter their pricing or product design to avoid higher taxes. Consumers can also employ tax avoidance, most commonly by crossing borders to buy products in jurisdictions with lower taxes. There are numerous examples of gaps in tobacco and alcohol taxation systems, both in the United States and internationally, that have left open possibilities for use of tax avoidance strategies.[43,44]

Tax evasion, in contrast, involves illegal activities to avoid tax payments. Similar to tobacco products, cannabis products are relatively lightweight (compared with alcohol) and therefore easier to smuggle than alcohol.[43] As the number of states that legalize cannabis for nonmedical use increases, this will likely become more of a concern, with cross-border smuggling of product and/or illegal production of products occurring without tax payments. The fields of alcohol and tobacco enforcement often have specialized agents trained to investigate tax evasion.

The seed-to-sale tracing systems that states have set up to monitor cannabis from cultivation through retail sales are designed, in part, to help prevent tax evasion and to facilitate investigations and audits when tax evasion (or other issues) are suspected. These systems (described in Chapter 9) have faced a variety of challenges in implementation and data sharing but offer a promising approach to tracking cannabis through the supply chain.

TAXATION AND THE ILLEGAL MARKET

Proponents of low taxes often make the argument that the cannabis industry needs lower prices, and thus lower taxes, to combat the illegal market. Experience from the alcohol and tobacco fields suggests that gradual implementation of higher taxes will over time squeeze out the illegal market if accompanied by enforcement actions that are sufficiently costly to the illegal marketeers that they raise the cost of doing business above a viable level. Historically across the nation, however, efforts to eliminate the illegal market through enforcement have had little success.

In addition, many factors beyond price go into a consumer's decision about whether to purchase from a legal supply or the illegal market, including product safety, reliable product information, avoidance of illegal markets, and range of available products. One survey of cannabis users found that they consider legal cannabis superior to illegal cannabis and are willing to pay higher prices for what they view as a safer product as a result of regulatory oversight. Survey respondents—adult cannabis users recruited using online crowdsourcing—considered $10 per gram of legal cannabis to be roughly equivalent to $7 per gram of illegal cannabis. They also said that they would pay up to $14 per gram for a legal product before turning to the illicit market.[52] As discussed in Chapter 4, early estimates from Colorado, Oregon, and Washington State indicate that 40% to 80% of the consumer market in these states is in the legal market.[53-55] Results from Canada's National Cannabis Survey also indicate that as of the third quarter of 2019, 28% of cannabis users reported obtaining all the cannabis they consumed from the legal market and 53% of cannabis users were getting at least some of their cannabis from the legal market.[56]

HOW HIGH TO TAX?

At least two principles may apply to setting the appropriate level of tax from a public health perspective. The first aims to reduce cannabis demand by setting the tax rate and thus the price of cannabis high enough that it is expensive relative to comparable consumer goods (e.g., alcohol or tobacco). The second seeks a tax rate high enough to cover the costs of cannabis to society—including costs for regulation, monitoring, surveillance, and enforcement, as well as losses in productivity, costs of injury and physical illness, property damage and criminal justice costs from cannabis-impaired driving, and mental and behavioral health costs.

The need to tax cannabis sufficiently to keep up with costs over time tilts the scale in favor of ad valorem taxes, whose real value and revenues will tend to rise with inflation. Alcohol taxes offer an object lesson in that they have not kept up with inflation and have lagged far behind the alcohol-related costs that states incur. Alcohol costs society nearly $250 billion each year in the United States. This works out to approximately $2.05 per drink, of which $0.80 is paid directly by government. In contrast, state and federal alcohol-specific taxes total approximately 20 cents per drink.[57] Without careful tax planning, a similar shortfall will occur for nonmedical cannabis. This can be relatively easy to address with the inclusion of an automatic adjustment for inflation; some countries do this for tobacco taxes,[43] and Minnesota tied an annual inflation adjustment to its cigarette tax from 2013 until 2017.[58]

While some have criticized Washington State's 37% cannabis tax rate, economists have found that the high taxes did not result in either lower revenue or a substantial black market. In fact, the average markup by retailers in the state ranged from 33% to 67%,[59] substantially higher than typical margins in retail settings, indicating that even with the tax rate factored in, retailers can make a considerable profit.

Tobacco provides a model for how high cannabis taxes could become over time. Excise and other taxes applied to cigarettes account for 75% or more of the retail price of cigarettes in 38 countries, with a total population of one billion protected by these taxes.[60]

REVENUE ALLOCATION

While cannabis taxes may someday account for as much of the retail price of the product as tobacco taxes, at the outset cannabis tax revenues should at a minimum be sufficient to cover the costs of funding a robust cannabis control agency. Such an agency should have enforcement powers to ensure cannabis industry compliance with all relevant laws and the capacity to monitor and evaluate the public health and safety impact of legalization. Beyond minimal oversight of the industry, a Best Practices for Comprehensive Tobacco Control Programs guide developed by the Centers for Disease Control and Prevention (CDC) suggests an integrated programmatic structure for implementing interventions that consists of five key areas:

1. State and community interventions
2. Mass-reach health communications interventions
3. Cessation interventions
4. Surveillance and evaluation
5. Infrastructure administration and management

The report by CDC also provides a recommended level of state investment to successfully implement each of these areas.[61] This approach could serve as a model for the development and funding of essential cannabis control programs and builds upon the American Public Health Association's recommendation (see Box 8-2) that the majority of cannabis tax revenue be used to fund cannabis and other substance use prevention, education, treatment, research, and regulatory efforts.[62]

Box 8-2. American Public Health Association Recommendations

> The American Public Health Association recommends that the majority of cannabis tax revenue be used to fund cannabis and other substance use prevention, education, treatment, research, and regulatory efforts.[62]

In August 2019, the Pew Charitable Trusts released a report on state revenues emanating from cannabis taxes that included a table detailing the allocation formulae mandated by each of the legalizing states[63]; that table is reprinted as Appendix 3. The report cautions that forecasting revenue has been difficult, with projections generally too high because of underestimation of the time it takes to establish an orderly marketplace and an effective tax collection regime. A report that analyzed 2018 revenue per capita from the six states with available data at that time found that it ranged from $5.30 in California to $49 in Washington.[59]

Best practice from tobacco and alcohol points to the importance of statutorily designating a portion of cannabis tax revenues to support cannabis prevention and recovery programs and counter-marketing activities (see Chapter 6), as well as ongoing data collection and cannabis-related research and evaluation. Funds can also be earmarked to assist communities disproportionately affected by the War on Drugs, but these funds should not be tied to establishing more cannabis-related businesses (see Chapter 5).

POLICY RECOMMENDATIONS

- Cannabis tax regimes need to be flexible to respond to and influence patterns of initiation and consumption.
- Cannabis taxes should be set high enough to increase prices post-legalization, more than countering the drop in price likely to occur in the wake of legalization.
- Specific taxes should be set based on potency to discourage excessive consumption. Potency ranges may be set and adjusted as laboratory and testing technologies and research on the effects of potency evolve.
- Specific taxes on cannabis should adjust automatically to account for inflation.
- Minimum pricing, minimum markup, and tax floor policies should be implemented.
- Price promotions, bulk purchases, coupons, and bundling of products with services should be prohibited.
- The tax administration structure should be efficient and facilitate ease of tax collection, possibly by collecting taxes at the producer, cultivator, or wholesale level instead of at the retail level.
- Cannabis taxes should generate sufficient revenue to provide adequate funding for a robust cannabis control agency with the capacity to evaluate the health and safety impact of legalization of nonmedical cannabis.

- A portion of cannabis tax revenues should also statutorily be placed in a fund to support state and local as well as mass-reach interventions, substance use prevention, cessation and treatment, counter-marketing, surveillance, and evaluation.
- As discussed in Chapter 5, if taxes are sufficiently high, revenues from them may be used to mitigate community-level damage from the War on Drugs, provided this is not tied to increasing cannabis businesses in those communities.

As the preceding list makes clear, supporting robust enforcement, monitoring, and surveillance is a key function of cannabis taxation. The final substantive chapter of this book provides greater detail on why such a function is needed and what it should look like based on research and experience to date.

REFERENCES

1. McCullough J. In economic crisis, Texas Democrats push to legalize marijuana. Key Republicans likely stand in the way. *Texas Tribune.* November 12, 2020. Available at: https://www.texastribune.org/2020/11/12/texas-marijuana-legalization-legislation. Accessed March 30, 2021.

2. Stearns JM, Borna S. The ethics of lottery advertising: issues and evidence. *J Business Ethics.* 1995;14(1):43–51.

3. Zavattaro SM, Fay DL. Social media in state lotteries: exploring the role of technology in program marketing. *Int J Org Theory Behav.* 2017;20(1):100–122.

4. Mäkelä K, Viikari M. Notes on alcohol and the state. *Acta Sociologica.* 1977;20:155–178.

5. Wagenaar AC, Salois MJ, Komro KA. Effects of beverage alcohol price and tax levels on drinking: a meta-analysis of 1003 estimates from 112 studies. *Addiction.* 2009;104(2):179–190.

6. Elder RW, Lawrence B, Ferguson A, et al. The effectiveness of tax policy interventions for reducing excessive alcohol consumption and related harms. *Am J Prev Med.* 2010;38(2):217–229.

7. Sharma A, Sinha K, Vandenberg B. Pricing as a means of controlling alcohol consumption. *Br Med Bull.* 2017;123(1):149–158.

8. US Department of Health and Human Services. 2000 surgeon general's report: reducing tobacco use. 2000. Available at: https://www.cdc.gov/tobacco/data_statistics/sgr/2000/complete_report/index.htm. Accessed April 5, 2021.

9. US Department of Health and Human Services. *Preventing Tobacco Use Among Youth and Young Adults: A Report of the Surgeon General.* Atlanta, GA: US Dept of Health and Human Services, Centers for Disease Control and Prevention, National Center for Chronic Disease Prevention and Health Promotion, Office on Smoking and Health; 2012.

10. Sharbaugh MS, Althouse AD, Thoma FW, Lee JS, Figueredo VM, Mulukutla SR. Impact of cigarette taxes on smoking prevalence from 2001–2015: a report using the Behavioral and Risk Factor Surveillance Survey (BRFSS). *PLoS One.* 2018;13(9):e0204416.

11. Chaloupka FJ, Yurekli A, Fong GT. Tobacco taxes as a tobacco control strategy. *Tob Control.* 2012;21(2):172–180.

12. US National Cancer Institute and World Health Organization. *The Economics of Tobacco and Tobacco Control.* Bethesda, MD and Geneva, Swizerland: US Dept of Health and Human Services, National Institutes of Health, National Cancer Insitute, and World Health Organization; 2016.

13. Community Preventive Services Task Force. Tobacco use: interventions to increase the unit price for tobacco. November 2012.

14. Wagenaar AC, Tobler AL, Komro KA. Effects of alcohol tax and price policies on morbidity and mortality: a systematic review. *Am J Public Health.* 2010;100(11):2270–2278.

15. Center for Public Health Systems Science. *Pricing Policy: A Tobacco Control Guide.* St. Louis, MO: Center for Public Health Systems, Science, George Warren Brown School of Social Work at Washington University in St. Louis and the Tobacco Control Legal Consortium; 2014.

16. Golden SD, Smith MH, Feighery EC, Roeseler A, Rogers T, Ribisl KM. Beyond excise taxes: a systematic review of literature on non-tax policy approaches to raising tobacco product prices. *Tob Control.* 2016;25(4):377–385.

17. Xu X, Pesko MF, Tynan MA, Gerzoff RB, Malarcher AM, Pechacek TF. Cigarette price-minimization strategies by US smokers. *Am J Prev Med.* 2013;44(5):472–476.

18. Choi K, Hennrikus D, Forster J, St Claire AW. Use of price-minimizing strategies by smokers and their effects on subsequent smoking behaviors. *Nicotine Tob Res.* 2012;14(7): 864–870.

19. DeLong H, Chriqui J, Leider J, Chaloupka F. *Tobacco Product Pricing Laws: A State-by-State Analysis, 2015.* Chicago: Tobacconomics Program, Institute for Health Research and Policy, School of Public Health, University of Illinois at Chicago; 2016.

20. Tynan MA, Ribisl KM, Loomis BR. Impact of cigarette minimum price laws on the retail price of cigarettes in the USA. *Tob Control.* 2013;22(e1):e78–e85.

21. Huang J, Chriqui JF, DeLong H, Mirza M, Diaz MC, Chaloupka FJ. Do state minimum markup/price laws work? evidence from retail scanner data and TUS-CPS. *Tob Control.* 2016;25(suppl 1):i52–i59.

22. O'Donnell A, Anderson P, Jane-Llopis E, Manthey J, Kaner E, Rehm J. Immediate impact of minimum unit pricing on alcohol purchases in Scotland: controlled interrupted time series analysis for 2015-18. *BMJ.* 2019;366:l5274.

23. Stockwell T, Zhao J, Giesbrecht N, Macdonald S, Thomas G, Wettlaufer A. The raising of minimum alcohol prices in Saskatchewan, Canada: impacts on consumption and implications for public health. *Am J Public Health.* 2012;102(12):e103–e110.

24. Stockwell T, Auld MC, Zhao J, Martin G. Does minimum pricing reduce alcohol consumption? the experience of a Canadian province. *Addiction.* 2012;107(5):912–920.

25. Davis AJ, Geisler KR, Nichols MW. The price elasticity of marijuana demand: evidence from crowd-sourced transaction data. *Empirical Econ.* 2016;50(4):1171–1192.

26. Pacula RL, Lundberg R. Why changes in price matter when thinking about marijuana policy: a review of the literature on the elasticity of demand. *Public Health Rev.* 2014;35(2): 1–18.

27. Williams J, Liccardo Pacula R, Chaloupka FJ, Wechsler H. Alcohol and marijuana use among college students: economic complements or substitutes? *Health Econ.* 2004;13(9): 825–843.

28. Gallet CA. Can price get the monkey off our back? a meta-analysis of illicit drug demand. *Health Econ.* 2014;23(1):55–68.

29. Pacula RL, Grossman M, Chaloupka F, O'Malley P, Johnston LD, Farrelly MC. Marijuana and youth. In: Gruber J, ed. *Risky Behavior Among Youths: An Economic Analysis.* Chicago, IL University of Chicago Press; 2001:271–326.

30. van Ours JC, Williams J. Cannabis prices and dynamics of cannabis use. *J Health Econ.* 2007;26(3):578–596.

31. Ben Lakhdar C, Vaillant NG, Wolff FC. Price elasticity of demand for cannabis: does potency matter? *Addict Res Theory.* 2016;24(4):300–312.

32. Caulkins JP, Kilmer B, Kleinman MAR. *Marijuana Legalization: What Everyone Needs to Know.* 2nd ed. New York: Oxford University Press; 2016.

33. Davenport SS, Caulkins JP. Evolution of the United States marijuana market in the decade of liberalization before full legalization. *J Drug Issues.* 2016;46(4):411–427.

34. Hunt P, Pacula RL. Early impacts of marijuana legalization: an evaluation of prices in Colorado and Washington. *J Prim Prev.* 2017;38(3):221–248.

35. Caulkins JP, Bao Y, Davenport S, et al. Big data on a big new market: insights from Washington State's legal cannabis market. *Intl J Drug Policy.* 2018;57:86–94.

36. Humphreys K. Marijuana is getting cheaper. For some states, that's a problem. *Washington Post.* November 16, 2018.

37. Smart R, Caulkins JP, Kilmer B, Davenport S, Midgette G. Variation in cannabis potency and prices in a newly legal market: evidence from 30 million cannabis sales in Washington State. *Addiction.* 2017;112(12):2167–2177.

38. Firth CL, Davenport S, Smart R, Dilley JA. How high: differences in the developments of cannabis markets in two legalized states. *Int J Drug Policy.* 2019;75:102611.

39. Davenport S. Price and product variation in Washington's recreational cannabis market. *Int J Drug Policy.* 2019.

40. Rolles S, Murkin G. *How to Regulate Cannabis: A Practical Guide.* 2nd ed. Bristol, UK: Transform Drug Policy Foundation; 2016.

41. Caulkins JP, Kilmer B, Kleiman MAR, et al. *Considering Marijuana Legalization: Insights for Vermont and Other Jurisdictions.* Santa Monica, CA: RAND Corporation; 2015.

42. Davis C, Hill ME, Phillips R. Taxing cannabis. Institute on Taxation and Economic Policy; January 2019.

43. World Health Organization. *WHO Technical Manual on Tobacco Tax Administration.* 2011. Geneva, Switzerland: World Health Organization; 2011. Available at: https://www.who.int/tobacco/publications/tax_administration/en/. Accessed March 30, 2021.

44. Sornpaisarn B, Shield KD, Österberg E, Rehm J, eds. *Resource Tool on Alcohol Taxation and Pricing Policies.* Geneva, Switzerland: World Health Organization; 2017.

45. Government of Canada. Cannabis duty—Calculate the excise duty on cannabis. 2019; https://www.canada.ca/en/revenue-agency/services/tax/businesses/topics/excise-duties-levies/collecting-cannabis.html. Accessed March 30, 2021.

46. National Institute on Alcohol Abuse and Alcoholism. Alcohol Policy Information System (APIS). Recreational use of cannabis. Vol 1. 2019. Available at: https://alcoholpolicy.niaaa.nih.gov/cannabis-policy-topics/recreational-use-of-cannabis-volume-1/104. Accessed March 30, 2021.

47. Prieger J, Hampsher SC, Oglesby P, Davenport S, Manning C, Hahn R. Cannabis potency tax feasibility study: a report for the Washington State Liquor and Control Board. BOTEC Analysis; January 2019.

48. Spindle TR, Bonn-Miller MO, Vandrey R. Changing landscape of cannabis: novel products, formulations, and methods of administration. *Curr Opin Psychol.* 2019;30:98–102.

49. Chaloupka F, Tauras JA. *Taxation of Emerging Tobacco Products.* Chicago: Institute for Health Research and Policy, University of Illinois at Chicago; February, 2020.

50. Doogan NJ, Wewers ME, Berman M. The impact of a federal cigarette minimum pack price policy on cigarette use in the USA. *Tob Control.* 2018;27(2):203–208.

51. Oglesby P. Supplemental thoughts about revenue from marijuana in Vermont. Rand Corporation. January 16, 2015.

52. Amlung M, Reed DD, Morris V, Aston ER, Metrik J, MacKillop J. Price elasticity of illegal versus legal cannabis: a behavioral economic substitutability analysis. *Addiction.* 2019;114(1):112–118.

53. Kilmer B, Davenport S, Smart R, Caulkins J, Midgette G. After the grand opening: assessing cannabis supply and demand in Washington State. RAND Corporation. 2019. Available at: https://www.rand.org/pubs/research_reports/RR3138.html. Accessed April 1, 2021.

54. Oregon Liquor Control Commission. Recreational marijuana supply and demand. January 31, 2019.

55. McCoy J. As Colorado's medical market finds a plateau, adult-use climbs 2x higher. *Cannabyte* blog. August 11, 2019. Available at: https://newfrontierdata.com/cannabis-insights/blog-as-colorados-medical-market-finds-a-plateau-adult-use-climbs-2x-higher. Accessed March 30, 2021.

56. Statistics Canada. National Cannabis Survey, third quarter 2019. October 30, 2019. Available at: https://www150.statcan.gc.ca/n1/daily-quotidien/191030/dq191030a-eng.htm. Accessed March 30, 2021.

57. Blanchette JG, Chaloupka FJ, Naimi TS. The composition and magnitude of alcohol taxes in states: do they cover alcohol-related costs? *J Stud Alcohol Drugs*. 2019;80(4):408–414.

58. Van Wychen J. Minnesota's shrinking cigarette tax. North Star Policy Institute. August 8, 2017. Available at: https://northstarpolicy.org/minnesotas-shrinking-cigarette-tax. Accessed March 30, 2021.

59. Hollenbeck B, Uetake K. Taxation and market power in the legal marijuana industry. September 23, 2018. Updated March 11, 2021. *RAND J Econ*. Forthcoming 2021. Available at: SSRN: https://ssrn.com/abstract=3237729. Accessed April 1, 2021.

60. World Health Organization. WHO report on the global tobacco epidemic 2019. July 25, 2019. Available at: https://www.who.int/teams/health-promotion/tobacco-control/who-report-on-the-global-tobacco-epidemic-2019. Accessed April 5, 2021.

61. Centers for Disease Control and Prevention. *Best Practices for Comprehensive Tobacco Control Programs—2014*. Atlanta, GA: US Dept of Health and Human Services, Centers for Disease Control and Prevention, National Center for Chronic Disease Prevention and Health Promotion, Office on Smoking and Health; 2014.

62. American Public Health Association. A public health approach to regulating commercially legalized cannabis. October 24, 2020. Policy 20206. Available at: https://www.apha.org/Policies-and-Advocacy/Public-Health-Policy-Statements/Policy-Database/2021/01/13/A-Public-Health-Approach-to-Regulating-Commercially-Legalized-Cannabis. Accessed April 5, 2021.

63. The Pew Charitable Trusts. Forecasts hazy for state marijuana revenue. 2019. Available at: https://www.pewtrusts.org/-/media/assets/2019/08/marijuana-brief_v2.pdf. Accessed August 11, 2021.

9

Enforcement, Monitoring, and Surveillance

SUMMARY AND INTRODUCTION

- Emerging cannabis regulatory regimes require both data collection and effective enforcement systems if they are to be amenable to evaluation over time.
- Existing national surveys of adult and youth drug use should add questions about mode, frequency, and quantity of cannabis consumption.
- Scientifically valid evaluation of the impact of legalization of cannabis for non-medical use requires a detailed national database that tracks policies and changes over time.
- States have required seed-to-sale tracking systems for cannabis production and sales. The information in these systems is not consistent across states, and researchers often are unable to access the information needed for monitoring and surveillance.
- Without evidence-based levels of cannabis impairment and accurate and reliable testing to determine them, cannabis-impaired driving laws will be difficult to enforce.

Regulatory systems are only as good as their implementation, and enforcement and evaluation are critical elements of implementation. As discussed in the previous chapter, if done right, cannabis taxation has the potential to provide sufficient resources for proper oversight, cannabis prevention and recovery programs, counter-marketing activities, ongoing data collection, and cannabis-related research and evaluation, as well as community reinvestment funds. To the degree that states are experimentally creating structures in an entirely new arena for state action, evaluation will be a critical element in promoting learning and course corrections along the way. Evaluation in turn requires effective monitoring and surveillance of patterns of use, outcomes, and how effectively regulations are being enforced.

This chapter begins by reviewing from a public health perspective the monitoring and surveillance needs of an effective cannabis regulatory system. It then summarizes the enforcement recommendations laid out in previous chapters and closes with a focus on a key area that brings together needs for both measurement and enforcement: cannabis-impaired driving.

CURRENT DATA SYSTEMS FOR MONITORING AND SURVEILLANCE

Prevalence and Patterns of Use

Researchers primarily use four national data sets to monitor cannabis use over time: the National Survey on Drug Use and Health (NSDUH), the Youth Risk Behavior Surveillance System (YRBS), the Monitoring the Future (MTF) survey, and the Behavioral Risk Factor Surveillance System (BRFSS). These data sets use repeat cross-sectional designs[*1] (i.e., they use the same questions but survey different people every year), as well as methodologies and measurements that have been fairly consistent over time. The NSDUH data provide important insights into adult as well as youth cannabis use and changes over time. Every two years, NSDUH provides state-level estimates of select measures that combine two years of data.[2] NSDUH also included a cannabis market module with price information from 2001 through 2014, dropped it from 2015 to 2017, and included it again in 2018. However, the 2018 module does not include any information on purchases at commercial cannabis retail outlets in states that have legalized cannabis for nonmedical use.[3] YRBS provides information on youth cannabis use; participation by states, however, is voluntary, and the number of states participating varies from year to year. Some states omit some of the questions in some years. Nonparticipants include Oregon and Washington State, two locales that have legalized cannabis use. These states conduct their own youth surveys, using questions similar to those included in YRBS.[4]

The MTF survey has measured drug and alcohol use and related attitudes among adolescents nationwide since 1975. The BRFSS surveys adults age 18 and older; however, its sampling methodology changed in 2011, and its cannabis questions have also changed slightly over the years. In 2016, the BRFSS added an optional three-question "marijuana module" that states can elect to include; some of the questions have changed over the three years that the module has been offered. In 2018, 13 states, Guam, and Puerto Rico incorporated the module into the survey.[5] Finally, the National Epidemiologic Survey on Alcohol and Related Conditions (NESARC), the National Longitudinal Survey of Youth, and the National Comorbidity Survey also have gathered data that researchers have used to analyze cannabis use.[6,7]

Cannabis Policies

In addition to tracking cannabis use, it is important to understand cannabis law and policy variables. As researchers have documented, cannabis policies (both medical and nonmedical) vary greatly. States should not be classified solely as having medical cannabis, cannabis for nonmedical use, decriminalization policies, or all or none of the above,

---

*Monitoring the Future does conduct longitudinal follow-up with a representative subsample of each 12th grade class annually through age 30 and at five-year intervals through age 60.

because in practice each state has a unique variant of these categories.[7] The Alcohol Policy Information System (APIS), developed by the National Institute on Alcohol Abuse and Alcoholism to aid in research on state alcohol policies, has added cannabis policy topics. The legal researchers who staff it code more than 20 cannabis policy variables, tracking and recording changes in law over time.[8] As of February 2020, this information was current through January 2019. While helpful, more research is needed to develop current, detailed databases both on the variables covered by APIS and the ones it does not monitor.

The Cannabis Industry

States that have legalized cannabis for nonmedical use have required seed-to-sale tracking systems, to varying degrees, for cannabis production and sales. These can go hand in hand with licensing systems, which also are an essential data component for outcome evaluations of cannabis outlet information. However, these systems are not always integrated, and sometimes multiple systems are used by different agencies within a state or by local jurisdictions.[9] Researchers have been able to access these data in some states but not others, and in some states the data that are available are not overly useful for public health–focused analyses (Steven Davenport, PhD, Aperture Research, phone interview, November 5, 2019). The seed-to-sale and licensing systems also do not appear to be comparable across states, as multiple IT companies have won contracts to set up state monitoring systems. This lack of uniformity further hampers comparative evaluations of state-level cannabis policies.

MONITORING AND SURVEILLANCE NEEDS

Prevalence and Patterns of Use

As numerous researchers and policymakers have acknowledged, there are major gaps in the data available for research and evaluation as well as monitoring and surveillance for emerging cannabis trends or issues.[10,11] Two leading researchers summarized some of the areas needing better measures of consumption:[10]

- Total use days or, ideally, total grams (total mg of THC) consumed, in addition to standard prevalence questions currently in use.
- Time of use per session within a day, amount consumed per use, and types of cannabis products consumed.
- Categorical measures about perceived potency or, ideally, actual information about THC and other cannabinoids.
- Surveys that make distinctions between medical and nonmedical consumption.
- Surveys that ask about multiple substance use during the same occasion.

Cannabis Harms

Assessing the effectiveness of a cannabis regulatory system from a public health perspective requires data on the specific harms that may emanate from nonmedical use of cannabis. Population surveys such as those described above may provide some insight into problem cannabis use and cannabis use disorder (CUD); however, there will also be a need to develop more detailed population-level surveillance of CUD, using the criteria laid out in *DSM-5*. Similarly, there will be a need for longitudinal surveillance of cohorts of young people, monitoring the specific cannabis products they consume, as well as how they consume those products, and what the physical and mental health outcomes are over time. Young people's patterns of cannabis use are changing rapidly. Without current knowledge of these youth patterns, regulators and service providers will have difficulty mitigating harms and developing effective youth prevention and treatment programs.[12]

Additional data are also needed in the areas of substance use and mental health disorders, hospitalizations, injuries, and long-term health outcomes.[13] In particular, trends in incidence and prevalence of psychosis will be important indicators of how effective cannabis regulation is from a public health perspective.[14] Tracking vulnerability to homicide victimization when under the influence of nonmedical cannabis may require standardization of assessment and testing by law enforcement.

With regard to impaired driving, the National Highway Traffic Safety Administration (NHTSA) has made the following recommendations for data and records system improvements:[15]

1. States should develop records systems that distinguish among alcohol, drugs, or both in impaired driving cases, and these records should be integrated into computerized data systems.
2. State records systems should document which drugs are used by drug-impaired drivers.
3. Standard toxicological screening and confirmation procedures are needed and should confirm the presence of drugs that impair driving and include standard analytic procedures and minimum thresholds.

The Cannabis Industry

Cannabis production itself has the potential for negative environmental impacts, as discussed in Chapter 3. Research is needed on plant growth cycles, wastewater streams, and outdoor and indoor air quality across the growing process to inform regulatory action. States will also need to create standards for laboratory testing of cannabis products to monitor product safety and potency and to inform taxation systems if they are to be based on product strength.

A licensing, enforcement, and adjudication system that tracks detailed license information over time, as well as enforcement actions and administrative penalties, is essential to monitoring outlet density changes, youth access, and criminal and administrative violations that have public health and public safety impacts. These data should be publicly available and kept for historical purposes; researchers in the alcohol field have learned that this is often not the case and that changes over time are not easily documented.

One group of researchers has developed a "marijuana retail surveillance tool," which can be used to assess multiple variables within retail cannabis environments, such as security features, promotions, product availability, and price.[16,17] These kinds of tools that create standardized surveillance methods for researchers are also essential for understanding the larger cannabis policy environment within and across states.

It is becoming clear in the tobacco and alcohol fields that the strategies and tactics of the industries that produce and market potentially harmful substances require public health surveillance and analysis. There has been sufficient research on tobacco industry[18] and alcohol industry[19] responses to public health initiatives to merit systematic reviews. Researchers have begun to document how the legal cannabis industry is using similar strategies to justify its actions in opposition to public health-oriented measures and to weaken cannabis-relevant regulations.[20]

A technical report published in 2020 by the European Union lists the variables that should be tracked for effective evaluation of cannabis policies, under the subheadings of health, crime and criminal justice, economics, and other (e.g., public opinion, advertising, and promotion). The lists comprise a useful and comprehensive guide to monitoring and surveillance needs.[21]

ENFORCEMENT

I think having a dedicated unit dealing with nothing but cannabis is important. [Washington is forming] a cannabis unit that focuses on producers, processors, and retailers. It will be comprised of about 38 officers total including command staff.

–Justin Nordhorn, BA, Washington State Liquor and Cannabis Board,
in person interview, August 13, 2019

Previous chapters have provided the outlines of an effective enforcement system. Independent, robust enforcement agencies are needed to ensure effective and consistent enforcement and compliance within the regulatory system and to maintain a stable marketplace. In addition to strong policies, proactive and routine enforcement is essential to protect public health and safety.[22] Enhanced enforcement and checks of the compliance of retail outlets with laws limiting youth access to tobacco have clearly reduced cigarette sales to minors.[23] For alcohol, the Task Force on Community Preventive Services, based on its systematic review of the research literature, has recommended enhanced enforcement of laws prohibiting sale of alcohol to minors as an effective intervention.[24]

The theory of general deterrence posits that the effectiveness of deterrent strategies rests on three legs: certainty of apprehension, swiftness of sanctions, and severity of sanctions.[25] Businesses in industries with the potential to cause public health harms require consistent monitoring of compliance with regulations, combined with increasing administrative sanctions for successive violations including fines, suspensions, and license revocations when necessary. Lessons from the alcohol and tobacco control fields indicate that it is most effective to focus on the providers/suppliers of the products versus going after individuals (especially young people).[24,26-28] Enforcement issues are more complex, however, when it comes to cannabis-impaired driving.

DRIVING UNDER THE INFLUENCE OF CANNABIS

As described in Chapter 2, cannabis use impairs the ability to operate a motor vehicle, and driving under the influence of cannabis was reported by almost 5% of the population age 16 and above in 2018.[29] As is the case with alcohol, the likelihood of cannabis involvement increases with the severity of the crash: in Washington State, the proportion of cannabis-positive drivers involved in fatal crashes doubled after legalization, and as of 2017, 21% of drivers involved in fatal crashes in that state were THC-positive.[30] The risks associated with co-use of cannabis and alcohol seem to be greater than for either substance on its own.[31]

Despite substantial evidence to the contrary, cannabis organizations favoring legalization for nonmedical use continue to put forward the position that cannabis use "is seldom a causal factor in automobile accidents."[32] In contrast, the National Institute on Drug Abuse has stated, "Marijuana significantly impairs judgment, motor coordination, and reaction time, and studies have found a direct relationship between blood THC concentration and impaired driving ability."[33]

Setting and enforcing laws governing cannabis-impaired driving raises significant and difficult measurement and surveillance issues.

Determining Impairment

Unlike blood alcohol content (BAC) levels for alcohol, THC levels that definitively pinpoint impairment for cannabis have not been determined, although some experts suggest a range of 7 to 10 nanograms per milliliter (ng/mL) for an initial nonzero per se limit.[34] The difficulty in setting a threshold is in part because THC can be detected in blood and urine samples for hours or even months following cannabis use.[34-37] In addition, THC concentration is likely affected by whether a person is a periodic or frequent cannabis user.[36]

There are at least four distinct types of drug-impaired driving laws in the United States that specify what evidence is needed to establish a violation:

- **Effect-based** (32 states and the District of Columbia): The driver's cannabis consumption must be shown to have impaired the driver's ability to operate the motor vehicle safely. Effect-based laws are often difficult to enforce because of the lack of standardization in assessing drug-induced impairment.[38]
- **Per se** (6 states): The driver is assumed to be impaired if a "specified amount of the cannabis is found in the driver's body while operating a motor vehicle without the need of additional evidence." Per se blood levels in the six states that have these laws range from 1 ng/mL to 5 ng/mL.[39]
- **Zero tolerance** (12 states): The driver is assumed to be impaired if there is any amount of cannabis (or a minimum reliably detectable level) in the driver's body. Zero tolerance is thus a form of per se law, with the limit set at zero. Nine states have zero tolerance laws for THC or a metabolite,*[15] and three states have zero tolerance for THC but no restriction on metabolites.[39]
- **Reasonable inference** (1 state): There is a permissible inference that the driver is impaired if a specified amount of cannabis is found in the driver's blood. The driver can present additional evidence to show that he or she was not actually impaired (Colorado). Colorado sets the reasonable inference level at 5ng/mL or higher.

Oral fluid testing, which involves swabbing the inside of an individual's mouth, has been considered a promising approach for testing for cannabis. It is less invasive than taking blood or urine samples, easier to obtain on site, and lowers the biohazard risks during collection. Studies from the mid-2010s have begun to show promise in the sensitivities of some oral fluid testing devices, but there appear to be wide ranges between different devices, and detection times can be as long as 26 hours in occasional smokers and more than 72 hours in frequent ones.[40,41]

The problem remains that unlike with alcohol, THC concentration in a blood sample does not necessarily correlate with impairment. Peak impairment may not happen when the THC concentration in a blood sample is at or near peak levels, and impairment may still occur when the THC level is low (see Figure 9-1).[15]

In its Report to Congress, NHTSA notes that "peak impairment occurs at 90 minutes after smoking while the THC level has declined over 80 percent from the peak level at that point in time." The report concludes that THC levels in blood or oral fluids do not appear to be accurate and reliable predictors of impairment and that per se limits appear

---

*As noted in NHTSA's Report to Congress, "drug metabolites are detectable in urine for several days after the drug has been used (and sometimes for weeks). Urine test results cannot be used to prove that a driver was under the influence of the drug at the time of arrest or testing." Thus, while impaired-driving laws may mandate zero tolerance for metabolites, the presence of metabolites does not necessarily mean that the driver is impaired.

Time Course of Standardized THC Concentration in Plasma, performance Deficit and Subjective High after Smoking Marijuana

(Adapted from Berghaus et al. 1998, Sticht and Käferstein 1998 and Robbe 1994)

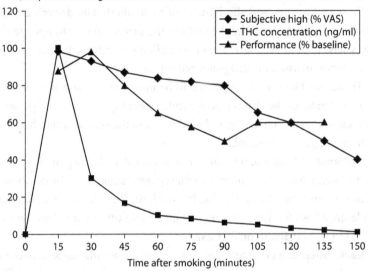

Figure 9-1. Time Course of Standardized THC Concentration in Plasma, Performance Deficit, and Subjective High After Smoking Marijuana

to have been based on something other than science. As such, in "rebuttable presumption" states such as Colorado, these laws may keep consequences from being certain by providing drivers with a basis for challenging the validity of per se levels when making a case to a judge or jury.[15]

Enforcement Strategies

Current training for law enforcement on impaired driving consists of three increasingly detailed levels:

- **Level 1:** NHTSA has developed an eight-hour course, Drugs That Impair Driving, which can be used in conjunction with Standardized Field Sobriety Test training. This program provides a general overview, but it likely would not enable an officer to determine impairment by drug category.
- **Level 2:** The 16-hour Advanced Roadside Impairment Driving Enforcement (ARIDE) course certifies officers to make arrests based on probable cause, founded in general knowledge of alcohol and drug impairment.[15]
- **Level 3:** The Drug Evaluation and Classification (DEC) program with drug recognition experts (DREs) requires nine days of classroom learning with additional days of

field certification testing. A DRE is a law enforcement officer trained in DEC and certified to conduct examinations, using a standardized 12-step procedure, of drug-impaired drivers.

There are approximately 8,000 certified DRE officers in the United States.[15] Officers trained in ARIDE would likely summon a DRE officer to conduct the DEC program if they suspected someone of driving under the influence of cannabis.[15]

DREs are the most reliable arbiters of impairment, but they are not infallible. A study of DREs in Canada found that their accuracy rate was 95%,[42] and an accompanying review of DEC evaluations (in the field and in labs) concluded that DREs are able to identify persons under the influence of drugs and identify which category of drugs with a high degree of accuracy, although a substantial proportion of drug-positive cases are missed or miscategorized. This underscores the importance of corroborating DREs with toxicology results.[43] Assessments by DREs are time-consuming, requiring between 45 and 60 minutes to complete.[44]

Some researchers have recommended that officers initially focus on a more limited set of key signs and symptoms to make assessments less cumbersome and more efficient.[43,44] Pupil size, rebound dilation, lack of convergence tests, bloodshot or watery eyes, eyelid tremors, impaired performance on the one-leg standing test, and elevated pulse are key variables in cannabis identification.[44,45] An algorithm weights the various components of the DEC program and assesses the probability of the case being representative of a certain class or classes of drugs. The model yielded sensitivity levels greater than 60% and specificity levels greater than 90% for impairments caused by cannabis.[46] Tools like these could be developed to support DRE officers in the field.

In 2010, Belgium instituted a new approach for evaluating potential drugged drivers, combining a 10- to 15-minute limited field sobriety test with oral fluid screening, followed by blood samples if necessary. Evaluations of the new approach indicated that the percentage of false positives decreased from 17% to 8% (as confirmed by the blood samples), and the data suggest that more recent drug use is being detected.[47]

Adding an initial oral fluid test during the field sobriety process could help indicate whether blood samples or additional DRE assessments are necessary. Oral fluid testing may indicate more recent use of cannabis, while nonpsychoactive cannabis metabolites remain detectable in blood or urine samples for days. Because THC can drop significantly within the first hour after smoking,[15,36,48] blood samples should be collected as early as possible to obtain the most accurate and reliable results, with the caveat that per se cutoff rates have shown limited relevance in establishing cannabis impairment.[45]

NHTSA has recommended as a best practice that states amend their statutes to provide separate and distinct offenses and sanctions for alcohol- and cannabis-impaired driving. This would enable officers to more readily pursue a separate cannabis-impaired driving charge even if there is a BAC of .08 g/dL or more.[15]

Many of the interventions recommended in previous chapters (taxation, limits on physical availability, minimum purchase age, etc.) have been shown to be effective in reducing alcohol-impaired driving,[49] and these are anticipated to reduce cannabis-impaired driving as well. Ideally, enforcement would be supported by environmental interventions such as these that reduce the likelihood of cannabis-impaired driving in the first place.

Social Justice Concerns

In enforcement of traffic safety laws, as across the panoply of law enforcement activities, there is evidence of discrimination against Black and Latinx drivers. The largest recent study analyzed data from nearly 100 million traffic stops across the country between 2011 and 2018. It concluded that police stops suffered from persistent racial bias. The authors also looked at pre-legalization and post-legalization stops of nonmedical cannabis for adult use in Colorado and Washington State and compared these to stops in 12 states where legalization had not occurred. Stops and searches for contraband declined for all drivers in Colorado and Washington State following legalization, but the relative gap between White drivers and Black and Latinx drivers persisted, suggesting the need for broader reforms to police practices to address persistent racial bias.[50]

POLICY RECOMMENDATIONS

Dr. Julie Johnson, director of research for the Massachusetts Cannabis Control Commission, stated, "As we have learned from the tobacco and alcohol industries and regulation, once science discerns differential effects of laws and specific provisions, evidence-based prevention mechanism(s) can be built into legalization policy and regulations."[13] Following are recommendations regarding monitoring and surveillance:

- Existing national surveys, in consultation with leading cannabis researchers, should add questions about mode, frequency, and quantity of cannabis consumption.
- The federal government should fund the creation of a detailed legal database tracking policies and changes over time, again in consultation with leading cannabis policy researchers.
- State licensing, enforcement, and adjudication data systems should be made easily accessible to researchers and the public at large. These systems should include race and ethnicity of persons involved in cannabis businesses as well as track outcomes from social equity initiatives. The federal government should fund a centralized database of this information from all states tracking information over time.
- States should require publicly available seed-to-sale tracking systems for cannabis production and sales, with data as consistent as possible across states.
- States should adopt NHTSA's suggested records systems changes and additions, including creating separate offenses for cannabis-impaired and alcohol-impaired driving.

- Research into effective means of determining and measuring the causal role of cannabis use in traffic crashes should be a high priority and should include an examination of alcohol and drug use across all crashes to identify co-use or substitution effects.
- A key focus of this research should be establishment of an impairment standard for driving under the influence of cannabis and development of a validated standardized field sobriety test to assess driving under the influence of cannabis.
- Until such a standard is developed and agreed on, states should increase funding for training law enforcement personnel to detect cannabis impairment and increase the use of technologies such as oral fluid screening when feasible and science-based.

With regard to enforcement of cannabis regulatory systems, in addition to the enforcement needs and priorities regarding cannabis availability listed in Chapter 7, states that legalize cannabis for nonmedical use should put in place the following enforcement systems and mechanisms:

- Sufficient funding, resources, and expertise for enforcement of cannabis laws.
- Policies and practices to ensure that enforcement operations and priorities are not influenced by revenue or cannabis industry pressures.
- Clear enforcement guidelines and protocols to ensure fair and consistent enforcement.
- A comprehensive records management system that allows researchers and the public to track enforcement actions (e.g., number of complaints, investigations, verbal or written warnings, citations) and administrative adjudication decisions that include warnings, fines, suspensions, and revocations. This system should also be able to track the length of time from enforcement actions to adjudication decisions.
- Inclusion in such a system of data by income, race, sex, and location to facilitate public monitoring of equity in enforcement practices.

Finally, in light of the significant natural experiments in cannabis policy currently being permitted at the state level by the federal government, the National Academies of Sciences, Engineering, and Medicine should regularly update their 2017 summary of the state of the research literature on cannabis benefits and harms and should couple this with a periodic review of lessons learned by the states in these ongoing policy experiments.

REFERENCES

1. Johnston LD, O'Malley PM, Schulenberg J, Bachman JG, Miech R, Patrick ME. *The Objectives and Theoretical Foundation of the Monitoring the Future Study.* Ann Arbor, MI: Institute for Social Research, University of Michigan; 2016.

2. Substance Abuse and Mental Health Services Administration. State data tables and reports from the 2017–2018 NSDUH. 2019. Available at: https://www.samhsa.gov/data/nsduh/state-reports-NSDUH-2018. Accessed March 30, 2021.

3. Substance Abuse and Mental Health Services Administration. *2018 National Survey on Drug Use and Health Public Use File Codebook*. Rockville, MD: Center for Behavioral Health Statistics and Quality; 2019.

4. Guttmannova K, Jones AA, Johnson JK, Oesterle S, Johnson RM, Martins SS. Using existing data to advance knowledge about adolescent and emerging adult marijuana use in the context of changes in marijuana policies. *Prev Sci.* 2019;20(2):291–299.

5. Centers for Disease Control and Prevention. CDC-BRFSS-2018 modules used by category. Updated August 28, 2019. Available at: https://www.cdc.gov/brfss/questionnaires/modules/category2018.htm. Accessed March 30, 2021.

6. Leung J, Chiu CYV, Stjepanović D, Hall W. Has the legalisation of medical and recreational cannabis use in the USA affected the prevalence of cannabis use and cannabis use disorders? *Curr Addict Rep.* 2018;5(4):403–417.

7. Pacula RL, Powell D, Heaton P, Sevigny EL. Assessing the effects of medical marijuana laws on marijuana use: the devil is in the details. *J Policy Anal Manage.* 2015;34(1):7–31.

8. National Institute on Alcohol Abuse and Alcoholism. Alcohol Policy Information System, Recreational Use of Cannabis, Volume 1. 2019. Available at: https://alcoholpolicy.niaaa.nih.gov/cannabis-policy-topics/recreational-use-of-cannabis-volume-1/104. Accessed July 14, 2019.

9. Miller B. Making it legal: the tech implications of regulating recreational marijuana. Government Technology. March 2017. Available at: https://www.govtech.com/policy/Making-It-Legal-Tech-Implications-of-Regulating-Recreational-Marijuana.html. Accessed March 30, 2021.

10. Kilmer B, Pacula RL. Understanding and learning from the diversification of cannabis supply laws. *Addiction.* 2017;112(7):1128–1135.

11. American Public Health Association. *A Public Health Approach to Regulating Commercially Legalized Cannabis.* American Public Health Association. October 24, 2020.

12. Knapp AA, Lee DC, Borodovsky JT, Auty SG, Gabrielli J, Budney AJ. Emerging trends in cannabis administration among adolescent cannabis users. *J Adolesc Health.* 2019;64(4):487–493.

13. Johnson JK, Doonan SM. Building evidence-based prevention mechanisms into cannabis legalization policy and regulations. *Am J Public Health.* 2019;109(9):1165–1166.

14. Murray RM, Hall W. Will legalization and commercialization of cannabis use increase the incidence and prevalence of psychosis? *JAMA Psychiatry.* 2020;77(8):777–778.

15. Compton R. *Marijuana-Impaired Driving—A Report to Congress.* Washington, DC: National Highway Traffic Safety Administration; 2017.

16. Berg CJ, Henriksen L, Cavazos-Rehg P, Schauer GL, Freisthler B. Point-of-sale marketing and context of marijuana retailers: assessing reliability and generalizability of the marijuana retail surveillance tool. *Prev Med Rep.* 2018;11:37–41.

17. Berg CJ, Henriksen L, Cavazos-Rehg P, Schauer GL, Freisthler B. The development and pilot testing of the marijuana retail surveillance tool (MRST): assessing marketing and point-of-sale practices among recreational marijuana retailers. *Health Educ Res.* 2017;32(6): 465–472.

18. Savell E, Gilmore AB, Fooks G. How does the tobacco industry attempt to inflluence marketing regulations? a systematic review. *PloS One.* 2014;9(2):e97389.

19. McCambridge J, Coleman R, McEachern J. Public health surveillance studies of alcohol industry market and political strategies: a systematic review. *J Stud Alcohol Drugs.* 2019;80(2):149–157.

20. Subritzky T, Lenton S, Pettigrew S. Legal cannabis industry adopting strategies of the tobacco industry. *Drug Alcohol Rev.* 2016;35(5):511–513.

21. European Monitoring Centre for Drugs and Drug Addiction. *Monitoring and Evaluating Changes in Cannabis Policies: Insights From the Americas.* Luxembourg: European Monitoring Centre for Drugs and Drug Addiction; 2020.

22. Wagenaar AC, Toomey TL, Erickson DJ. Preventing youth access to alcohol: outcomes from a multi-community time-series trial. *Addiction.* 2005;100(3):335–345.

23. Friend KB, Lipperman-Kreda S, Grube JW. The impact of local US tobacco policies on youth tobacco use: a critical review. *Open J Prev Med.* 2011;1(2):34–43.

24. Elder R, Lawrence B, Janes G, et al. Enhanced enforcement of laws prohibiting sale of alcohol to minors: systematic review of effectiveness for reducing sales and underage drinking. *Transportation Res.* 2007;(E-C123):181–188.

25. Stafford MC. Deterrence Theory: Crime. In: Wright JD, ed. *International Encyclopedia of the Social & Behavioral Sciences.* 2nd ed. Oxford: Elsevier; 2015:255–259.

26. Babor T, Caetano R, Casswell S, et al. *Alcohol: No Ordinary Commodity: Research and Public Policy.* 2nd ed. Oxford University Press; 2010.

27. Lantz PM, Jacobson PD, Warner KE, et al. Investing in youth tobacco control: a review of smoking prevention and control strategies. *Tob Control.* 2000;9(1):47–63.

28. Mosher JF. The merchants, not the customers: resisting the alcohol and tobacco industries' strategy to blame young people for illegal alcohol and tobacco sales. *J Public Health Policy.* 1995;16(4):412–432.

29. Azofeifa A, Rexach-Guzman BD, Hagemeyer AN, Rudd RA, Sauber-Schatz EK. Driving under the influence of marijuana and illicit drugs among persons aged >/=16 years—United States, 2018. *MMWR Morb Mortal Wkly Rep.* 2019;68(50):1153–1157.

30. Tefft BC, Arnold LS. *Cannabis Use Among Drivers in Fatal Crashes in Washington State Before and After Legalization.* Washington, DC: AAA Foundation for Traffic Safety; 2020.

31. Hartman RL, Huestis MA. Cannabis effects on driving skills. *Clin Chem.* 2013;59(3):478–492.

32. Armentano P. Cannabis and driving: a scientific and rational review. 2011. Available at: https://norml.org/library/item/cannabis-and-driving-a-scientific-and-rational-review. Accessed March 30, 2021.

33. National Institute on Drug Abuse. Does marijuana use affect driving? 2020. Available at: https://www.drugabuse.gov/publications/research-reports/marijuana/does-marijuana-use-affect-driving. Accessed April 5, 2021.

34. Grotenhermen F, Leson G, Berghaus G, et al. Developing limits for driving under cannabis. *Addiction.* 2007;102(12):1910–1917.

35. Ashton CH. Pharmacology and effects of cannabis: a brief review. *Br J Psychiatry.* 2001;178: 101–106.

36. Desrosiers NA, Himes SK, Scheidweiler KB, Concheiro-Guisan M, Gorelick DA, Huestis MA. Phase I and II cannabinoid disposition in blood and plasma of occasional and frequent smokers following controlled smoked cannabis. *Clin Chem.* 2014;60(4):631–643.

37. Bergamaschi MM, Karschner EL, Goodwin RS, et al. Impact of prolonged cannabinoid excretion in chronic daily cannabis smokers' blood on per se drugged driving laws. *Clin Chem.* 2013;59(3):519–526.

38. Wong K, Brady JE, Li G. Establishing legal limits for driving under the influence of marijuana. *Inj Epidemiol.* 2014;1(1):1–8.

39. Governors Highway Safety Association. Marijuana-related laws. 2020. Available at: https://www.ghsa.org/sites/default/files/2020-01/marijuanalaws_jan2020.pdf. Accessed March 30, 2021.

40. Strano-Rossi S, Castrignano E, Anzillotti L, et al. Evaluation of four oral fluid devices (DDS(R), Drugtest 5000(R), Drugwipe 5+(R) and RapidSTAT(R)) for on-site monitoring drugged driving in comparison with UHPLC-MS/MS analysis. *Forensic Sci Int.* 2012;221(1–3):70–76.

41. Desrosiers NA, Huestis MA. Oral fluid drug testing: analytical approaches, issues and interpretation of results. *J Anal Toxicol.* 2019;43(6):415–443.

42. Beirness DJ, Beasley E, LeCavalier J. The accuracy of evaluations by drug recognition experts in Canada. *Can Soc Forensic Sci J.* 2009;42(1):75–79.

43. Beirness DJ, LeCavalier J, Singhal D. Evaluation of the Drug Evaluation and Classification program: a critical review of the evidence. *Traffic Inj Prev.* 2007;8(4):368–376.

44. Porath AJ, Beirness DJ. Predicting categories of drugs used by suspected drug-impaired drivers using the Drug Evaluation and Classification Program tests. *Traffic Inj Prev.* 2019;20(3): 255–263.

45. Hartman RL, Richman JE, Hayes CE, Huestis MA. Drug Recognition Expert (DRE) examination characteristics of cannabis impairment. *Accid Anal Prev.* 2016;92:219–229.

46. Schechtman E, Shinar D. Modeling drug detection and diagnosis with the "drug evaluation and classification program." *Accid Anal Prev.* 2005;37(5):852–861.

47. Van der Linden T, Wille SM, Ramirez-Fernandez M, Verstraete AG, Samyn N. Roadside drug testing: comparison of two legal approaches in Belgium. *Forensic Sci Int.* 2015;249:148–155.

48. Toennes SW, Kauert GF, Steinmeyer S, Moeller MR. Driving under the influence of drugs—evaluation of analytical data of drugs in oral fluid, serum and urine, and correlation with impairment symptoms. *Forensic Sci Int.* 2005;152(2–3):149–155.

49. National Academies of Sciences, Engineering, and Medicine (NASEM). *Getting to Zero Alcohol-Impaired Driving Fatalities: A Comprehensive Approach to a Persistent Problem.* Washington, DC: NASEM; 2018.

50. Pierson E, Simoiu C, Overgoor J, et al. A large-scale analysis of racial disparities in police stops across the United States. *Nat Hum Behav.* 2020;4(7):736–745.

10

Looking Forward

This book provides a public health perspective on and public health evidence for policy debates regarding the status of cannabis production and use in the United States. As described in previous chapters, cannabis policy in this country has been influenced by commercial interests and by a range of other factors, including racism, xenophobia, and periodic drug panics (that had little to do with cannabis use). Policies have been little influenced by health data despite claims being made on both sides of the legalization debate for the benefits and harms that emanate from cannabis use.

Researchers have examined the health impact of cannabis and cannabinoids, as well as the health impact of efforts to prevent cannabis use and related problems. There is substantial research support for the finding that cannabis and cannabinoid use can reduce chemotherapy-induced nausea, symptoms of chronic pain, multiple sclerosis–related spasticity, and seizure frequency in two rare forms of epilepsy. A similar level of evidence exists for a range of harms related to cannabis use: increased risk of motor vehicle crashes, development of schizophrenia and other psychoses, respiratory symptoms (coughing, wheezing, and phlegm), and lowered birth weight of offspring. There is also substantial evidence of harms arising from cannabis use during adolescence, including greater risk of poor educational outcomes, cannabis dependence, psychotic symptoms, anxiety, and suicide attempts.

Cannabis prohibition has not eliminated these harms, and it has brought with it harms of its own. As discussed in Chapter 5, cannabis law enforcement historically and in the present day has disproportionately affected poor, and particularly Black, communities. The legacy of hundreds of thousands of drug arrests in the 1990s, most of them for cannabis possession, endures in the form of denial of opportunities for housing and employment, the right to vote, and the ability to build wealth. Along with incarceration itself, these in turn have health consequences—numerous studies show that unstable housing, inadequate income, and unemployment all contribute to a shorter life span and poorer health.[1-3]

A growing number of states are moving to legalize nonmedical cannabis for adult use, but it is not too late for state-level policymakers to learn from what has been tried so far, both in this country and elsewhere. Next steps regarding cannabis regulation must navigate between the Scylla of cannabis harms and the Charybdis of social injustice. Recent efforts to address a history of racist policing and social injustice through cannabis law reform have yielded mixed results: arrests have gone down, but disparities persist. Communities disproportionately harmed by cannabis prohibition are now at risk of disproportionate harm from legalization, as cannabis outlets cluster within their borders.

Regarding cannabis use and harms, states that have legalized cannabis for nonmedical use have seen an increase in adult prevalence, which some studies find accompanied by a rise in youth use. Prevalence of cannabis use disorder among adolescents has increased following legalization for adult nonmedical use, as adult treatment admissions for cannabis use disorders have increased in states that have passed laws permitting medical cannabis use. And as states have increased cannabis availability, presence of cannabis in drivers in fatal crashes has nearly tripled nationwide; in Washington State, prevalence of cannabis-positive drivers involved in fatal crashes doubled after full legalization, with more than one in five drivers testing positive for THC.

A public health approach requires working from the available data toward the goals articulated at the start of this book: preventing youth use; controlling prevalence, frequency, and intensity of use; reducing cannabis-related harms to individuals and communities; disseminating accurate information about the risks of cannabis use; and minimizing the influence of the profit motive in setting cannabis policies.

In light of these goals and the data thus far, full commercial legalization of cannabis for nonmedical use is not the best approach from a public health perspective. There are ways—some of which states are discovering—to decriminalize cannabis possession and offer controlled access to cannabis for a limited number of medical conditions that can remove many of the harms associated with cannabis prohibition without the increase in use and problems that apparently accompany full legalization.

This book has discussed these options but has focused primarily on the situation in which many states find themselves: facing enormous public pressure to liberalize cannabis availability. While looking for the best way to do more than decriminalize and medicalize, states seek to avoid the negative consequences seen in the legalized states as well as the more dire outcomes associated with the nation's two most deadly and widely available legal drugs, tobacco and alcohol.

A thoughtful legislative approach—rather than the blunt instrument of most ballot initiatives—one that learns from alcohol and tobacco experiences as well as cannabis regulatory systems in place in other countries, will begin with the right regulatory system. The evidence is clear: such systems will limit or eliminate the degree to which distribution is driven by profit-making interests. Cannabis social clubs provide small-scale models of how to do this. On a larger scale, government monopolies (and their close cousins, public authorities) are the most reliable means of maintaining sufficient control over availability that public health and social justice concerns may outweigh commercial interests.

Beyond the right system, a public health approach to cannabis regulation entails using multiple policy levers, across government departments, to create physical, fiscal, and information environments supportive of public health goals. Limiting the type, number, and location of outlets; setting retail outlet practices such as days and hours of sale, amount that may be purchased in a single transaction, and use of security personnel; and curtailing youth access are key elements of health-enhancing physical availability. All require clear policies and consistent enforcement with meaningful sanctions.

Fiscal policies should discourage heavy consumption and employ policy levers such as taxation, minimum pricing, and bans on couponing and other discounts to keep prices at a level that is protective of public health. Overreliance on revenues from cannabis sales to rectify past injustices from cannabis prohibition can place states in a conflicted position. These past injustices need to be rectified, but making states dependent on cannabis revenues to do so can create a state-level motive for increasing consumption and sales. Displacement of illegal markets will take time; taxes and other controls over pricing should anticipate this and look to safe marketplaces and reliable products more than lower prices to displace illegal trade.

Abundant experience from alcohol and tobacco indicates that marketing will influence rates and patterns of cannabis use and related problems. Minimal marketing in the hands of a public health–oriented government monopoly is the safest approach; if states opt for a different system, such as commercialized licensing, then states should explore using their tax codes to discourage marketing expenditures by denying them deductibility as business expenses. Such an approach should be accompanied by as thorough a ban on cannabis marketing as is constitutionally feasible. Self-regulation by cannabis marketers will be ineffective; studies find widespread violation of the relatively minimal marketing regulations in place in states that have legalized nonmedical cannabis for adult use.

Finally, effective cannabis control will require the creation and maintenance of effective systems of enforcement, monitoring, and surveillance and research. The list of pressing research and monitoring topics is lengthy and includes study of the environmental impact of cannabis production; development of accurate and uniform measures of cannabis potency; databases that track with precision cannabis policies and changes to them over time; seed-to-sale tracking systems for cannabis products; product and packaging standards; youth and adult patterns of use and problems; monitoring of advertising and marketing practices and compliance; compliance checks on retail sales to minors, particularly in jurisdictions permitting home delivery; and creation of evidence-based standards for detecting and discouraging cannabis-impaired driving.

The world is changing rapidly, and cannabis law reform is and will continue to be part of those changes. Public health researchers have compiled the data, done the analyses, and produced results that should inform an approach to cannabis law that enhances health and safety and promotes justice and equity. This book summarizes and synthesizes the available public health data and uses it to create a road map for policymakers.

Almost 90 years ago, the authors of *Toward Liquor Control* closed their report with these words:

> A new spirit is in the air—a new belief in the power of human intelligence to plan a social order in the interests of a saner and more balanced life. It is this revived faith, this impatience with abuses which have so long seemed inevitable, this willingness to experiment, that constitute the hope of a new era.[4]

A renewal and revival of that faith in the coming decade, and the courage to experiment and to follow public health data and science, can produce policies toward cannabis that will facilitate a "saner and more balanced life" for all.

REFERENCES

1. Daniels N, Kennedy BP, Kawachi I. Why justice is good for our health: the social determinants of health inequalities. *Daedalus.* 1999;128(4):215–251.

2. Adler NE, Glymour MM, Fielding J. Addressing social determinants of health and health inequalities. *JAMA.* 2016;316(16):1641–1642.

3. Massoglia M. Incarceration, health, and racial disparities in health. *Law & Society Rev.* 2008;42(2):275–306.

4. Fosdick R, Scott A. *Toward Liquor Control.* New York: Harper and Brothers; 1933; reprint Alexandria VA: The Center for Alcohol Policy, 2011.

APPENDICES

Cannabis Harms and Therapeutic Effects— Findings From *The Health Effects of Cannabis and Cannabinoids: The Current State of Evidence and Recommendations for Research*

The Health Effects of Cannabis and Cannabinoids: The Current State of Evidence and Recommendations for Research,[*] a 2017 report from the National Academies of Sciences, Engineering, and Medicine (NASEM), utilized key features of a systematic review process to yield more than 24,000 articles, of which the committee considered more than 10,000 abstracts to determine relevance for study of 11 prioritized health endpoints.[1]

The full report presents nearly 100 conclusions related to the health effects of cannabis and cannabinoids and uses standardized language to categorize the weight of evidence. The categories are defined below. The table (Table A1-1) that follows highlights key findings for both harms and therapeutic effects by evidence level:

Excerpts from Box 1-4: Weight-of-Evidence Categories in *The Health Effects of Cannabis and Cannabinoids: The Current State of Evidence and Recommendations for Research*[1]

Conclusive Evidence (Strong evidence from randomized controlled trials)
There are many supportive findings from good-quality studies with no credible opposing findings. A firm conclusion can be made, and the limitations to the evidence, including chance, bias, and confounding factors, can be ruled out with reasonable confidence.

Substantial Evidence (Strong evidence)
There are several supportive findings from good-quality studies with very few or no credible opposing findings. A firm conclusion can be made, but minor limitations, including chance, bias, and confounding factors, cannot be ruled out with reasonable confidence.

Moderate Evidence (Some evidence)
There are several supportive findings from good- to fair-quality studies with very few or no credible opposing findings. A general conclusion can be made, but limitations,

---

[*]The NASEM report also reviewed studies on risk and protective factors for problem cannabis use (Chapter 13), which are not included in Table A1-1.

including chance, bias, and confounding factors, cannot be ruled out with reasonable confidence.

Limited Evidence (Weak evidence)
There are supportive findings from fair-quality studies or mixed findings with most favoring one conclusion. A conclusion can be made, but there is significant uncertainty due to chance, bias, and confounding factors.

No or Insufficient Evidence to Support the Association
There are mixed findings, a single poor study, or a health endpoint has not been studied at all. No conclusion can be made because of substantial uncertainty due to chance, bias, and confounding factors.

Cannabis-Derived and Cannabis-Related Medications

Many of the NASEM conclusions are based on either cannabis-derived or cannabis-related drug products. Cannabinoids are a group of psychoactive chemical compounds found in the cannabis plant. There are more than 100 different cannabinoids in cannabis.[2] Other compounds identified include terpenoids, flavonoids, nitrogenous compounds, and more common plant molecules. Different cannabis-related medications may comprise a variety of cannabinoids.

The US Food and Drug Administration (FDA) has approved one cannabis-derived and three cannabis-related drug products. Dronabinol (marketed under the trade name Marinol as well as Syndros, which is a liquid formulation) and nabilone (marketed under the trade name Cesamet) are approved by the FDA.[3] These medications are clinically indicated to counteract nausea and vomiting and to stimulate appetite, specifically in anorexia associated with weight loss in AIDS patients or nausea associated with chemotherapy. In 2018, the FDA approved Epidiolex, a CBD oral solution for the treatment of seizures associated with two rare forms of epilepsy. One additional cannabinoid-based medication has been examined by the FDA but not approved for use in the United States. Nabiximols (marketed under the trade name Sativex) is indicated in the symptomatic relief of multiple sclerosis and for pain relief in cancer patients. Nabiximols are available in at least 15 countries.[1] Some of these medications are referenced in Table A1-1 of Appendix 1.

Table A1-1. Cannabis Harms and Therapeutic Effects—Findings From the NASEM Report *The Health Effects of Cannabis and Cannabinoids: The Current State of Evidence and Recommendations for Research*

Scientific Evidence Level	Harms	Therapeutic Effects
Conclusive Evidence		Oral cannabinoids • Effective antiemetics in the treatment of chemotherapy-induced nausea and vomiting
Substantial Evidence	Cannabis use • Increased risk of motor vehicle crashes • Development of schizophrenia or other psychoses, with the highest risk among the most frequent users Long-term smoking • Worse respiratory symptoms and more frequent chronic bronchitis episodes (moderate evidence of improvement in respiratory symptoms if cannabis smoking ceases) Maternal cannabis smoking • Lower birth weight of offspring	Cannabis • Effective treatment for chronic pain in adults Oral cannabinoids • Effective treatment for improving patient-reported multiple sclerosis spasticity symptoms
Moderate Evidence	Cannabis use • Increased risk of overdose injuries, including respiratory distress, among pediatric populations in US states where cannabis is legal • Increased symptoms of mania and hypomania in individuals diagnosed with bipolar disorders (regular cannabis use) • Small increased risk for the development of depressive disorders • Increased incidence of suicidal ideation and suicide attempts with a higher incidence among heavier users • Increased incidence of suicide completion • Increased incidence of social anxiety disorder (regular cannabis use) • Impairment in the cognitive domains of learning, memory, and attention (acute cannabis use) • Development of substance dependence and/or a substance abuse disorder for substances, including alcohol, tobacco, and other illicit drugs Problem cannabis use • A history of psychiatric treatment • Increased severity of posttraumatic stress disorder symptoms No statistical association between cannabis use and • Incidence of lung cancer • Incidence of head and neck cancers	Cannabinoids • Primarily nabiximols, as an effective treatment for improving short-term sleep outcomes in individuals with sleep disturbance associated with obstructive sleep apnea syndrome, fibromyalgia, chronic pain, and multiple sclerosis Cannabis use • Better cognitive performance on learning and memory tasks among individuals with psychotic disorders and a history of, but not recent, cannabis use • No statistical association with worsening of negative symptoms (e.g., blunted affect) among individuals with psychotic disorders Cannabis smoking • Improved airway dynamics, such as bronchodilation and higher forced vital capacity with acute use, but these short-term benefits are offset by the effects of long-term smoking

(Continued)

Table A1-1. (Continued)

Scientific Evidence Level	Harms	Therapeutic Effects
Limited Evidence	**Cannabis use** • Increase in positive symptoms of schizophrenia (e.g., hallucinations) among individuals with psychotic disorders • Likelihood of developing bipolar disorder, particularly among regular or daily users • Development of any type of disorder, except social anxiety disorder • Increased symptoms of anxiety (near daily cannabis use) • Increased severity of posttraumatic stress disorder symptoms among individuals with post-traumatic stress disorder • Increased risk of ischemic stroke or subarachnoid hemorrhage • Increased risk of prediabetes • Impaired academic achievement and educational outcomes • Increased rates of unemployment and/or low income • Impaired social functioning or engagement in developmentally appropriate social roles • Initiation of tobacco use • Changes in the rates and use patterns of other licit and illicit substances **Sustained abstinence from cannabis use** • Impairments in the cognitive domains of learning, memory, and attention **Cannabis smoking** • Triggering of acute myocardial infarction **Current, frequent, or chronic cannabis smoking:** • Non-seminoma-type testicular germ cell tumors **Occasional cannabis smoking** • Increased risk of developing chronic obstructive pulmonary disease when controlled for tobacco use **Maternal cannabis smoking** • Pregnancy complications for the mother • Admission of the infant to the neonatal intensive care unit	**Cannabis and oral cannabinoids** • Effective in increasing appetite and decreasing weight loss associated with HIV/AIDS **Oral cannabinoids** • Effective treatment for improving clinician-measured multiple sclerosis spasticity symptoms **THC capsules** • Effective treatment for improving symptoms of Tourette syndrome **Cannabidiol** • Effective treatment for the improvement of anxiety symptoms, as assessed by a public speaking test, in individuals with social anxiety disorder **Cannabinoids** • Better outcomes (i.e., mortality, disability) after a traumatic brain injury or intracranial hemorrhage **Nabilone** • Effective for improving symptoms of posttraumatic stress disorder **Cannabis use** • Decreased risk of metabolic syndrome and diabetes • No statistical association with the progression of liver fibrosis or hepatic disease in individuals with viral hepatitis (daily cannabis use) **Cannabis smoking** • Decrease in the production of several inflammatory cytokines in healthy individuals **Cannabis use is ineffective for** • Improving symptoms associated with dementia • Improving intraocular pressure associated with glaucoma • Reducing depressive symptoms in individuals with chronic pain or multiple sclerosis

(Continued)

Table A1-1. (Continued)

Scientific Evidence Level	Harms	Therapeutic Effects
Insufficient Evidence or No Evidence (No Evidence marked with an *)	To support or refute a statistical association between • Self-reported cannabis use and all-cause mortality • General, nonmedical cannabis use and occupational injuries • Cannabis use and death due to cannabis overdose • Cannabis smoking and the incidence of esophageal cancer • Cannabis use and the incidence of prostate cancer, cervical cancer, malignant gliomas, non-Hodgkin lymphoma, penile cancer, anal cancer, Kaposi's sarcoma, or bladder cancer • Parental cannabis use and subsequent risk of developing acute myeloid leukemia/acute non-lymphoblastic leukemia, acute lymphoblastic leukemia, rhabdomyosarcoma, astrocytoma, or neuroblastoma in offspring • Cannabis smoking and hospital admissions for COPD • Cannabis smoking and other adverse immune cell responses in healthy individuals (besides the decrease in production of inflammatory cytokines included in the limited evidence benefits) • Cannabis or dronabinol use and adverse effects on immune status in individuals with HIV • Regular cannabis use and increased incidence of oral human papilloma virus • Maternal cannabis smoking and later outcomes in the offspring (e.g., sudden infant death syndrome, cognition/academic achievement, and later substance use) • *Chronic cannabis use and the increased risk of acute myocardial infarction • Cannabis smoking and asthma development or asthma exacerbation • *Cannabis use and changes in the course or symptoms of depressive disorders • *Cannabis use and the development of post-traumatic stress disorder	For the treatment of • Cancers, including glioma • Cancer-associated anorexia-cachexia syndrome and anorexia nervosa • Symptoms of irritable bowel syndrome (dronabinol) • Epilepsy • Spasticity in patients with paralysis due to spinal cord injury • Symptoms associated with amyotrophic lateral sclerosis • Chorea and certain neuropsychiatric symptoms associated with Huntington's disease (oral cannabinoids) • Motor system symptoms associated with Parkinson's disease or levodopa-induced dyskinesia • Dystonia (nabilone and dronabinol) • *Achieving abstinence in the use of addictive substances (cannabis and tobacco) • Mental health outcomes in individuals with schizophrenia or schizophreniform psychosis

Source: Based on NASEM.[1]

REFERENCES

1. National Academies of Sciences, Engineering, and Medicine. *The Health Effects of Cannabis and Cannabinoids: The Current State of Evidence and Recommendations for Research.* Washington, DC: National Academies Press; 2017.

2. American Herbal Pharmacopoeia. *Cannabis Inflorescence: Cannabis spp.: Standards of Identity, Analysis, and Quality Control.* Scotts Valley, CA: American Herbal Pharmacopoeia; 2014.

3. US Food and Drug Administration. FDA regulation of cannabis and cannabis-derived products, including cannabidiol (CBD): questions and answers. 2019. Available at: https://www.fda.gov/newsevents/publichealthfocus/ucm421168.htm#approved. Accessed April 5, 2021.

Examples of State Cannabis Advertising Policies: California, Colorado, and Washington

State	Content Restrictions			Placement Restrictions		Penalties
	General Prohibitions	Health Claims	Youth Provisions	Prohibited Locations	Distance Requirements for Outdoor Ads	
California[1]	A licensee shall not advertise or market in a manner that is false or untrue in any material particular, or that, irrespective of falsity, directly, or by ambiguity, omission, or inference, or by the addition of irrelevant, scientific, or technical matter, tends to create a misleading impression.	A licensee shall not include on the label of any cannabis or cannabis product or publish or disseminate advertising or marketing containing any health-related statement that is untrue in any particular manner or tends to create a misleading impression as to the effects on health of cannabis consumption.	A licensee shall not advertise or market cannabis or cannabis products in a manner intended to encourage persons under 21 years of age to consume cannabis or cannabis products or publish or disseminate advertising or marketing that is attractive to children.	Any advertising or marketing placed in broadcast, cable, radio, print, and digital communications shall only be displayed where at least 71.6% of the audience is reasonably expected to be 21 years of age or older, as determined by reliable, up-to-date audience composition data. Any advertising or marketing involving direct, individualized communication or dialogue controlled by the licensee shall utilize a method of age affirmation to verify that the recipient is 21 years of age or older before engaging in that communication or dialogue controlled by the licensee. A licensee shall not advertise or market on a billboard or similar advertising device located on an Interstate Highway or on a State Highway which crosses the California border.	A licensee shall not advertise or market cannabis or cannabis products on an advertising sign within 1,000 feet of a day-care center, school providing instruction in kindergarten or any grades 1 to 12, inclusive, playground, or youth center.	Each citation may contain either order(s) of abatement, monetary fine(s), or both, and shall fix a reasonable time for abatement of the violation if the citation contains an order of abatement, or assess an administrative fine of up to $5,000 if the citation contains a fine. The Bureau may also file an accusation to suspend or revoke a license where grounds for such suspension or revocation exist. (From California Code of Regulations, Title 16, Division 42. Bureau of Cannabis Control)

(Continued)

(Continued)

State	Content Restrictions			Placement Restrictions		Penalties
	General Prohibitions	Health Claims	Youth Provisions	Prohibited Locations	Distance Requirements for Outdoor Ads	
Colorado[2]	A regulated marijuana business shall not engage in advertising that is deceptive, false, or misleading and shall not make any deceptive, false, or misleading assertions or statements on any product, any sign, or any document provided to a patient or consumer.	No regulated marijuana business may engage in advertising or utilize signage that asserts its products are safe because they are regulated by the State Licensing Authority or because they are tested by a medical marijuana testing facility or retail marijuana testing facility.	Branding may not be used to target minors. A retail marijuana business shall not include in any form of advertising or signage any content that specifically targets individuals under the age of 21, including but not limited to cartoon characters or similar images.	A retail marijuana business may advertise in television, radio, a print publication, or via the internet only where at least 71.6% of the audience is reasonably expected to be at least age 21. A retail marijuana business may sponsor a charitable, sports, or similar event, but a retail marijuana business shall not engage in advertising at, or in connection with, such an event unless the retail marijuana business has reliable evidence that 71.6% of the audience at the event and/or viewing advertising in connection with the event is reasonably expected to be at least age 21.	A regulated marijuana business shall not advertise on any outdoor sign that is within 500 feet of established and conspicuously identified elementary or secondary schools, places of worship, or public playgrounds.	The range of penalties for utilizing advertising material that is misleading, deceptive, or false, or advertising violations directly targeting minors may include license suspension, a fine per individual violation, a fine in lieu of suspension of up to $100,000, and/or license revocation depending on the mitigating and aggravating circumstances. Sanctions may also include restrictions on the license.

(Continued)

(Continued)

State	Content Restrictions			Placement Restrictions		Penalties
	General Prohibitions	Health Claims	Youth Provisions	Prohibited Locations	Distance Requirements for Outdoor Ads	
				A regulated marijuana business shall not engage in advertising via marketing directed toward location-based devices, including, but not limited to, cellular phones, unless the marketing is a mobile device application installed on the device by the owner of the device who is 18 years of age or older for medical marijuana, 21 years of age or older for retail marijuana, and includes a permanent and easy opt-out feature. A regulated marijuana business shall not utilize unsolicited pop-up advertising on the internet.		The range of penalties for advertising violations that do not directly impact patient or consumer safety may include, but are not limited to, license suspension, a fine per individual violation, a fine in lieu of suspension of up to $50,000, and/or license revocation depending on the mitigating and aggravating circumstances. Sanctions may also include restrictions on the license. (From Colorado Department of Revenue, Marijuana Enforcement Division, Colorado Marijuana Rules, CCR 212-3, Part 8.)

(Continued)

(Continued)

State	Content Restrictions			Placement Restrictions		Penalties
	General Prohibitions	Health Claims	Youth Provisions	Prohibited Locations	Distance Requirements for Outdoor Ads	
Washington[3]	No statements or illustrations that are false or misleading or promote over-consumption. No outdoor advertising signs, including billboards, may contain depictions of marijuana plants or marijuana products.	No statements or illustrations that represent the use of marijuana has curative or therapeutic effects.	No statements or illustrations that depict a child or other person under legal age to consume marijuana, or includes the use of objects, such as toys, inflatables, movie characters, cartoon characters suggesting the presence of a child, or any other depiction or image designed in any manner to be likely to be appealing to youth or especially appealing to children or other persons under legal age to consume marijuana; or is designed in any manner that would be especially appealing to children or other persons under 21 years of age.	Outdoor advertising is prohibited on signs and placards in arenas, stadiums, shopping malls, fairs that receive state allocations, farmers markets, and video game arcades.	No advertising in any form or through any medium whatsoever within 1,000 feet of the perimeter of a school grounds, playground, recreation center or facility, child-care center, public park, library, or a game arcade admission to which is not restricted to persons age 21 or older.	First violation: $1,250 monetary fine. For subsequent violations within a two-year window: Second: Five-day license suspension or $2,500 monetary fine. Third: 10-day license suspension or $5,000 monetary fine. Fourth: 30-day license suspension or $10,000 monetary fine.

Note: This table may not be all-inclusive of policies related to cannabis marketing restrictions in these states. A full legal review was not conduced; as such, other policies may apply that are not included in this table. For example, warning labels and symbols that may be required on advertising are not included in this table. Prohibitions that directly relate to false branding or origin of product are not included, nor are restrictions on other aspects of marketing such as price and product.

REFERENCES

1. California Business and Professions Code. Division 10. Cannabis. Chapter 15. Advertising and Marketing Restrictions [26150-26156]. 2019.

2. Code of Colorado Regulations. Colorado marijuana rules. In: Department of Revenue MED, ed. *1 CCR 212-3*2020.

3. Washington Administrative Code. Title 314 WAC. Liquor and Cannabis Board. 2020.

Tax Revenue Distributions by State, As of FY 2019

State	Distribution
Alaska	50% to Recidivism Reduction Fund, split between public safety, health and social services, and corrections departments 25% to health education 25% to general fund
California	$10 million to $50 million to Community Reinvestment Grant Program $10 million to public universities to evaluate effects of ballot measure and $2 million to study medical cannabis $3 million to California Highway Patrol Remaining revenue: 60% to Youth Education, Prevention, Early Intervention, and Treatment Account 20% to Environmental Restoration and Protection Account 20% to State and Local Government Law Enforcement Account
Colorado	90% of special sales tax to general fund (72% to the Marijuana Cash Fund and 13% to the state public school fund, 15% retained) 10% of special sales tax to local governments that allow retail sales First $40 million or 90% of excise tax to Building Excellent Schools Today Fund Remainder to public school fund
Maine	Excise and sales tax to general fund Once a month, 12% of general fund marijuana sales and excise tax revenue is transferred to the Adult Use Marijuana Public Health and Safety Fund
Massachusetts	Excise tax revenue goes to Marijuana Regulation Fund Local option revenue goes to the municipality Sales tax revenue follows conventional sales tax allocation rules: 16% to Massachusetts Bay Transportation Authority 16% to School Modernization and Reconstruction Trust 68% to Commonwealth General Fund
Michigan	Amount needed to cover costs of implementation, administration, and enforcement, then: $20 million to clinical trials studying efficacy of marijuana in treating veterans 30% of remaining to municipalities and counties with retail sales 35% to School Aid Fund and 35% to transportation fund
Nevada	Excise tax revenue to fund administrative costs; $5 million to local governments, remainder to Distributive School Account Retail tax revenue to rainy day fund

(Continued)

(Continued)

State	Distribution
Oregon	40% to education and 20% to mental health treatment or alcohol and drug abuse prevention, early intervention, and treatment 15% to state law enforcement 10% to cities and 10% to counties 5% to drug abuse prevention, early intervention, and treatment
Vermont	Undecided; Marijuana Advisory Commission proposed using current statutory guidelines to allocate sales and local option tax (sales tax goes to education fund; local option goes to administrative fees, towns with local option tax, and state PILOT special fund)
Washington	Majority to health-related programs, including Department of Health, health plan trust account, and state health care authority; remainder to general fund and local governments

Source: Adapted with permission from Pew Charitable Trusts.[1]
Note: Sources provided in the original.

REFERENCE

1. Pew Charitable Trusts. Forecasts hazy for state marijuana revenue. 2019. Available at: https://www.pewtrusts.org/-/media/assets/2019/08/marijuana-brief_v2.pdf. Accessed June 2, 2021.

Cannabis Terminology

Blunt: Cannabis wrapped in tobacco or cigarillo paper.

Bud: The unfertilized flower of the female cannabis plant.

Budder: An extract that has a viscous, spreadable texture.

Butane Hash Oil (BHO): A THC extract created through use of solvents. BHO products typically have a much higher THC concentration than traditional flower cannabis.

Cannabidiol (CBD): One of the active cannabinoids identified in cannabis. It is generally considered non-intoxicating.

Cannabinoids: A group of active chemical compounds found in cannabis. Among the more than 100 types of cannabinoids are tetrahydrocannabinol (THC) and cannabidiol (CBD).

Cannabis: a broad term that is used to describe the various products and chemical compounds derived from the *Cannabis sativa*, *Cannabis indica*, or *Cannabis ruderalis* species.

Clone: A cutting from a mature cannabis plant.

Concentrates: Accumulation of trichomes usually made without solvents. Examples include kief, dry-sift hash, charas, bubble hash.

Dab(s): The amount of extract used for one inhalation or hit.

Dabbing: The consumption of cannabis by inhaling the vapor of heated cannabis extract oil.

Dronabinol: A synthetic cannabinoid for oral administration (active ingredient in Marinol and Syndros), both of which are FDA approved for the treatment of nausea associated with cancer chemotherapy and anorexia associated with weight loss in AIDS patients.[1]

Dual extraction method: The pairing of a butane extraction with an alcohol wash. Butane is used as a solvent for the first run and alcohol is used for the second run.

Edibles: Food products (including drinks) that have been infused with cannabis, and usually includes THC and/or CBD.

E-pen: Handheld electronic device used for vaporizing extracts.

Epidiolex: FDA approved medicine containing a purified form of CBD, for the treatment of seizures associated with Lennox-Gastaut or Dravet syndrome.[1]

Extracts: Specific type of concentrates usually created using solvents (BHO, carbon dioxide, alcohol), although there can be solventless extracts (made through the use of dry sifting or ice water). Examples of extracts include budder, crumble, honeycomb, shatter.

Flower: The most commonly used portion of the female cannabis plant, known to have the highest concentration of cannabinoids.

Hash (or hashish): The concentrated resin collected from the flowers of the cannabis plant.

Hemp: Under US law, cannabis plants with less than 0.3% THC are regulated as an agricultural product. Hemp is grown primarily for its fiber, oil, and seed.

Honeybuds: Cannabis buds that have been infused with BHO.

Honeycomb: A crumbly cannabis extract with a spongiform appearance and dry texture. Also referred to as crumble wax.

Kief: A selection of trichomes that have been separated from the cannabis flower and stored as a loose powder-like substance.

Marijuana: Colloquial term for the cannabis plant, considered by some to be racist due to its history (see Chapter 5).

Nail: A hollow rod used in place of a bowl to use concentrates. Nails are usually made of titanium, but glass and quartz are also used.

Nabilone: A synthetic cannabinoid for oral administration (active ingredient in Cesamet) indicated for the treatment of nausea and vomiting associated with cancer chemotherapy.[1]

Nabiximol: Pharmaceutical drug that is a botanical extract of naturally occurring constituents in cannabis (THC and CBD) indicated for the relief of multiple sclerosis symptoms. Not approved in the US, but available in Europe as Sativex.

Shatter: A form of BHO with a solid, glasslike appearance.

Synthetic cannabinoids: Products containing synthetically produced cannabinoids which typically mimic the effects of THC.

Terpene: Aromatic compounds found in plant resins (trichomes). There are more than 100 terpenes found in cannabis.

Tetrahydrocannabinol (THC): (also known as delta-9-tetrahydrocannabinol) A cannabinoid known as the main psychoactive constituent of cannabis.

Tincture: A liquid solution containing the active compounds in cannabis. Often consumed sublingually with a dropper.

Track and trace system: A program used by cannabis control agencies to record the inventory and movement of cannabis and cannabis products through the commercial cannabis supply chain. Agencies can require that all cannabis-related businesses (including cultivation, manufacturing, retail, distribution, testing labs, and microbusinesses) participate in the system.

Trichome: A small hair or other outgrowth from the epidermis of a plant, typically unicellular and glandular.

Vaporizer: A device that heats cannabis buds and/or concentrates to 315-440°F, which causes the cannabinoids stored in the plant's trichomes to evaporate into a gas without combusting any plant material.

Wax: An extract with a sticky, pasty consistency. Also referred to as earwax.

REFERENCE

1. US Food and Drug Administration. FDA and Cannabis: Research and Drug Approval Process. 2020. Available at: https://www.fda.gov/news-events/public-health-focus/fda-and-cannabis-research-and-drug-approval-process. Accessed July 21, 2021.

ADDITIONAL READING

1. American Herbal Pharmacopoeia. *Cannabis inflorescence: Cannabis spp.: Standards of identity, analysis, and quality control.* Scotts Valley, CA:American Herbal Pharmacopoeia; 2014.

2. National Academies of Sciences, Engineering, and Medicine. *The health effects of cannabis and cannabinoids : the current state of evidence and recommendations for research.* Washington, DC: The National Academies Press; 2017.

3. Stogner JM, Miller BL. Assessing the dangers of "dabbing": Mere marijuana or harmful new trend? *Pediatrics.* 2015. 136(1):1-3.

4. UCLA Cannabis Research Initiative. Terminology. 2021. Available at: https://cannabis.semel.ucla.edu/terminology/. Accessed July 21, 2021.

Index